Praise for The Ban...

"... is a riveting ac................................... .... drug kingpin Ike Atkinson. In his latest book, Chepesiuk has once again used his investigative journalist skills to unearth the true story behind the Atkinson drug band and to dispel the many myths that have been purported by the media and Hollywood regarding the Asian-American heroin trade. Using exclusive interviews with Atkinson himself, as well as numerous agents who investigated him, Chepesiuk takes the reader inside the mind of a drug trafficker as he establishes his empire."

— David Weeks, author of *Death at the Ballpark: A Comprehensive Study of Game-Related Fatalities of Players, Other Personnel and Spectators in Amateur and Professional Baseball, 1862-200*

"As a 25-year veteran of the DEA, I congratulate Ron on setting the record straight on the true story of the "American Gangster." By interviewing former DEA agents, drug kingpins and reviewing public documents, Ron has accurately captured the role of the gangsters and the investigative strategy implemented by the DEA that led to the dismantling of this complex international heroin organization. This is a must read for anyone interested in the true story of the chess game between the international drug kingpin the 1970s and the DEA agents who took him down."

—Lew Rice, former DEA Special Agent in Charge and author of *DEA Special Agent: My Life on the Front Line*

First published as *Sergeant Smack* in the USA. This edition published in 2011 by MAVERICK HOUSE PUBLISHERS, Office 19, Dunboyne Business Park, Dunboyne, Co. Meath, Ireland.

info@maverickhouse.com
http://www.maverickhouse.com

ISBN: 978-1-905379-74-3

5 4 3 2 1

The paper used in this book comes from wood pulp of managed forests. For every tree felled, at least one tree is planted, thereby renewing natural resources.

The moral rights of the author have been asserted.

A CIP catalogue record for this book is available from the British Library.

THE
BANGKOK
CONNECTION

Trafficking Heroin from Asia to the USA

Ron Chepesiuk

'Crime is no more easily hidden than in a crowd.'
—Anonymous

For Magdalena, my wife, my love and my inspiration

CONTENTS

PROLOGUE

Strange Encounters of a Cadaver Kind

DECEMBER 9, 1972—It was to be a routine flight, one of dozens the retired U.S. Army Master Sergeant had taken since 1966 when he first arrived in Bangkok, Thailand. Given the colorful nickname 'Sergeant Smack' by the U.S. Drug Enforcement Administration (DEA), 47-year old Leslie 'Ike' Atkinson, the squat retired U.S. Army master sergeant, was dressed appropriately for the long flight to the U.S. mainland: khaki pants, casual loafers and a loose white short sleeve sports shirt. With his short cropped curly black hair and military bearing, Atkinson looked like one of the scores of American servicemen, active and retired, black and white, who came to Bangkok in search of romance and excitement. With Atkinson in the black Mercedes that sped through the chaotic streets of Bangkok was 30-year old Thomas Southerland, a friend and fellow African American from Wilmington, North Carolina, whom Atkinson had known for nearly a decade. Like his companion, the trim, tight-lipped Southerland, or Sonny, as friends knew him, was a gambler—a card shark and hustler—and, their paths had crossed often in the numerous craps and poker games common in the black communities of eastern North Carolina. Southerland had visited Bangkok frequently, and over time Atkinson had become almost like an older brother to him.

Relaxing in the car, Ike assessed Southerland and could not help but admire what he saw. Fitted resplendent in an Army uniform complete with battle and service ribbons, Sonny looked like a war hero. He carried a military card that identified his rank as Sergeant. His special orders explained that he had served a 12-year hitch in the Army, and they instructed anyone reading the orders to please accord all privileges worthy of such service. In reality, Southerland's orders were totally bogus, forged by Atkinson himself, who, as a retired 20-year service veteran, knew the military system inside and out. His 'privileges' made obtaining military uniforms, NCO stripes and badges as easy as shopping for groceries. Forging IDs was so easy to do, in fact, that Atkinson did it himself in the comfort of his bungalow on a klong (a small canal), located in the heart of Bangkok.

Southerland could spend several years in prison for impersonating a U.S. military non-commissioned officer; it was a serious criminal offense. But he looked confident; after all, he had performed this role before—as a courier, carrying heroin in the standard army AWOL bags. Specifically designed for military travel, the bags looked like gym bags, except that they folded out like an accordion and contained hidden pockets. The false bottom of the AWOL bag had been stitched and fitted to carry two kilos each of a potent type of heroin commonly known on the 'street' as 'China White.' On this particular flight, Atkinson and Southerland each carried an AWOL bag, in addition to a suitcase. One kilo of heroin could fetch as much $50,000 in the U.S. Not bad for a $16,000 investment and a flight's work.

Military servicemen can fly on a military flight or 'hop', so long as space is available. The delays between flights can vary from an hour or two to as many as 24 hours. At times the wait and uncertainty can be aggravating, but invariably, the serviceman will get to his destination safely. And, of course, the best thing about the hops—they are free.

On this typically sweltering Bangkok day, the two travelers found space available for a grueling transatlantic flight that would take them to Honolulu, Hawaii, via a relatively short hop to Okinawa and on to Travis Air Force Base in the San Francisco Bay area before flying across continent to the airbase at Dover, Delaware. The tired travelers would then rent a car and drive the ten-hour trip to Goldsboro, North Carolina, Atkinson's hometown.

Bangkok's Don Muang airport had a U.S. military air base, but Atkinson preferred to fly from the U-Tapao air base in Sattihip, Thailand, located 100 miles to the south of Bangkok. Don Muang was always frantically busy and it was much easier to get a hop out of U-Tapao. Sure enough, space was available at U-Tapao, at least for the first leg to Okinawa, and Ike and Sonny had no problem moving through security. There were no x-rays machines in those days and security guards often did not hand-check the luggage. Besides, it was almost impossible to detect the contraband stitched into the bottom of the AWOL bags. They boarded a large Lockheed C-5A Galaxy double decker transport cargo plane, an enormous bird that could carry a payload of 125,000 pounds over a distance of 8,000 miles, take off and land in relatively short distances and taxi on substandard surfaces during emergencies. Shortly, Ike Atkinson would be very happy that he had flown this fortress-like military transport aircraft, which seemingly had an inexhaustible fuel supply.

AFTER THE PLANE reached cruising speed, the two pilots began taking turns coming back to chat with the passengers. Fresh from a war zone, the passengers had some first-hand knowledge of the situation, and the pilots were eager to learn what they knew. The United States Air Force (USAF) had deployed combat aircraft in Thailand since 1961, and its units trained annually with other Asian air forces. The U-Tapao base was activated in June 1966, and the following April, as the American presence in Southeast Asia increased, the number of aircraft based there swelled. B-52 bombers began raids over Vietnam. In fact, more than 80 percent of all USAF air strikes over North Vietnam originated from there and from other air bases in Thailand, and by 1970 Thailand had become part of the secret bombing of Cambodia.

A month before this flight, republican Richard Milhaus Nixon won the presidential election over democrat George McGovern in the biggest landslide in U.S. history. Three weeks later, the U.S. troop withdrawal from Vietnam was completed under Nixon's watch, although 16,000 military advisors and other government and civilian administrators remained to assist South Vietnamese military forces. Two days after Atkinson's flight was scheduled to land at Dover Air Force Base, the U.S.-North Vietnam peace negotiations collapsed in Paris.

So it was a pivotal time in the Vietnam War and inquiring pilots wanted to know: Do you think we are winning the war? How long do you think the war will last? Nobody on board really discussed the merits of the seemingly never-ending war because most of the passengers, given their backgrounds, supported it. For Ike Atkinson, the war was more of an opportunity—that is, something to be exploited as he pursued his criminal objectives. He ignored the conversation around him and napped, dreaming of the stuff that drug trafficking empires are made of.

It was a typical flight, but then as the plane approached the Okinawa air field and the pilots prepared for landing, Atkinson was jolted out of his reverie by an announcement that came over the intercom: 'We have problems with our landing gear, but we expect to correct the problem shortly.' A collective gasp rippled through the cabin. Never completely comfortable with flying, Atkinson asked himself: 'Did the Lord bring me up here to die?' Ike looked at Sonny; his friend was so cool and collected he looked as if he had taken a tranquillizer.

The passengers tried to stay calm as the plane flew in circles, seemingly endlessly. Then another announcement came: the crew was dropping fuel. Thinking about the consequences was chilling. 'Why are they telling us all this bad news,' Ike thought? 'Because they think we are brave, tough military people?' But he concluded—it's better to meet one's fate with eyes wide open. Finally, a few minutes later another announcement was made: the landing gear is free and the plane will be landing shortly. Some of the passengers cheered; others clapped. Ike and Sonny looked at each other and both flashed a chest-high thumbs-up sign.

The landing was smooth and the big bird taxied down the landing strip before coming to a stop about 100 yards from the terminal of the Kadena Air Base. The base, which dates back to just before the Allies invaded Okinawa in 1945, spreads across Kadena Town, Chatan Town and Okinawa City in the central part of the main island of Okinawa. It is the largest and most active U.S. air base in the Orient, and today it is home to the 18th Wing, a subordinate of the U.S. Fifth Air Force. Kadena is an airport Ike had seen often on his journeys to and from Bangkok and the U.S. In fact, Eddie Wooten, one of his best pals, had a bar in Okinawa. On his flights, Ike would stop to visit his old friend and at times plot a scheme or two on how to smuggle heroin into the U.S. But on this trip Ike knew Wooten was not in Okinawa.

A bus came to retrieve the passengers and their luggage. Moving into the terminal, some of them joked about their harrowing trip. Ike and Sonny went to the service counter to check the flights. They were told space was available on the next leg of their flight, but they would have to change planes. 'We want to make sure the landing gear is working properly, and it's going to take some time to do it,' they were told. 'Put your name on the flight manifest and we will get you home.' The next flight would leave early in the morning, so the travelers went looking for a nearby hotel. On the way, Atkinson told Sonny they would have paid Eddy Wooten a visit if he had been in Okinawa.

When Ike and Sonny arrived at the airport early the next morning, they could see a number of mechanics looking over the landing gear of the C-5A they had flown from Thailand. They saw a different plane taxing up the runway. Built by Lockheed, the C-141 was more of a troop carrier than a cargo plane. In the early 1960s, Uncle Sam introduced the C-141 to replace the slower cargo planes. One of the existing C-141s, the so-called 'Hanoi Taxi,' would be used in 1973 as part of Operation Homecoming, a series of diplomatic negotiations that in January 1973 made possible the return of 591 American prisoners of war held by North Vietnam.

Ike was happy to ride a different plane. He would not have to worry so much about meeting his maker somewhere over the Pacific Ocean. An airman came into the airport terminal, calling out the names of those who were traveling 'space available.' 'Yes sir! That's us,' Ike said cheerfully, and he and Sonny picked up their AWOL bags, checked their suitcases and headed for the door and their flight to Honolulu. On board, Ike noted a lot of friendly faces. It seemed everybody on last night's flight was on this one as well. Two of the faces were new though. They belonged to two high-ranking, uniformed airmen with somber expressions, who sat at the plane's rear.

ONCE THE PLANE was airborne and reached cruising speed, one of the somber airmen came to the front of the plane and made an announcement. 'The curtain at the back of the plane is drawn for a reason,' he said. 'On board are the bodies of two of our brave service men who have given their lives in Vietnam. Do not go to the back of the plane for any reason. If you must use the rest room, please use the one at the front of plane.' This would be a new experience for Atkinson. He had never knowingly flown with the bodies of dead GIs aboard. He knew that, given the heavy toll in the Vietnam War, the military had flown thousands of corpses back to the U.S. for burial. But why the announcement?

Most of the dead bodies were 'processed' at the main military mortuary at the Tan Son Knut Air Base just outside Saigon. On June 20 1967, the U.S. Army opened a second, less active mortuary at the Da Nang Air Base. The U.S. withdrawal from Vietnam led to the deactivation of the Da Nang Mortuary by February 1972. By this time, the number of bodies processed at Tan Son Knut Mortuary had decreased significantly because of the declining U.S. troop strength in Vietnam.

Having two corpses on board gave Ike a creepy feeling. It did not help that the airmen came back repeatedly during the flight to issue their blunt admonition: don't go behind the curtain! 'What's up with those damn fools?' Ike thought. 'Why would we want to go behind the curtain?' What with his earlier near-death experience, Ike thought this was turning out to be one weird flight indeed.

From Okinawa, the plane flew to Hickam Air Force Base in Honolulu, Hawaii. Unlike the initial leg, the flight was uneventful, but when the plane reached the tarmac at Hickam, the airport swarmed with military vehicles and personnel. Atkinson had never seen security like that before on a hop. However, after a 24-hour layover, the plane was on its way to the U.S. mainland.

THE TRIP GOT more bizarre once the flight landed at Travis Air Force Base. Situated in the San Francisco Bay area and known as 'The Gateway to the Pacific,' Travis handles more passenger and air traffic than any other military airbase in the U.S. On this pleasant California day in December, the tarmac swarmed with military personnel and vehicles, which moved into position around the C-141. Ike's stomach churned; after all, he and Sonny were carrying four kilos of heroin. But would the authorities use an entire military police unit to make a bust? Ike relaxed a little when he saw that two buses had come to pick up the passengers. They were directed to a holding area inside the terminal, where the passengers could see the C-141 through a big terminal window. Floodlights lit up the plane, and the military police remained in place. The hours slipped by; finally someone came and began to check the passenger's identification cards.

Ike had time to think. "This trip is getting stranger and stranger. Should we switch to a civilian plane?" Ike asked Sonny. "We are almost home, man," said Sonny. "Why should we spend the money?" Later, Ike wished he had followed his instincts instead of listening to his friend.

Once again, the C-141 was airborne, this time heading cross-country for Dover Air Force Base, located two miles south of Dover, Delaware's capitol. Once again, the bodies of the two dead GIs were on board and the same airmen took turns pronouncing the same stern admonition. But about an hour from Dover, an announcement was made. The plane would not land as scheduled. Instead it was going to be re-directed to Andrews Air Force Base, southeast of Washington, DC, near the town of Morningside. 'I thought what the hell is going on?' Atkinson recalled. 'Why's our flight being re-directed? The trip was getting more like the Twilight Zone by the minute.

It was enough to make me think that maybe I should buy my own plane.'

The landing was routine but when the door was opened, the passengers were surprised to see several military police standing at the bottom of the walk. With them were some men in black suits, who looked like FBI types. The passengers were directed off the plane to two waiting buses. Ike's mind raced. A military police (MP) jeep led the buses to a small terminal, where the passengers were told to disembark and go to a spartanly furnished room containing nothing but cold steel chairs to sit on. Four MPs stood guard; Ike moved quickly to take a seat besides Sonny.

'What do you think is going on?' Ike asked his friend.

'I don't know but it can't be good,' Sonny replied.

Ike glanced at the floor and the two AWOL bags that carried the heroin.

'Let's stay cool,' Ike said. Sonny nodded.

Then one of the FBI types came in and said, 'Excuse me, ladies and gentlemen. I have some instructions. No one is to talk. When I call your name, come with me.' One by one, the passengers were led away. A few hours passed, and Sonny was called out. Then a MP came back and picked up Sonny's AWOL bag. Ike's heart nearly fell to his stomach, but he knew Sonny would not panic and could be counted on to keep his mouth shut, no matter the circumstances.

Finally, Ike was the last one left and they came for him. It was after midnight. Ike was taken to an office that contained a chair, desk, filing cabinet and a big American flag under which hung a picture of a smiling President Nixon. Behind the desk, sat one of the men in dark suits.

'I see from the manifest that you are Sergeant Leslie Atkinson, retired. Good evening, Mr. Atkinson,' the type said. 'It's been a long journey. You must be tired. Would you like a cup of coffee?' Atkinson declined the offer, wondering if the interview was about to become a mind game.

'My name is Mr. Marr and I am the Assistant U.S. Attorney for the District of Maryland. Let me get to the point. We believe you are smuggling heroin from Thailand. Where is it?'

Atkinson did not flinch; he looked Marr right in the eye. 'I don't mess with drugs. I don't know what you are talking about.'

Michael Marr made cold eye contact with Atkinson and began squeezing. 'Mr. Atkinson. What did you do with the heroin on the two corpses that were on the flight coming from Travis?'

Atkinson looked at the man as if he was crazy and snapped, 'What?' In a strange way, he felt a little relieved. So this was not about the heroin in the AWOL bags.

Atkinson said nothing more. Marr stopped the interrogation, realizing it was going nowhere. 'We have been taking the plane apart, panel by panel,' Marr said. 'We will find it.'

About a half hour of awkward silence ensued and then the phone rang. Atkinson could see by Marr's expression that he did not like the news. 'What? Are you sure?' Marr asked. He listened to the answer and then hung up the phone. Marr looked at Atkinson intently; then he sighed. 'You can go now.'

SONNY WAS GONE by then. Outside in the street, Atkinson found a waiting cab and hopped in. He pulled a handkerchief from his back pocket and wiped his brow. He thought about the interrogation, the dead bodies and the heroin that was supposed to be in them. It made absolutely no sense, but obviously, a high ranking U.S. official would not waste his time on him unless he thought he was on to something. In the intensity of the moment, Atkinson had forgotten about Sonny and he wondered where he was. Ike concluded that his friend would have waited for him at the airport, so something must have happened. Maybe he was arrested. Atkinson told the cabby to take him to a nice hotel.

He remembered that a friend, a well-known drug dealer, lived in the Washington, DC area. At the hotel, he thumbed through his address book and made a call to his friend.

'I believe a friend of mine is in jail,' Atkinson explained. 'I need you to find him and bail him out.'

'No problem,' said the friend. 'What is his name and the charge?'

'I'm not sure, but it could be possession of heroin.'

It was the wee hours of the morning, but Ike could not sleep. He was exhausted and worried about Sonny. About noon, Ike heard a knock at the door. It was the drug-dealing friend who had gone looking for Sonny. With him was a man the friend identified as a bail bondsman. 'We located Southerland,' Atkinson's friend said. 'He is in jail charged with using false military documents and impersonating a military non-commissioned officer. The bail hearing is tomorrow.'

'What about his AWOL bag?' Ike asked anxiously.

'His bags are at a local police station, stored in the property room. You can go down to the station and try to get them released to you.'

Ike was relieved about the heroin but concerned about Sonny. He would not talk, no matter what charges he faced, but Ike was certain the charges would be serious. How serious, Atkinson learned later at the bond hearing. Southerland was being held on a $50,000 bond in a Baltimore jail, and magistrate Clarence E. Goetz had denied a bail reduction after military and Customs agents told him at the hearing that Southerland was involved in a 'large international conspiratorial organization.' Furthermore, he had flown aboard a plane headed for Dover Air Force Base in Delaware that carried the corpses of two dead GIs, which, an informant had told authorities, might be packed with heroin.

Having to explain why the authorities did not find any heroin, Marr told the court—and later the press—that during the stopover in Honolulu, the bodies had been left in a hangar, unguarded for 16 hours. Marr further told the court that one of the bodies exhibited a recent incision and stitching.

THE PRESS JUMPED on the sensational 'Cadaver Connection' and the headlines screamed: 'Top people part of ghoulish heroin ring,' 'Body heroin smuggling a puzzler' and 'Feds trace route of GI bodies.' The press speculated in numerous articles, based largely on anonymous sources, theorizing that Southerland was accompanying bodies as a dry run to test the efficiency of Federal law enforcement. After all, the press concluded erroneously, he could have taken a commercial plane and not have to take the risk of wearing a military uniform and carrying bogus documents.

Since that flight, the story of the 'Cadaver Connection' has persisted. More than three-and-half decades later, the speculation was rekindled with the release of the blockbuster movie, *American Gangster*, starring Denzel Washington and Russell Crowe. The movie depicted the life of former Harlem gangster Frank Lucas, an Atkinson associate. In interviews hyping the movie, Lucas embraced the 'Cadaver Connection.' In its open and shut conclusion about things cadaver, the *Associated Press*, which did absolutely no investigative reporting on the subject, reported in November 2007 that Lucas 'bought his dope in the jungles of Vietnam, and to get his drugs back into the U.S., Lucas established the infamous "Cadaver Connection."'

Meanwhile, the press reports made Ike Atkinson guilty by association. In response, Atkinson described the cadaver connection as 'the big lie…the biggest hoax ever perpetuated,' and he asked, 'Will we ever know who is responsible for the hoax?'

It is a question that Ike Atkinson has asked himself often since that fateful transpacific flight in December 1972.

MY SEARCH FOR the answer to that intriguing question helped spawn this tale of the international drug trade. The story of Ike Atkinson and his band of brothers spans three continents and is largely set in the 1960s and '70s, but it began on a bright warm day in June 2006 when I visited the sprawling Federal Penitentiary in Butner, a small rural town in the heart of North Carolina tobacco country. Several notorious Americans have spent time in Butner, including John Hinckley, Jr., the would-be assassin of President Ronald Reagan, and Jonathan Pollard, the unrepentant Jewish-American spy for Israel.

Ike Atkinson, the inmate who agreed to see me, is not as well known as some of the high profile prisoners at Butner, but in his own right he has made an indelible mark on criminal history. The man, whom the Drug Enforcement Administration (DEA) nick-named 'Sergeant Smack' when he shipped thousands of kilos of heroin from Bangkok, Thailand, to military bases in the U.S. at the height of the Vietnam War, happens to be the biggest American drug lord ever to operate out of Asia. When I visited Atkinson, he had already spent nearly 31 years in prison.

I came to see Atkinson to verify information I had gleaned through interviews I had conducted with Frank Lucas. Lucas was the subject of a profile I was writing for a book about organized crime in Harlem, New York City (*Gangsters of Harlem*). I knew and worked with Atkinson, Lucas told me; in fact, he is my cousin. Ike helped me to develop my Southeast Asia heroin connection. At the time of my visit to Butner, Lucas was about to become a household name among filmgoers.

Frank Lucas became legendary in the drug trade by purporting to be the first African American drug lord truly to break with La Cosa Nostra at that time the U.S. drug trade's major source of heroin supply, and to develop the Southeast Asia heroin pipeline. The former Harlem gangster has promoted himself —and is promoted in the media—as a swashbuckling drug lord who had the foresight and nerve to transform the drug trade by going to Bangkok on his own and connecting with a shadowy English speaking Chinese character he had colorfully code named '007'. Lucas's story is filled with tales of unsolved gangland killings, coffins—and perhaps corpses—carrying heroin from the killing fields of Vietnam to the streets of America, a drug empire run at times from behind prison bars, a controversial career as an informant and an ambiguous relationship between drug lords—in short, the stuff of Hollywood manufactured legends.

Yet, what about the claims Lucas made in our interviews? Did he establish a heroin distribution route that allowed him to bypass his La Cosa Nostra connection and to buy his supply directly from Southeast Asia's famed drug production center, the Golden Triangle, an area encompassing rugged parts of Thailand, Laos and Myanmar (formerly Burma). Such 'smack' was sold in the U.S. for as much as $316,000 per kilo, 'Superfly' had also told me.

Some law enforcement officials who investigated Lucas believe he indeed did have a strong, direct connection to Thailand and the Asian heroin supply. 'If you can bypass the middle man, you have power, and Lucas was a big time drug dealer,' one source explained to me. Lucas's connection to Thailand and Asian heroin, initially at least, was said to be Ike Atkinson. Lucas has also played up the Atkinson connection in the past. In a 2000 *New York* magazine article, Lucas told the author, Mark Jacobson: 'Ike knew everyone over there, every black guy in the Army, from the cooks on up.' Jacobson concluded: 'It was this 'army inside an Army' that would serve the Country Boys' (Lucas's organization) international distribution system, moving heroin shipments almost exclusively on military planes routed to the military bases along the eastern seaboard.'

Other law enforcement officials had a different take on Lucas's source of supply. Retired DEA Special Agent Joe Sullivan recalled what he knew about who controlled the heroin supply at the time. 'All the big drug traffickers, including Lucas, were getting their heroin from the Italians,' he said. 'The French Connection was in the process of being dismantled and the supply was tight and expensive. Lucas was getting it for about $200,000 a kilo.'

Law enforcement's conflicting opinion of Lucas's source of heroin supply, as well as some of the intriguing but unsubstantiated claims the former drug kingpin made in our interviews, made me want to dig deeper into his story. Fortunately, Ike agreed to see me and share what he knew about Frank Lucas.

At 81 years of age and near release from prison, Atkinson was confined in the low-risk section of the Butner Federal Penitentiary. He looked eager to see me, as we sat down for our interview in a cubicle under the watchful eye of the deputy warden. Retired DEA agents who investigated Atkinson in the 1970s had cautioned me that Ike was a 'real smooth charmer,' who excelled at manipulating a situation and was cool under pressure. Don Ashton, a retired DEA agent who headed the agent's Wilmington, North Carolina office and investigated Atkinson's drug ring, recalled the night he and some other DEA agents had Atkinson's house in Goldsboro under surveillance. 'Ike spotted us and came out to see us. He said to us: "It's a cold winter night, so why don't you guys come in and have bowl of soup?" He was almost likable.'

Later, when interviewing sources, friends and investigators for the Ike Atkinson story, one word would invariably pop up to describe Atkinson: gentleman. Christine Whitcover Dean, a retired federal prosecutor for North Carolina, recalled the time in 1976 when she was prosecuting Atkinson and several of his associates in what is perhaps the biggest drug trafficking trial in the State's history. 'At the court-house there was a side door the marshals used to bring the prisoners in,' Dean recalled. 'We would use that side door ourselves because we could avoid the crowds and it was an easier way to get in. Ike was ahead of us a couple of times, accompanied by marshals. He always opened the door for us with a smile. He was a real gentleman. We were trying to put him away for life, but he never took it personally.'

DRESSED IN A light brown prison jumpsuit for our interview, Atkinson retained much of his military bearing, although he walked with a slight shuffle, the result of many years living in confined quarters. Ignore the age spots and Atkinson looks to be at least ten years younger than his actual age. He greets me like I am a long-lost friend. He is indeed charming, and I listened as he caressed our conversation with a smooth engaging tone until the subject of Frank Lucas popped up. I told Atkinson the gist of what Lucas remembered about their relationship. Atkinson listened intently and then got agitated as he challenged Lucas's story. At times, Atkinson rolled his eyes and looked at me with the stare of one who believes the messenger must be high on something.

Atkinson, however, acknowledged meeting with Lucas and even being his friend, and dealing drugs with him. At one point, the former big-time drug trafficker, whose demeanor was once described as 'Buddha-like,' leaned forward, and in a measured tone, told me, 'Frank never brought any drugs into this country. He only spent three or four days in Bangkok, and he slept most of the time. I told Frank I would take him anywhere he wanted to go in the city. The only thing he wanted to do was go to the zoo and look at the snakes.' Atkinson roared with laughter; at that moment he did indeed look like a laughing Buddha.

At one point, Atkinson summed up his feelings about his former criminal colleague. 'Frank,' he says, his voice rising, 'is the dumbest guy I ever met in the drug business.' Atkinson could not insist spinning a yarn at Lucas's expense. According to Atkinson, he took Lucas to a Buddhist temple on his second or third day in Bangkok. When Lucas saw people bringing food and gifts for Buddha and leaving it at the temple, he said that he had to go and buy some apples and leave them for the Buddha. Then he commenced crying and asked Atkinson, 'Does Thailand border the Holy Land?'

While startled by Atkinson's candor, I am fascinated by his revelations about the man whom the movie *American Gangster* would soon make famous. I saw the Deputy Warden glancing at his watch, and I knew that, in a few minutes, I would have to end the interview. Yet, I had many more questions that begged answers. Then Atkinson dropped a bombshell. 'I woke up one morning about twenty years after I went to jail and it hit me,' Atkinson recalled, his voice rising. 'I realized why Frank had come to Bangkok: to get information that would help put me behind bars.'

I was stunned by the revelation. The interview ended with a bang, but it turned out to be a mere prologue to the beginning of what became an informative relationship when Ike Atkinson finally decided he needed to tell his story. But as my adrenalin pumped that day, I was already plotting how to dig up, what I knew would be, this journalist's 'story of a lifetime.'

CHAPTER 1

The Formative Years

GOLDSBORO IS A small, eastern North Carolina city located halfway between Raleigh, the state capital, and the coast, in an agricultural region marked by gentle rolling uplands and tobacco; historically, tobacco has been its principal cash crop. The town is conservative, rural and proud of the role it has played in southern history. Read the local tourism and travel literature, and one would have to agree that Goldsboro has had its fling with history. Among other claims to small town fame, the world's longest railroad once ran through the Goldsboro area. The city played its part for the southern cause in the Civil War, or the 'War between the States' as many white southerners still refer to the seminal historical event. The city was an important railroad junction and the scene of the Battle of Goldsborough Bridge, and today 800 confederate soldiers are buried in a mass grave at Willow Dale Cemetery. Not publicized in the literature is the fact that Goldsboro was the headquarters for Union General William Tecumseh Sherman who once referred to the South as 'the hell hole of secession.'

Locals will explain that the construction of the Seymour Johnson Air Force Base (AFB) on June 12 1942, was one of the best things that ever happened to the city economically. The base is named in honor of the U.S. Navy Lieutenant Seymour A. Johnson, a Goldsboro native and test pilot, who was killed in a March 1941 crash near Norbeck, Maryland.

During World War II, the air base's prime mission was to train pilots for the P-47 Thunderbolt aircraft. Today, Seymour Johnson AFB is home of the 4th Wing and the 916th Air Refueling Wing. A gigantic set of air force pilot wings in the form of adorned columns overlooks the downtown area near city hall, signifying the tight Goldsboro-Seymour Johnson relationship.

Goldsboro is described as an 'old river town,' given its proximity of the Neuse River; more than 1.5 million people live in the river's watershed that extends from the sprawling suburbs of the Raleigh-Durham area to the upscale communities of New Bern near the Carolina coast. The entire state of North Carolina is situated in so called the 'Hurricane Alley' and such powerful hurricanes as Floyd, Emily and Diana have swept through the state. Yet, remarkably, for more than 150 years, Goldsboro managed to survive extensive flooding. Then in 1996 Hurricane Fran struck Goldsboro and wiped out parts of the city near the Neuse River, including Neuse Heights, a predominantly African American neighborhood of 60 homes.

NEUSE HEIGHTS IS now history, nothing more than a forest, the houses demolished and the residents long gone, bought out by FEMA (Federal Emergency Management Agency), the U.S. Government agency responsible for dealing with hurricanes and other natural disasters relief. But in the 1970s, this quiet middle class neighborhood was home to Leslie "Ike" Atkinson and his family at the time Ike's actions became the object of U.S. drug law enforcement's attention. Ike lived at 127 Neuse Circle in a split-level, seven-bedroom home that had a color TV-set in every room, a game room and master bar. Walnut paneling lined the master bedroom and a large swimming pool rested in the back yard. Ike Atkinson, however, kept a low profile and no local could have gauged his wealth, especially after seeing his battered 1964 Chevy station wagon parked in the driveway. Atkinson liked to shroud himself in anonymity. In the town of about 6,000 residents at the time, many of the locals would later recognize his name but few ever saw him. 'I was gone so much that I understand some people thought I was federal employee working overseas,' Ike Atkinson explained. 'When they did see me, I was doing what they were doing—cutting the grass, fixing the house, driving my wife to buy groceries. I was being a good family man and neighbor.'

Milton Best, who today is a jeweler in Atlanta, Georgia, lived in Ike's neighborhood and grew up with Ike's children in the late 1960s and early 1970s. 'I dated Ike's daughter, Ann, and she was one of the smartest kids in high school,' Best recalled. 'His kids dressed well and some of them had cars in high school. Ike would work in his garden and give a friendly wave when he saw me. I would see him driving an old station wagon, but I knew he could drive something better. There were rumors that Ike was dealing drugs, but at the time I didn't know how big (a drug trafficker) he was.'

In the mid 1970s, Michael Hooks was a kid, not yet into teens, who lived across the street from the Atkinsons. Michael's father was a retired serviceman like Ike, and the two vets were the best of friends. Ike became Michael's godfather, and Ike's wife, Atha, became almost like a second mother to the boy. Michael went to school with some of Ike's eight children and enjoyed going to the movies and playing softball in the streets with them. Once a week Michael would go over to the Atkinson home and watch the Tom Jones variety show on the tube.

'I was accustomed to Ike being gone for extended periods of time,' Hooks recalled. 'When I did see Ike, he reminded me of a farmer. He wore overalls and a T-shirt or a short sleeve sports shirt…totally unpretentious. He loved his garden and would always be working on his home. I remember seeing his new swimming pool. It was really something special for the neighborhood. One day, he bought a pool table, and I would go over to the Atkinsons nearly every day to play. I'm an only child and Ike's children became like brothers and sisters to me. We would eat often at each other's house. Ike was one of the most personal guys I've ever met. A gentleman's gentleman.'

Hooks also recalled the day the Atkinson family fortunes changed dramatically. 'I was in my house and walking down the hallway to the door that led to the carport. The door was open and I could see Ike talking to my mother. I walked toward him and into the carport. I looked across the street and could see a bunch of cops and suited white men in the street and in his yard. Ike said good-bye to my mother, smiled at me and walked slowly towards the cops. I think he wanted to prevent the scene from becoming a spectacle. The children were moved down the street to the duplex where Ike's mother lived that Ike had bought for her. My parents and I were shocked; the neighborhood, disheartened. The Atkinsons were good neighbors and nobody wanted to see Ike go away."

THE COMFORTABLE LIFESTYLE that Ike Atkinson enjoyed in the 1970s was much different than the one he experienced growing up. He was born on November 19 1925, in Johnston County, the son of Preston and Rosetta Jones Atkinson and the youngest of a large family of three brothers (Dallas, Edward and Essell) and two sisters (Pearl and Nelly Mae). Today, anybody who grew up with Ike or knew him well in Goldsboro during his formative days, calls him 'Stimp,' not Ike.

'I had a friend named Willie Wesby who would go swimming with me at the Neuse River,' Ike recalled. 'One day out of the blue he started calling me 'Stimp.' I really don't know why he did it, but everybody in Goldsboro started calling me by that nickname, and it stuck. Then about 1959 while I was in the military, I got transferred to Ramstein Air Force Base in Germany. I met a man there who would eventually have a big impact on my life. His name was Ellis Sutton, a hulking heavyset man who looked like a grown up Fat Albert. He was a military policeman at the time. One day, Sutton saw me at the NCO (non commissioned officer) club and asked someone: "Who is that guy?" "That's Stimp," someone said. For whatever reason, which I still don't know, Sutton started calling me 'Ike.' The next thing you know, everybody who wasn't from Goldsboro started calling me Ike. It never bothered me, but you just don't have any control over some things in life.'

At an early age, Ike moved with his family to Goldsboro, where his mother found work as a domestic at the county courthouse and his father as a sawmill operator for M.E. Robinson Lumber Company. 'We lived in a rented house. At the time, it was not common for blacks to own property, but in our neighborhood one black guy owned his own house. His name was Doyle Baker. I remember him well because my family and neighbors identified him as the man with the steady job on the railway. He was like a star athlete, a real celebrity. He was just a worker on the train who stoked the coal while the engineer drove, but it was one of the best jobs blacks could find at the time. The truth was—everybody in our neighborhood felt lucky if they had a job.'

One day, when Ike was about five or six years old, his father walked out on the family. His father would come around the family house, bringing his friends to talk and drink alcohol. At times he would even have some money for his family, but his support could not be counted on. Ike saw little evidence that his father tried to help his family, and Ike never became close to his father. Money was so scarce that brother Essell went to live with a couple on the other side of town who did not have any children. After that, Ike did not see much of him.

Ike's two oldest brothers, Dallas and Essell, worked at the sawmill with their father, and they helped supplement their mother's meager income. 'My brothers did all they could to keep the family together,' Ike recalled. 'Later, I had major differences with Dallas and Ed; they stole dope from me when I was in prison, so I didn't put them on my visitor's list. But when I lay in my prison bed at night, I would think about how they tried to keep food on the table. I never disliked or resented them.'

At age nine or ten, Ike got a job at a drug store delivering prescriptions. He was able to save enough money to buy an Ivory Johnson bicycle, a popular bicycle at the time. Juanita Atkinson, who was born in 1920 and married Ike's brother Dallas in 1942, remembered Ike as an ambitious boy, full of energy, popular among his friends, who, at an early age, showed that he had a head for business. 'He was a mama's boy who tried to take care of his mother when he got old enough to work,' Juanita explained. Ike stayed down at the river all summer, swimming, so he was lean and fit, as a young boy should be.

Ike's mother was his role model and his relationship with her helps to explain Ike's courteous and gentlemanly manner.

'She believed good manners were important,' Ike said. 'She always treated people with respect when they came around the house or when I saw her in public talking to them. I was taught to take my hat off when I entered a home or building, and I still do today.'

In the early twentieth century, life was difficult for African-Americans, especially so for a large black family in rural North Carolina. It was the age of Jim Crow, when the laws, in effect, mandated segregation of all public facilities, and blacks had to live and operate within a system that treated them as second-class citizens. Thousands of blacks eked out a living as tenant farmers, but outside of agriculture, employment opportunities were limited to what was considered 'traditional' Negro jobs, such as railroad maintenance, construction and lumbering; those in the better paying textile and furniture industries were off limits.

Juanita Atkinson recalled how the Depression of the 1930s made life even worse for black people. 'What jobs there were dried up and the unemployment rate was terrible. The only opportunities we had were in the tobacco factory, the state hospital and sawmill, but the work didn't pay much. I found work as a domestic for $7 a week.'

The lack of opportunity for North Carolina Blacks extended to education. In 1916, Professor Charles H. Moore, a respected African American educator in North Carolina, conducted a survey of the state's black schools. Professor Moore's conclusion: 'The average Negro school house is a real disgrace to an independent civilized society.' The Great Depression only exacerbated this dire situation. In their book, *A History of African Americans in North Carolina,* Jeffrey J. Crow and Paul D. Escott provide these grim statistics: 'Some Black classrooms have 60, 70 or even 100 students. Only seven percent of Black students—compared to a meager 17 percent of White students—attended high school.'

Ike attended the elementary School Street School and Dillard High School, a free school for Goldsboro black children that opened in 1869 when the Quakers offered to provide a school for African American children, if their parents could furnish a building. The land where School Street School is now located was purchased and the school opened as the Goldsboro Normal and Classical Institute. Ike, like other black children, had to trek across town to get to school. Still, the boy took his schoolwork seriously and became a good student. 'If you can find anyone in Goldsboro who is alive today and went to school with me, they will tell you I was an outstanding history student. The teacher would always call on me to answer questions about history.'

Reading history and learning about far off places stimulated the young boy's imagination, and Ike dreamt of leaving Goldsboro and finding adventure. 'My life in Goldsboro was oppressing. I don't remember the Ku Klux Klan running around in white sheets, but everything was segregated: schools, water fountains, bathrooms, restaurants and movies… thinking back to those days, the symbol of segregation for me was the community center that the city built right in the heart of Goldsboro. It included a big beautiful swimming pool, but only the white kids could use it. The black kids would go up to the fence and look in, but the white folk would chase us away. We had to swim in the Neuse River or a river that ran into it called the Little River. There were no lifeguards and we took a risk when we jumped into the water. Logs from the sawmill upstream could break away at any time and kill us. That swimming business was one of the major things that helped me make up my mind not to stay in the South. I wanted to go anywhere in the world where I thought I would be accepted for who I was. So from a very young age I dreamt of leaving Goldsboro. I wanted to change my life.'

One program at Dillard High helped Ike to make the big move. Dillard was the only black high school in North Carolina to have ROTC (Reserve Officer Training Corp)-like training. 'Professor Hugo Victor Brown introduced the program,'

Ike recalled. 'He was a former commissioned officer in the army during World War I, who had come to Goldsboro from Louisiana. We learned how to use a .45 pistol and assemble a M1 rifle, and we studied how the military was organized and what it expected from recruits. I got really good at the military drills. Professor Brown became one of the biggest influences on my life; I really liked the man. Later, when I joined the military, I knew what was expected of me. That was why I adapted so well to military life.'

Ike's first opportunity to leave the South came in the summer of 1942 when he traveled to Brooklyn to visit his cousin Leonard Peacock. A few years older than Ike, Leonard had a friend who had a contract to hire people to work in Ithaca, New York, on the construction of the Sampson Naval Base. Ithaca sits on the southern shore of Cayuga Lake in Central New York State and, with its Cornell University and Ithaca College, the town is a bastion of higher learning. The town has some notable African American connections. On December 4 1906, for instance, seven black Cornell students recognized the need for a strong bond of brotherhood among African descendants in the US and established Alpha Phi Alpha, the first intercollegiate Greek-letter black fraternity. Noted African-American writer Alex Haley, the author of *Roots: A Saga of an American Family*, was born in Ithaca in 1921. In 1942, Ithaca was far removed from Ike's rural conservative hometown, not only by distance but also by culture.

The Japanese had bombed Pearl Harbor on December 7 1941, and the World War II effort was in high gear. The naval construction project was hurting for manpower. Anybody who wanted to work, blacks as well as whites, were welcome. Ike called home and his brother Dallas and Juanita Atkinson headed for Ithaca. Construction began on May 13 1942, and was completed 270 days later at a cost of about $56 million.

The Sampson Naval Base covered 2,535 acres, and during its three-and-a-half-years of operation, the base trained 411,429 recruits.

'Ithaca was such a great experience', Ike recalled. 'I can honestly say there was no racial discrimination. We did our job in constructing the base and we were paid the same as whites. I was the youngest of the group I came with, but I didn't cause any problems. I had my first interracial girl friend. We were just friends. Back home, our friendship would have been a big problem, but not in Ithaca. Our group lived in a boarding house on the same block as the girl's family. Her mother was friendly towards us.'

When the first payday came around, Ike and his brother Dallas sent money to their mother who was having a serious health problem. Her bad teeth were poisoning her system; in fact, her health got so bad she had to learn how to walk again.

'That summer was a fabulous experience,' Ike added. 'I made more money than I had seen in my life. Before I returned to Goldsboro, Leonard took me shopping and I bought clothes that were in style in New York City. I was really something with the girls at school. Nobody in Goldsboro had my "New York" clothes. All girls love a sharp-dressed man, and they were real friendly towards me. I told the girl in Ithaca I would miss her but would return, but I never saw her again. I was in Ithaca for just three months, but the experience really helped mold my character. I got to see white people in a different light."

UPON RETURNING TO Goldsboro, the town seemed much smaller and parochial to Ike. The Ithaca experience had given the young man a taste for travel and adventure, and he figured the best way to find it was to join the military.

In November 1942, Ike went to the local military recruiting station to inquire about joining. The Navy recruiter took one look at the eager young boy and told him he needed to provide a birth certificate because a recruit had to be 18 years of age to join. Ike was barely 17, and he told the recruiter that he did not have a birth certificate on him. Ike began to walk away, dejected, when a recruiter from the Army overheard the conversation and called Ike over to his recruiting table. 'If you can provide a signed letter from your mother that says you are 18, I will accept your application,' the recruiter told the teenager. Ike knew his mother would never give him that letter. Boys were dying overseas and she wanted her son to stay in school. Besides, Essell had already joined, and one son was enough to give to Uncle Sam.

Undeterred, Ike simply forged the letter and brought it back to the recruiting station. The army recruiter looked at the letter and did not blink. 'Okay, be ready to go to Fort Bragg for your physical next Thursday,' he instructed. 'My mother was upset, but she never knew I had to be 18 to join the service,' Ike recalled. 'I guess you can say it was the beginning of the life of a guy who would make up stuff and manipulate the military system for a very long time. The strange thing—no one ever said anything about it.'

ON NOVEMBER 25 1942, Ike Atkinson was sworn into the Army at nearby Fort Bragg, North Carolina. Established in 1918 and named for native North Carolinian General Braxton Bragg who fought in the Civil War. The base was just a few miles from Ike's home. With the outbreak of the war, the population of Fort Bragg ballooned to 67,000 and eventually reached 159,600 military personnel later into the war. Various famous units trained at Fort Bragg, including the 9th Infantry

Division, The 2nd Armored Division, the 82nd Airborne Division and the 100th Infantry Division.

Given Fort Bragg's vital mission and its swirl of activity, Ike found the base and military life exciting, and he was proud as a peacock to be a part of the war effort. 'I felt really special. They gave me a field jacket, boots, socks and a khaki uniform. I couldn't stay away from the mirror. I would strut and pose.'

Ike became part of the largest segregated army in U.S. history, and at times he wondered if the U.S. Government really appreciated his desire to serve his country. The U.S. military had initially resisted having blacks participate in World War II, but then relented and agreed to ban racial discrimination in so far as ensuring that every tenth man inducted into the armed forces would be black. But it was still not certain whether blacks would be allowed to perform meaningful service in defense of the homeland. Black leaders adopted a so-called 'Double V' campaign: victory against fascism abroad and discrimination at home. 'Blacks would serve in all-Negro units and possibly as parts of larger white units,' wrote A. Russell Buchanan, the author of *Black Americans in World War II*. 'There were differences of opinion concerning mixing of units, but it was agreed that the races would separate within the small units: officers for Negro units could be Negro or white, but Negro officers would be placed in command of only Negro units. Facilities for Negro and white troops would be of equal quality.'

The military's policy reflected that of mainstream American society: separate but equal. 'The majority of black troops continued to be employed in service units around the world, performing important duties, but ones that tended to reinforce old stereotype about blacks as soldiers,' Ulysses Lee explained in his book *The Employment of Negro Troops*. Operating through the Advisory Committee on Negro Troop

Policies, John J. McCloy, the Assistant Secretary of War, and General George C. Marshall, two powerful figures in the U.S. war effort, were able to shake the status quo somewhat. By war's end, two black Infantry Divisions, as well as a number of separate tank and artillery battalions and combat support troops, saw action in the ground war.

DESPITE THE RACISM and discrimination, Ike assumed his military duties with enthusiasm and determination. He took basic training at Fort Huachuca in Arizona. A product of the Indian Wars of the 1870s and 1880s, the fort, beginning in 1913, was home to the famous Buffalo soldiers for 20 years. During the World War II years, the troop strength at Huachuca reached 30,000. Ike did not mind the dry heat and loved the training and the education, even though it put him in class for four weeks. 'The military was so easy for me; I think I was born to it. I could take apart a 30-calibre machine gun and do it blind folded. I could hardly wait to get overseas.'

Ike was assigned to the all-black Veterinarian Company at Fort Bliss, Texas, a vast military outpost that sprawls from Texas into New Mexico and makes the base comparable in size to Rhode Island. The young recruit was not there too long before his company was sent to the infantry school at Fort Carson. Established in 1942, following Japan's attack on Pearl Harbor, and located in El Paso County, Colorado, Camp Carson was named in honor of the legendary Army scout, General Christopher 'Kit' Carson, who explored much of the West in the 1800s. The 89th Infantry Division was the first major unit to be activated at Fort Carson. During World War II, over 100,000 soldiers trained at the camp, including the 71st Infantry Division, 89th Infantry Division, 104th Infantry Division and 10th Mountain Division.

Ike wanted to join the all-black paratroop battalion, the 555th better known as the 'Triple Nickel,' that was being organized, but the number of applications was overwhelming. So Ike volunteered for the all-black 372nd Infantry Regiment, 93rd Infantry Division, which was activated in the spring of 1942 and based at Fort Huachuca. Rumors swirled that the division would actually be going overseas.

In 1943, Ike's sister Nelly Mae got in a car accident, and he was granted a six-day emergency leave to return home. His sister recovered, but while on leave, Ike married Helen, his high school sweetheart, whom he had known since age ten and was in his class at Dillard High. 'Helen was a light skinned girl with a nice personality and fine hair. She lived about a block from us. It was a spur of the moment thing that many soldiers did during the war. Helen said: "Let's get married," and I said, "Okay." Marriage was great at first, but it didn't last. After the war, our relationship wasn't the same. I was traveling around and she had a boyfriend. We divorced in 1947.'

WHILE IKE FELT privileged to serve his country, he soon faced the harsh conditions all blacks experienced in the service of their country during the 'Good War'. 'Coming from the South, I was used to racism and being a second-class citizen, but it was still hard to take. We faced a hostile reception in many of the communities located near the military bases. There was definitely a morale problem among my brothers.'

The U.S. military tried to improve morale by recruiting black celebrities to meet with the troops. A highlight of Ike's World War II service was seeing two legendary boxers, Joe Louis and Sugar Ray Robinson, up close. Joe Louis, one of the greatest heavyweights of all-time, had reclaimed the heavyweight championship in 1937 by knocking out Max Schmeling, a German fighter praised by Adolph Hitler as the paragon of Teutonic manhood. As a World War II soldier, Louis traveled 20,000 miles and staged 96 boxing exhibitions before two million soldiers. Robinson, who is often hailed as, pound for pound, the greatest boxer in history, was inducted into the U.S. Army on February 27, 1943. While Louis maintained the status quo, Sugar Ray challenged it, refusing to fight exhibitions when he was told black soldiers would not be allowed to watch him.

'Every black soldier knew about Joe and Sugar Ray,' Ike recalled. 'When we learned that we would get a chance to see them box, that's all we could talk about when we got together. When Joe got in the ring, he looked like the fighter we saw on the movie reels: powerful but slow-footed and deliberate. When Sugar Ray did all that fancy footwork and showed off his hand speed, everybody went crazy. We admired the stance that Sugar Ray took for us. Joe Louis kept things to himself, but what the IRS did to Joe after he had served his country, and sacrificed his career, was criminal. Later, when I got to know Joe Louis through Frank Lucas, I could see that he was always in trouble with the IRS.'

Louis donated the purses from two fights to the Army and Navy, but the IRS would not let him deduct the money from his taxes. He could not even deduct the $3,000 worth of tickets he had donated for one of those fights. After the war, Louis spent the rest of his life struggling to pay off the $500,000 debt in back taxes he owed the IRS.

IN APRIL 1943, the division went on maneuvers in Louisiana, and Ike did go overseas later in the year, but it was not what he expected. 'Our morale improved a little because we thought we would fight the Japanese. But when we went to the Pacific Theater, all we did was sit out the war. We could tell the Army thought the black soldier was inferior. My answer to that opinion has always been the same—we were trained to kill, so why did you waste the taxpayers' money and not allow us to fight? We couldn't fight? I had five weeks of tough training and was a good shot. We were told the Japanese were going to invade Hawaii, and we laid down our fortifications and mortar positions. That was easy. But nothing happened. Our commander kept saying: "What the hell are we doing on this goddamn island?" Boredom set in, and it lasted until the war ended.'

But no matter where Ike was posted during his military service, the boondocks of the Pacific or on a military base in the South, he always made the best of the situation. Ike's nature is to be upbeat. That's why people have felt good around him. But Ike, an opportunist who could charm the makeup off the face of a harlot, always looked for ways to make a quick buck; the Army offered easy pickings, and pick he did.

To pass the time, his comrades in arms loved to gamble, but they were no match for the friendly young man from Goldsboro who literally cut his teeth on a pair of dice. In his early teens, Ike had begun frequenting the gambling establishments of Goldsboro with his brothers and family friend, Willie Simmons, who owned a pool room that was a center of gambling activity. Ike watched how they were able to con people into getting over their heads in a card or craps game. His mentors taught him how to play 'Skin,' the most popular card game among blacks in eastern North Carolina. One pot could reach $500, lots of money in the Depression and the war years.

Ike also learned how to bend the rules—that is, use marked cards in a poker game or loaded dice in craps game. 'Before I ever picked up a deck of cards or a pair of dice, I saw my older brother Dallas and his best friend, Lester Brock, marking a deck of cards. The deck they liked to mark was called Steamboat. It was a popular brand sold in the drugstore, and each card in the deck was covered with little four-leaf clovers. Dallas and Lester would make a particular mark or scratch a different four-leaf clover for each of the 52 cards so they could tell when, say, an ace or king was dealt. When I was about 14-years old, I started to hang out at Willie Simmon's pool room and watch my brother and Brock play. The guys would come to the pool room after work and play all evening. Anybody could get into a poker game so long as there were no more than five players. The players were all a lot older, but they let me play. I'd use my money from work at the drug store and win $10 to $12 from those guys. Some of them would get so embarrassed that they would high tail out of the pool room as soon they lost.'

The pool room experience of his youth was a kind of a boot camp that prepared Ike for the widespread gambling environment he encountered in the military. Ike could not wait for payday. 'The men would not only have to pay off the gambling debts they already owed me, they would start gambling again. I made enough money gambling in the military that I was able to buy my mother a five-room house near School Street. I took my mom over to see it, and she was ecstatic. She even changed her mind and agreed that I had made the right decision about joining the army.'

The Japanese surrendered to the Allies on August 10 1945. Ike Atkinson was one of 700,000 blacks who had volunteered to do his part for the U.S. war effort. Not yet twenty years old, the young man would now have to decide what to do with the rest of his life.

CHAPTER 2

In the Army

WHEN WORLD WAR II ended, Ike Atkinson's company was brought to Fort Bragg near Fayetteville, North Carolina, to be processed and released from active duty. At Fort Bragg, Ike, like other black soldiers and their families, lived in crowded army barracks in a segregated area called Spring Lake. Many of his Army buddies were planning to go back to school by taking advantage of the GI Bill (officially known as the Servicemen's Readjustment Act of 1944, PL 345), which provided World War II veterans with financial support for college or vocational school. Ike, however, was smitten with the military. He liked the sense of purpose the Army gave him, and the fact it had rewarded him for his service by promoting him to the rank of sergeant within 50 days of joining the military in November 1942. A month after the war ended, Ike was promoted again to the rank of technical sergeant, with five stripes. The young army veteran followed his heart and re-enlisted after his discharge, but he always felt education was important, so he studied on his own to earn a GED (high school equivalency diploma) in 1948.

While at Fort Bragg, the noisy sound of soldiers doing exercises awoke him at 5 A.M. every morning for several days. A fellow soldier told Ike that the noisemakers were members of the all-black paratroop battalion, the 555th Airborne, or the 'Triple Nickel', as the unit became commonly known. It was the same unit that Ike had tried to join soon after he initially enlisted, but the Army had rejected his application then.

The Triple Nickel had hoped to go to Europe and kill Nazis. But in May 1945, after exhaustive training and much waiting, the unit finally received its orders. The company was trimmed to 160 of its best-trained men, and they were secretly sent, not to Europe, but to Pendleton, Oregon, where they were re-trained as smoke fighters to battle forest fires. In the summer of 1945, the men of the Triple Nickel began jumping into forest fires, and by the late autumn, they had made 1200 jumps.

After the war ended, the Triple Nickel returned to Fort Bragg where it became part of the 82nd Airborne, which many military analysts consider to be the finest division of World War II. The 82nd was under the command of Major General James M. Gavin, the man who unlike many of his white military counterparts, had a reputation among black soldiers as being color-blind. Once again the competition to get into the Triple Nickel was intense, but this time, Ike was not a raw recruit. He had compiled an exemplary record, was in excellent physical condition, and had the ability to get along with his fellow soldiers, black and white, given his many connections in the military.

After his discharge in early 1946, Ike stayed a civilian for 90 days before his application for the Triple Nickel was accepted. In July 1946, he was one of 800 men who joined the 555th. By the following November, the Triple Nickel had reached a peak of 36 officers and 1309 men, making it the largest battalion in the U.S. Army, at the time, perhaps in the world. When Ike finished jump school as part of his training for the Triple Nickel, he was assigned Platoon Sergeant, Headquarters Company, 555 Parachute Infantry Battalion.

In January 1946, Ike met Herman Jackson, the man who would eventually become his best friend and his partner in crime. 'We were in the same weapons company of the Triple Nickel and were attending jump school together,' Ike recalled. 'An instructor was teaching a class about 81mm mortars. I asked a question and Jack, who was sitting behind me, answered it. I turned around to look at him and thought: "I've seen him somewhere before." After class, Jack came up to me and said: "Do I know you?" I thought about it and said: "Didn't I see you at a Goldsboro nightclub with a girl?" Jack said: "Yeah, that was Hilda and I hope she wasn't your girl." I laughed and we hit it off. Jack, who was about my age, told me he was from Alabama, and that at one time his family owned a farm there. He would ride with me from Fort Bragg to Goldsboro to see Hilda, who later became his wife. I ended up dating Hilda's sister, who was prettier than Jack's girl.'

Herman Jackson was tall, mustached and as charming as Ike. His gray eyes were unusual for a black man, and for that reason, Ike gave Jack the nickname 'Eyes.' Later, a U.S. Customs agent who investigated the Atkinson organization would insist in an interview with the author that the unusual color of Jack's eyes were the result of contact lenses. The Customs agent claimed to have seen Jack put them on in a prison cell. He said he read a report that indicated Jackson's eyes were blue, but when he went to interrogate Jackson, his eyes were gray. But Ike dismisses the agents' claims. 'The color of Jack's eyes was real; that's all I can say.'

Jack had a bad habit of getting married but not divorcing his previous wife. 'When Jack married Hilda, he was already married to a woman in Alabama,' Ike recalled. 'I didn't know that until a jury indicted him while we were at Fort Bragg. Jack was found guilty, and it looked as if he would be thrown out of the Army. I convinced the company commander to go to Jack's defense. He did, and it made a difference. Jack was fined and put on probation, but he wasn't kicked out of the Army.'

THE TRIPLE NICKEL was still all black and segregated, as were all the other units in the U.S. military, but that changed on December 9, 1947, a day that has become known as 'Integration Day.' The previous July, U.S. President Harry S. Truman had issued Executive Order 9981, which declared 'equality of treatment and opportunity for all persons in the armed forces without regard to race, color, religion or national origin.' 'Integration Day' was marked by a special ceremony at Fort Bragg. Ike and other members of the 555th were briefed and then marched out to the parade ground where an aide to General Gavin read an eight-line 'order of integration' while the soldiers stood at attention. General Gavin then told the men to stand at ease and welcomed them into the 82nd Airborne Division.

On July 31, 1948, the Chicago Defender, one of the country's most influential black-owned newspapers, published the headline: 'President Truman Wipes Out Segregation in the Armed Forces.' In reality, though, nothing changed immediately, and it was not until after the Korean War that full integration of the armed forces was achieved. Still, Ike was impressed. 'The Truman Declaration was a step in the right direction. Sure it took time for the military to change, but I knew it would never be the same. After that big event Truman became my president, and it was a real honor to serve under General Gavin. In fact, I had the pleasure of shaking his hand. All the blacks who served under General Gavin thought he was a saint. We respected and admired him for his fairness. No white commander had a better reputation than General Gavin.'

It would take more than an executive order from the commander-in-chief, however, to change the status quo. Discrimination and racism persisted in the military and got so bad that in May 1956, eight years after 'separate but equal' was banned in the military, Ike felt compelled to write a letter to Adam Clayton Powell, a leading African-American congressman from Harlem. In his letter, Ike, who, at the time was assigned to Fort Benning, Georgia, complained about discrimination in housing and in the assignments black soldiers received. 'An unwritten law of the Army is (that) a certain percentage of Negroes will be assigned to certain units in the Army,' Ike wrote. 'Certain commanders tell their classification officers they want so many Negroes in their unit.' He concluded his letter by charging that the Army 'is not doing enough toward integration. I think from experiences that the white soldier is as ready as he will ever be to accept integration. The only thing holding back integration is the diehard commanders who are getting by giving orders and no one will contest them.' Ike offered to go to Washington 'in the near future with facts and figures about this segregation here at Fort Benning.' But Congressman Powell never replied.

Ike's challenge to the military's status quo did not hurt his career, however. In September 1950, the Army promoted Ike to the rank of master sergeant with six stripes. Master sergeant, a non-commissioned army rank just above sergeant first class and before the position of sergeant major was created, was the highest rank an enlisted man could attain at the time. 'I felt really good. I was about to turn 25 years old, and I was one of the youngest master sergeants in the military. It was a promotion so I got a nice increase in pay, but as far as getting my fellow soldier's respect, it didn't change a thing. I always had it.'

The young master sergeant was already a kind of 'dispute mediator' who would be called upon by his superior officers to mediate the disputes of lack soldiers and their families. 'Mediating was a part of my unofficial duties and sometimes it could be a real headache. Once while assigned to a unit in Germany, I had a black superior officer, a captain whose name was James E. Hill. He was married but also had a German girlfriend on the side. His wife knew about her, got fed up and threw the captain out of the house. I had to go over to their place to settle them down because they were making all kind of noise. The captain was threatening to break down the door. The wife recognized me and let me into her apartment. She was calm at first, but then she got worked up and began cursing her husband and his German girlfriend, and only got madder. She had a fire extinguisher in her hand and was going to use it on Captain Hill. Finally, I calmed them down and got things back to normal. That was the kind of thing I was called on to mediate.'

MILITARY LIFE WAS beautiful. Yes, the marriage with Helen had not worked out, but Ike had a son with her, and in 1952 he married Atha, a woman from Goldsboro. 'I met Atha in 1949. She lived right across the street from my family. She was not as pretty as my first wife, but I liked her personality. I had dated Atha's older sister twice before Atha and I got together. Atha was pregnant when we got married. I didn't know it at the time, but Atha liked liquor. When she had that first drink she couldn't stop. Later, it became a dangerous situation when I was dealing drugs.'

Ike continued to find the military adventurous. When he was not performing his duties or spending time with his growing family, Ike played in the big craps games at payday and the two- to three-day poker marathons, and the money continued to roll in. Indeed, it never stopped flowing. Military pay amounted to a paltry couple of hundred dollars a month, but Ike always carried a fat wad of cash around with him. Marijuana was pretty easy to get in the military, and Ike was constantly offered it but declined. He never did try illegal drugs. His highs came through gambling.

THE BEAUTIFUL LIFE changed on December 1 1952, because of Ike's passion for gambling. Ike joined a craps game in the day room of the headquarters company, First Battalion, 30 Regimental Combat Team, at Fort Benning, Georgia. Ike was now a second lieutenant. 'With the Korean War on, the military academies were not graduating enough officers,' Ike recalled. 'I met the qualifications for second lieutenant, so it was a pretty easy move up in rank.'

Ike was a commissioned officer now, but the soldiers in the gambling games were enlisted men; fraternization with them was a serious violation of the Uniform Code of Military Justice. That was bad enough, but one night, Ike removed the second lieutenant insignia from his uniform, another serious violation. About thirty minutes into the craps game, First Lieutenant Carl Cooper, the battalion duty officer at the time, entered the day room and told the gambling soldiers to 'break up the game right now.' Cooper asked about the ownership of a certain automobile parked outside the building, but he received no reply. Then he noted that Ike was wearing a trench coat containing the insignia of the rank of second lieutenant on the right shoulder only.

'Are you a lieutenant,' Cooper asked Ike.

'No, my buddies are playing a trick on me,' Ike replied and he removed the insignia on the right shoulder and threw it on the floor. Then Ike coolly picked up the pot of money he had just won and left.

The Army, however, brought Ike before a military court of review. In testifying, Ike explained that, except for that instance, he had never been in any difficulty in military or civilian life, and that he wanted to remain in the military. Five officers, all having the rank of captain who knew Ike for a period extending from five months to five years, testified on his behalf. They said he performed his duties either 'very satisfactory or excellently,' that his reputation among his acquaintances was good or satisfactory, that 'he measured up with the best officers in terms of efficiency and moral character,' and that he 'was an all-around outstanding officer and gentleman.'

Not impressed, the board of review took a hard line and found him guilty of 'knowingly making a false statement with intent to deceive in violation of article 107 of the Uniform Code of Military Justice, and gambling with enlisted men, in violation of article 134 of the Code.' Ike's sentence—dismissal from the Army and a fine of $500.

Ike was now in a heap of trouble, but thanks to his exemplary military career and friends in the right places, he managed to get the conviction overturned. 'I was stripped of my second lieutenant rank, and instead of going back to the rank of master sergeant, I became a staff sergeant. I was assigned to infantry school, but I had to resign my commission and then re-enlist.'

AFTER RESIGNING HIS commission, Ike took 30 days off before re-enlisting; he ached for the military life and vowed that he would do his best to redeem himself in the eyes of the brass. In October 1954, Ike was off to Korea as part of the First Battalion, 32nd Infantry. The Korean War began in the pre-dawn hours of June 25 1950, when the North Korean Army crossed the 38th Parallel and invaded South Korea. U.S.

forces entered the war on the side of South Korea, but when the Americans pushed the North Koreans across the 38th Parallel into North Korea, China entered the conflict. The war reached a stalemate in July 1951 and remained so until July 1953. By the time Ike's unit reached Korea, the war had wound down.

Assigned to the operations section, Ike worked long hours reorganizing the section, hoping his hard work would help him make master sergeant once again. But there was no war; so the Army did not need any new master sergeants. Still, Ike's effort did get him noticed, and he was recommended for and received a commendation ribbon for meritorious service performed from September 13 1954, to July 27 1955.

Ike returned to his new assignment at the Infantry School in Fort Benning and served there until 1957 when he was transferred to the 82nd Airborne Division at Fort Bragg. After a couple of routine years at Fort Bragg, Ike got some exciting news: the Army would be sending his unit, the 505th Parachute Infantry Regiment, to Germany. Ike could not only take his family with him, but his personal possessions as well, including his beige top Pontiac convertible. While the Atkinsons got ready for Germany, Ike got some more good news. He had been promoted to his old rank of master sergeant.

When Ike arrived with his unit in Mainz, Germany, a picturesque city located on the West Bank of the Rhine River, political tensions were high. Yet, life for Ike remained largely routine as he adjusted to his new setting. He heard through the military grapevine that gambling flourished at the NCO clubs all across the European continent, so he looked forward to his tour in Germany, expecting it to be another bold adventure.

Winston Churchill, Great Britain's World War II leader, popularized the term 'Iron Curtain' to signify the ideological, symbolic and physical boundary dividing Europe into the two separate and distinct areas after the war. The Cold War had set in, and the Iron Curtain had divided Germany into West Germany and communist East Germany. And the divided city of Berlin was surrounded by East Germany. The U.S., France, Great Britain and the Soviet Union all occupied sections of the city. A new Joint United States European Command (USAREUR) was established on August 1 1952, with Heidelberg as its headquarters.

More than 85,000 U.S. troops were stationed in Europe. Ike was based at Lee Barracks in Mainz, but all of Western Europe would eventually be his oyster. 'I got off the plane, settled my family and headed to the local NCO club. When I got there, I did not see any poker or craps games going on. Where the hell was the gambling? Someone told me that I could find plenty of gambling at the Ramstein Air Force Base at Kaiserslautern, which was a small city about 60 miles from Mainz. I wasn't working yet, so I drove there in my convertible. Being black, I must have stuck out like a bubba in Harlem. Later, I would hear some brothers complain about racism, but the German people treated me good. I'm sure I must have had some bad incidents, but I really can't recall any.

'But, boy, was life good! The dollar was strong, so living was cheap. I knew I would soon be making money gambling, so I got my wife a maid to help her out. Times were still tough for a lot of Germans, so every time the maid came over she brought her son, daughter and her son's daughter with her, and I had to feed the entire lot. I had plenty of work to do at Lee Barracks, eight to ten hours a day during the week, but when the weekend came I hopped into my convertible and drove like a mad man to Ramstein.'

'I was in heaven. I never ran into a gambling den like the one they had at Ramstein. It had the biggest craps and poker games at any U.S. military base in Europe. It was loaded with GIs and the first three days after they got paid was a gravy train for me. On a good night, I could make $1,000 to $1,500. I built a bankroll of $20,000. I lived good and still saved money. For a change of pace, I went to Wiesbaden and Darmstadt, where a lot of gambling went on at the officers clubs on the U.S. bases there.'

U.S. soldiers, sailors, airmen and diplomats were not the only personnel gambling at U.S. military establishments. Wherever Ike went, he seemed to bump into defense contractors. 'Long before the public learned about Dick Cheney and his ties to Halliburton, I knew about defense contractors. The Cold War was big business, and wherever there were military bases you could find defense contractors. They always had money to burn, and they didn't care that my buddies and I were black. They only cared that our money be green.'

Ike had one thing to worry about, though. 'My wife didn't like Germany and she started drinking. I was gone all the time, either working or gambling, but Atha wanted me home; she was lonely. I gave her money but she was still not happy.'

IKE WAS NOT the only black gambler and hustler in Europe at the time, and being charismatic, Ike had no problem making friends with many of them, all of whom were like-minded adventurers. Many of his new friends were retired U.S. servicemen who stayed in Germany because of the gambling, friendly women and inexpensive lifestyle. Many of them lived in apartments near the U.S. military bases and became part of his informal social network. Ike could only marvel at some of their gambling skills.

The heavyset Eddie Wooten was an old friend whom Ike had known since 1952, having served with him in the same battalion at Fort Campbell, Kentucky. Ike considered Wooten, who had curly hair, dark skin and a broad nose, a gambling all-star; he played all the games of chance well—cards, craps and pool. Wooten was cocky, too. An associate recalled the time he went with Wooten to pick up a friend and had to wait in front of his apartment. The friend was late, and when he showed, Wooten blasted him in a high pitched, mocking voice; 'Hey, brother. What's going on? You know who I am? I am Eddie Wooten, and wherever I go, I am the biggest dude. So I don't wait for no one!'

Wooten was popular, and he introduced Ike to many of the brothers. There was Berlin (no one knew his real name), another all around card player who had been in Germany, drifting, one of the few in the group who had not served in the military. Berlin was a real chatterbox who could not shut his mouth, even during the most intense moments of a card or craps game. Ike would pick up Berlin occasionally and go gambling at Bitburg, 31 miles northeast of Luxembourg, where Bitburg Air Force Base and Spangdahlem Air Force Bases were located. The intelligent Ed Russell, who was married to a Dutch girl, had a photographic memory for the cards dealt in a poker game, so he didn't have to resort to cheating to get an edge. John Roy, a New Orleans native, balding, nondescript and always with a smile on his face, was a big time craps shooter and the only white man who regularly hung with the band of brothers.

The hulking Ellis Sutton, whom Ike met during his German tour and who gave him the nickname 'Ike,' was still in Europe. Sutton was the best 'swing' player Ike had ever seen, and he never seemed to miscalculate in a poker game. 'Sutton was a mound of a man with big hands, which gave him an advantage in a card game,' Ike recalled. 'So with his skill it was easy for him to mess with the deck. Deal him five cards and he would have six. He always hid an extra card and you would never know it.'

Ellis Sutton came to Germany about 1958, bringing with him Pratt Benthall, a slender, light-skinned gambler from New Jersey. Ike got to meet Benthall before he had a run-in with the German law. Benthall was speeding in the German countryside outside Kaiserslautern and killed a German kid who was walking along the road. Benthall was thrown in jail and his brother had to come from New Jersey and pay $10,000 to bail him out. Benthall returned to the U.S. and managed to avoid going to the jail.

Then there was Peter Rabbit, the nickname of Herman Lee Gaillard, but no one ever called him by that name. Born in La Grange, North Carolina, Peter Rabbit was nice looking, of medium height and build, and one of the best skin players around. Ike met Robert Johnson, a tall, pop-eyed, light skinned brother from Greensboro, North Carolina, at Johnny's Keller, a popular bar in Kaiserslautern owned by James Wilkins, a Pennsylvania native. When Johnson got excited, a vein would pop up in the middle of his forehead. Ike considered Johnson, a retired Air Force man, one of the biggest hustlers in Europe. He trafficked in contraband PX supplies and could count cards in a poker game like few other gamblers. That is why he drove a Mercedes and could be seen tooling around Germany and France with his good looking Corsican girlfriend.

Later, DEA intelligence and press reports claimed that Atkinson and Johnson were protégés of Wilkins who, the DEA further alleged, was involved in a variety of criminal activities from stealing PX supplies to prostitution to narcotics trafficking. Sources say there was a Black Masonic Club, based in Frankfurt, but according to Atkinson the club was not a front for Wilkins; it was totally legitimate. Its membership consisted of black GIs in Europe interested in Masonic activities. 'Both Jack and I did not belong to any Masonic Club,' Atkinson said. 'Johnny (James Wilkins) was a club member, but he did not organize it for criminal activities.' For a variety of reasons, some from the band of brothers would leave and head back to the U.S., while many others would stay with the group, motivated by the camaraderie and adventure it generated. Later when Ike moved to Bangkok, many of the brothers in his circle would become part of the international criminal enterprise he built.

IKE HAD DODGED the court marshal bullet once, in 1952, so it would seem highly improbable that military lightning would strike twice. But it did, in 1959, during Ike's German tour. During a two-month period, Ike and Eddie Wooten had gambled several times in the officers club at the U.S. military base at Wiesbaden. Wooten was no longer in the service and had never been an officer. Ike was in the Army but was not an officer at the time. They should not have been gambling there, but neither the club management nor the officers seemed to care. After all, green is green. Nothing would have happened except that one of the gamblers who had been steadily losing a lot of money to Ike and Wooten, became a sore loser and decided to blow the whistle on them. Wooten was arrested, convicted and spent five months in jail. Ike was court marshaled again. He was not thrown out of the military, but his rank was reduced from six to three stripes and his pay was docked accordingly. 'I had a good lawyer, who was recommended by some of the friends in my unit. It was not the type of charge that got a soldier with my record and length of service thrown out of the military.'

'It was another devastating blow to my military career. Captain Hill, the same man who had the dispute with his wife over the German girlfriend, said to me: '"What the hell were you thinking?" He told me that the military police had actually been watching me for a couple of months, collecting evidence against me. Demoted in rank, I now had to work under a soldier who had been under me. When I would see my new boss, he would say to me: "Well, if it isn't Mr. Operations himself." It didn't bother me, though; I just laughed. I really had no business in that officers club. I had done wrong. But worst of all, I got caught.'

Four years later, shortly after his retirement from the Army while visiting a friend at Fort Bragg, Ike felt the impact of the incident. At the security gate, Ike was told to park his car. After a 30-minute wait, a captain appeared and asked Ike to come to his office. When they got there, the captain asked:

'Are you Leslie Atkinson?'

'Yes, I am.'

The captain then pulled out some paperwork and began reading off a list of names.

'Do you know Eddie Wooten?'

'Uh, uh.'

'Do you know Ellis Sutton?'

'Yes.'

'Robert Johnson?'

'Yes.' Ike now sensed that the interrogation had something to do with gambling.

Then the captain said, 'I have an order from my commanding officer. You will not lose your commissary privileges, but every time you come here we will be watching you.'

For Ike, it was no sweat. He wrote off Fort Bragg like a bad debt and did not go there anymore. Little gambling was going on at Fort Bragg anyway.

IKE COMPLETED HIS two-year tour in Germany and then was reassigned back to Fort Bragg, the permanent home of the 82nd Airborne. He had spent 18 years in the military and was almost ready to retire. Since he had been around military bases all of his adult life and would, as a retiree, enjoy military privileges such as access to the PX, he began to look for a suitable house close to a military base. Finding nothing he liked, he decided to return to Goldsboro, the home of Seymour Johnson Air Force Base. Because of his gambling talents, Ike had saved from $40,000 to $60,000, and he used it to build his own home in the newly developed Neuse Heights.

After retiring, Ike had no intention of finding a steady, routine job in the civilian sector. Gambling was his chosen profession, and he would continue the adventurous life he had pursued in the military. Ike's pal Eddie Wooten had organized a regular high stakes poker game in Kaiserslautern, Germany, as well as in Madrid, Spain, where the players included U.S. Embassy staff and well-connected American businessmen and members of the Spanish elite who did not mind losing their money. Ike could go to Charleston, South Carolina, about 150 miles from Goldsboro, and take a first-class flight on the so-called Embassy Flight, which the U.S. diplomatic core used, and fly directly to Madrid, Spain, and then on to other major cities worldwide. In fact, one could travel around the world via the Embassy Flight. From Madrid, Ike often took a military hop to Ramstein Air Force Base near Kaiserslautern and usually head for Eddie Wooten's place in the city, unless, that is, he wanted to stay and gamble at the Ramstein Air Base's NCO club.

Ike would fly back and forth between Charleston and Madrid every few weeks. Sometimes he would hear of a big game in some exotic locale, such as Greece or Turkey, and he would use an Embassy Flight to fly there. He had a valid passport and a military ID and, of course, could fly on a military plane so long as space was available. If some of his buddies did not have military privileges, no problem. He would fix them up with phony military documents. 'When I came home to see my family, I put more money in our savings. I was doing more than okay; I was living the life of a Cool Hand Luke…a professional hustler.'

But Ike's hustle was not above board. To tilt the odds of winning in his favor, he went to New York City and bought loaded dice and a magnet that he could place under a craps table and influence the course of the game. 'From an early age, I knew that to win in gambling consistently, you have to give yourself an edge or leave the game alone. That's why I would never go to a casino and gamble where I have no control of the games and would not have the odds in my favor.'

Ike and Robert Johnson took their shady game to Rota, Spain, a town of about 27,000 people south of Madrid in the Andalusia region. Rota is the home of a joint Spanish-U.S. naval base and also hosts U.S. Marine and Air Force units. With so many military personnel, Rota was a hot gambling haunt that Ike and Johnson frequented when they could get away from Madrid. They hoped to break (clean out) a slick gambler known simply as Chief, a chief petty officer at the U.S. Naval Base at Rota. Heavyset and legendary for the amount of money he carried on him, Chief took on all gamblers but nobody could beat him; in fact, Ike and Johnson had earlier lost thousands of dollars to him. After half an hour and three huge bets, the hustlers broke Chief, taking him for $38,000. A magnet placed strategically under the gambling table helped Ike and Johnson achieve their objective.

IN RETIREMENT THE charismatic Atkinson continued to meet and befriend retired military servicemen who shared his gambling passion and enjoyed the life of a hustler. In 1964, Ike hit it off with Daniel Burch, a tall, slender light-skinned brother who sounded southern, although his hometown was Akron, Ohio. Born in 1940, Burch became the youngest member of the band of brothers. When he left the Army in 1961, he wanted to be a professional gambler, but did not know anything about it. 'In the Army, when payday came around, I'd gamble and lose every dollar I had earned,' Burch explained. 'I decided to stay in Germany because it was such an exciting place. I met a couple of hustlers named Jimmy Merrill and Norman Young, and they taught me the ropes about gambling. I specialized in craps and began hustling. I bought some magnetized dice and a magnet and I was in business.'

In 1964, Ike and Burch met Jimmy Smedley, a likeable laid back ex-soldier who was living in Kaiserslautern. Smedley was the odd man in the band of brothers, an old fashioned sucker who did not have a clue about gambling, except how to lose his money. Smedley's apartment became a hangout and crash pad for army buddies coming to town or passing through; a place they would gamble, drink and party all night long. Smedley always seemed to be at some stage of inebriation. When his pad got crowded, Smedley's Dutch girlfriend would have to make room in the bed she shared with Smedley for one of his buddies. Jimmy Smedley and Herman Jackson became two of Ike's closest friends. In a short while, all three would be operating in an exotic locale, using a different hustle.

CHAPTER 3

Bangkok Calling

HERMAN JACKSON HAD retired in December 1962, a little over a year before Ike did. The two old friends kept in touch, and whenever their paths crossed, they fraternized and enjoyed each other's company. Jack was not much of a gambler and what he knew about the game he learned from Ike. Yet Jack had a way of sniffing out opportunity, and this knack complemented Ike's social and entrepreneurial skills.

In early 1966, Jack hopped the Embassy Flight to visit a friend named Smitty in Korea, but upon arrival at Bangkok, he was bumped off the flight to make room for diplomatic personnel. Jack did not mind the idea of waiting for the next available flight. He had a liking for Thai women ever since he had ogled some attractive Thai international stewardesses in the Los Angeles airport, having noticed the emblem on their lapels indicating they were from Thailand.

In the mid-1960s, no place on Earth offered an American male traveler better opportunities for hustling women and having a good time than did Bangkok. Once considered a backwater of Asia—an exotic locale known for its friendly people, Buddhist temples, beautiful flowers and languid klongs, or canals, the city changed to become a major tourist destination. Most of the visitors came from the U.S., even though a war raged in neighboring Vietnam.

Arriving at Don Muang airport, 12 miles north of the city, visitors took a taxi and sped down a four-lane super highway that passed a mix of the old and the new, imposing advertising signs, rice fields with water buffalo, makeshift concrete office buildings and perhaps a fisherman or two casting their nets in one of the klongs, eventually reaching the chaotic and car-clogged city of Bangkok. In 1968, British writer Alex Waugh, who had not visited Bangkok since 1964, noted in an article he wrote for the National Review magazine that 'not only the appearance but the climate of the city has changed, with the heavy sunlight reflected from solid concrete.' He added that the tourist boom had included Bangkok as 'a five-day must in every package holiday. Every hotel, every restaurant was crowded.' At the time Bangkok had several hundred first class hotels.

The biggest reason for the tourist boom was Bangkok's trans-formation into a must visit rest-and-recuperation (R&R) center for American troops fighting the Vietnam War. Bangkok was a wide-open town, much like the Wild West of American history fame, but without the violence. Within Bangkok city limits, there were 2,000 nightclubs with entertainment that included everything from nude dancers and live sex acts to Filipino bands and big show business acts from Europe and the U.S. Most of the GIs headed for the neon-lit, garish nightclub and massage parlor strips along Patpong or New Petchaburi Road, which in the mid-1960s was on the city outskirts, virtually in the rice paddies. 'The Thai government had a sensible policy to handle the nightlife,' explained Peter Finucane, a native of Bath, England, who arrived in Bangkok in 1966 and eventually went to work as a journalist for the Bangkok Post, Thailand's leading English-language newspaper. 'It didn't want a lot of GIs going into the city center and potentially causing problems. So it built New Petchaburi Road on the city's outskirts to accommodate the nightlife. It worked out well. Many Thais didn't even know that a lot of American GIs were in the city.'

In the mid-1960s, New Petchaburi Road was a two-mile strip of bars and massage parlors that lined both sides of the road and beckoned the war-weary American soldier to come and enjoy the company of pretty, scantily clad young women eager and willing to serve the soldier's every physical need. 'The women treated men as kings,' Ike recalled. 'And a good time was not all you could find in Bangkok. The black market was booming, and you could buy anything…cigarettes, rifles, ammunition… even army trucks.'

JACK LIKED WHAT he saw and could experience in Bangkok. The first night in town, he stumbled upon La Fee's, a sweaty girl-jammed hole-in-the-wall bar located on New Petchaburi Road in the forecourt of the U.S. military-rented Siam Hotel. La Fee's rocked and with the Thai women vying to catch his attention, Jack was in good-time heaven. 'Jack was soon up to his old tricks,' Ike recalled. 'He eventually married three Thai women, and I'm not certain he divorced any of them.'

Jack bumped into the bar owner, Luchai Ruviwat, a clean-cut, polite, formal mannered Chinese Thai. Jack and Luchai struggled to be heard above the din of Motown music, but Jack got a sense that Luchai had a head for business. Luchai regaled Jack with stories about the moneymaking opportunities in Vietnam generated by the use of Military Payment Certificates (MPCs).

The U.S. military first issued MPCs (also known as 'script') in September 1946 as a response to the large number of U.S. dollars that American servicemen used and circulated in post-World War II Europe. Many local citizens in the countries where U.S. soldiers operated did not trust their own country's currency, given the unstable political and economic situation in post-World War II Europe, and preferred to accept payment for goods and services in dollars for less than the official conversion rates. So American troops being paid in U.S. dollars were able to get a much more favorable conversion rate by converting dollars on the black market for the local currency. However, this practice undermined the currencies of the countries involved.

In Vietnam, the use of MPCs served the same purpose as in post World War II Europe—to limit the number of dollars circulating in the local economy but was further designed to prevent the enemy from obtaining U.S. dollars that they could use to buy guns and other supplies on the open international market. Between August 31, 1965, and October 21 1968, the U.S. military issued a 641 series of MPCs in Vietnam in five cent, ten cent, twenty-five cent, one dollar, five dollar and ten dollar denominations.

Both Ike and Jack had served in Korea and were familiar with MPCs and had exchanged them for profit on the black market there. Ike remembered how every two weeks in Korea the military would change the MPC notes, so the old notes would need to be surrendered for new ones. If a GI was dealing with MPCs on the black market, his 'customers' would be stuck with the old, useless notes unless they had used them to purchase goods from the military Post Exchanges through proxies before the conversion. But easy money could be made by any U.S. person who had U.S. dollars to buy MPCs from these merchants and could convert them back to dollars at the official exchange rate upon leaving Vietnam

Excited by the prospect of making some big bucks, Jack called Ike whom he knew would be at Wooten's apartment in Spain. 'Jack was a smart guy who could recognize an opportunity, but he was not a leader,' Ike explained. 'He depended on me to get things going.' Ike was not at Wooten's apartment, but Jack left a message for Ike. 'Come immediately to Bangkok. You won't regret it.'

When Ike got the message, he thought: 'Why should I go to Bangkok? I'm making good money gambling here in Europe. Besides, I don't know much about Bangkok, or Southeast Asia for that matter.' But Ike trusted Jack's instincts and he knew something big could be up. When Ike finally caught up with Jack by phone, Jack told Ike about the thriving black market in MPCs. Ike knew he had to make the move. At this time, Ike was seeing a lot of his young pal, Daniel Burch, who had his own plans to go to Bangkok. Burch heard big money could be made at the card and craps games flourishing in Saigon and at the U.S. bases in Thailand, and he was itching to make a move.

BY 1966 THE U.S. had no better ally in Southeast Asia than Thailand, which it supported in an effort to repulse communist infiltration from North Vietnam. With its 35 million inhabitants, three million of whom lived in Bangkok, Thailand covered an area slightly larger than Spain. Strategically, Thailand was an important American ally. By 1970, the total U.S. aid for the country totaled $500 million.

As part of the deal with the U.S., Thailand, as early as 1961, agreed to allow the deployment of U.S. airplanes and the construction of U.S. bases on its soil. The U.S. Government asked Thailand to contribute to the Vietnam War effort against North Vietnam by permitting the U.S. to base its principal aerial attack force on its territory. Thailand willingly complied. The U.S. military establishment in Thailand initially consisted of five major air bases and eventually about 50,000 U.S. military personnel. The bases were located at Don Muang, the headquarters of the Royal Thai Air Force, adjacent the main civilian airport of Thailand, located about 17 miles north of Bangkok; Korat, located at Thailand's third largest city by the same name, about 117 miles northeast of Bangkok; Nakhon Phanom in northeast Thailand, next to the Laotian border in a politically unstable area; Tahkli, about 160 miles northeast of Bangkok, the smallest town adjacent to a United States Air Force-occupied base; and Ubon, a Royal Thai airbase also in the northeastern part of Thailand.

In 1967, a year after Atkinson and Burch arrived in Thailand, a new base, Utapao, was constructed at Sattahip Navy Base in southeast Thailand about 120 miles south of Bangkok. When President Lyndon Johnson's administration began operation Rolling Thunder, the U.S. aerial bombardment campaign conducted against North Vietnam from March 2 1965 to November 2 1968, several tactical fighter and reconnaissance wings moved into the bases. Thailand became the home to F-105 fighter wings whose primary mission was bombing targets in North Vietnam. Eventually, up to eighty percent of the North Vietnam-bound sorties flown by the U.S. originated from Thailand.

Most of the 50,000 U.S. troops were in Thailand to support the airbases and logistics network, but U.S. personnel also included counter-insurgency advisors, technical advisors, training consultants and professional consultants. To gain a military presence in Thailand, however, Uncle Sam had to agree to maintain a low profile. The Thais were hedging their bets on the Vietnam War's outcome and got the U.S. to agree that no mention of air raids against North Vietnam from their soil would be made.

Still, everybody who operated and lived around U.S. military bases, including Dan Burch, knew what was happening in Vietnam and Thailand, and rumors abounded about how gambling flourished there. Burch had a friend with whom he was planning to go to Southeast Asia, but that did not pan out. He heard that Ike was heading to Thailand and contacted him.

The friends agreed to go to Thailand together. Burch was in Kaiserslautern at the time and went to Frankfurt to see a man known as 'Mr. Personnel,' who could forge orders allowing military personnel to fly space available anywhere in the world, using the Embassy Flight. Burch flew from Frankfurt to Madrid and joined Ike for the Embassy Flight to Bangkok.

Ike had no doubt he had made the right move. Some buddies from his band of brothers had already moved or were planning to go to Bangkok. Robert Johnson, for instance, had opened a little bar called Johnny's Place, which Ike heard was doing quite well. Arriving in Bangkok on March 1 1966, Atkinson and Burch checked into the Bangkok Hotel on 49/4 New Petchaburi Road, close to Johnny's bar. Jackson had reserved a room for them. The travelers felt good after their long journey, which had included a stop in India. Coming from Western Europe, the heat of Bangkok was insufferable, but the hotel's rooms were air-conditioned, and they had a private bath, private phone and even an FM musical system.

Soon after their arrival, a man named Mr. Yeung came by the Bangkok Hotel and informed Ike that he was Mr. Jackson's lawyer. Yeung explained that Mr. Jackson was in Saigon on business and would be back in a couple of days. 'Please make yourself comfortable and let me know if you need anything.' Ike learned that Jack had purchased a part interest in La Fee's, and so Ike and Burch dropped by the bar to check out Jack's new investment. The bar was crowded and smoky but sizzling with action and crawling with many young girls. Despite La Fee's small size, Ike felt as if he was in a candy shop. 'I met Luchai Ruviwat, Jack's business partner the first day I was in Bangkok,' Ike recalled. 'We called him "Chai." He was reserved and didn't talk much; he liked to listen. But he was easy going and fit into our group. I never met a person in Bangkok who said he didn't like Chai."

When Jack returned from Vietnam, Ike introduced him to Burch. Jack described the MPC scene in Saigon and the amount of money he had made on his recent "business" trip. He confirmed that the gambling scene in Vietnam and on U.S. airbases in Thailand was red hot.

Jack agreed to go with Ike and Burch to the Korat air base and check out the gambling scene and then to Saigon to observe the MPC scam first-hand and do some more gambling. Johnson decided to come along as well. The four men won a few bucks at Korat and then headed for Saigon, where they experienced a side of Vietnam that had nothing to do with the war.

BY 1966 THE Vietnam War was raging, but Saigon was an odd kind of wartime city. With two million people living within 21 square miles, Saigon rivaled Tokyo for the dubious distinction of having the world's greatest population density. In addition to overcrowding, the city's 150,000 cars and a half-million bicycles and motorbikes clogged the transportation system, reducing vehicular movement to a crawl. Saigon's poor drainage and almost non-existent sewage and garbage collection system had turned the city into a cesspool. Everywhere, one saw beggars, many of whom were refugees from the war-torn battle areas in the countryside.

The U.S. impact on Saigon was enormous. About 25,000 U.S. troops and 5,000 American contractors were based in the city, and tight security measures were in effect around all U.S. facilities. One could see U.S. military police, rigid with attention and armed with shotguns, standing outside the American Embassy. In front of them were concrete-filled barrels firmly anchored to the sidewalk to prevent bomb-laden cars from ploughing through and hitting the Embassy. One U.S. military policeman told *Look* magazine in May

1966: 'I've been here for two years and I don't trust any of them (Vietnamese). I've caught old men with grenades and schoolboys with Claymore mines stashed in their book bags. I guess the bastards think they are some kind of hero to the people.'

Saigon was also awash with corruption. Just around the corner from the U.S. Embassy was the black market known as 'PX Alley,' where one could find everything from vintage champagne to exotic cameras to air conditioners. In November 1966, the Associated Press published a six-part series investigating the corruption. The authors estimated that a small number of Vietnamese and Americans were making a killing off the war, amounting to half-a-million dollars daily, perhaps more. They concluded that of the $1.2 billion in aid the U.S. poured into Vietnam, as much as 40 percent was wasted because of graft and corruption.

Many war-weary GIs streamed from their outlying jungle bases into Saigon for R & R, and at the height of the Vietnam War, some 500 bars with names like the Eve, Bunny Club, Blue Angel, San Francisco Bar, the King Bar and the Seattle Bar enticed the thrill-seeking American servicemen. Providing entertainment were an estimated 5,000 bar girls and dancers. At night the city crawled with black market money-changers, and with an estimated 29,000 prostitutes available, sex-hungry GIs could find one of nearly any age. To have a good time, though, a GI would have to get an early start. By 11 p.m. the bars were closed and a curfew took effect.

In May 1966, Secretary of State Dean Rusk and Secretary of Defense Robert McNamara squared off with Senator William Fulbright, Chairman of the Senate Foreign Relations Committee, one of the staunchest critics of the Vietnam War, before the Foreign Relations Committee, over Fulbright's charge that Saigon had become an 'American brothel.' 'It just isn't true,' Rusk insisted, while McNamara added this spin: 'I don't mean there are no prostitutes in Washington, but nobody has called Washington a brothel.' The statements of Rusk and McNamara reflected the myopia that characterized the U.S. Government's understanding of the situation in Vietnam.

In March 1966, about the time that Ike and Burch arrived in Bangkok, William Westmoreland, the U.S. Commander in Chief in Vietnam, initiated Operation Moose (Move Out of Saigon Expeditiously), an attempt to deal with the growing anti-Americanism in Saigon, exacerbated by the off-duty behavior of U.S. troops in the city. Henceforth, Saigon was off limits to combat soldiers on R & R. The move made Bangkok an even hotter destination for American GIs.

NEITHER IKE NOR any of his buddies were much concerned about the politics of Uncle Sam's battle with communism. They saw the large U.S. presence, not only in Vietnam but in all of Southeast Asia, and the disorder and the wide openness, particularly of Saigon, as providing another golden moneymaking opportunity, one that could potentially outstrip their 'Cold War' Western Europe experience. After a few days in Saigon, Ike and Burch were convinced that their future lay in the black market MPCs. Excited by the prospect, they returned to Bangkok, rented an apartment together and prepared to head back to Saigon. Loaded with American dollars, Ike began flying once a week on military aircraft, 'space available,' to the busy Tan Son Knut airbase in Saigon in pursuit of the new hustle. He rented part of a house from a friendly Vietnamese couple. The wife worked in the U.S. Embassy, and the husband, for the South Vietnamese government, while their daughter attended school in Europe.

Ike was happy to learn that the MPC certificates were not changed every couple of weeks as they had been in Korea. The

U.S. military did have rules requiring the GIs to exchange their dollars for MPCs only on U.S. bases, but Ike, Dan and the other brothers who got involved with MPCs, dealt off base with Indian exchange merchants who gave a better rate of return. For 100 American dollars, the Indian merchant gave Ike as much as $191 in MPCs.

Ike would put on his master sergeant uniform and hit the Army post offices (APOs) on Long Bin Road, a strategic transportation artery in Saigon. The Long Binh Army Depot served as the major supply base for U.S. Army personnel in Vietnam. The depot was more like a small city, replete with gift shops, snack bars, laundries, bowling alley and even a post office, where Ike used MPCs he bought on the black market to buy U.S. money orders at the official exchange rate and mail them back to Bangkok.

The road to Long Binh was a dangerous place to travel. Firefights with the Vietcong were frequent, and Ike would often hear the rat-tat-tat of gunfire. One day, he was riding down Long Bin Road on the back of a motorcycle taxi. He had dozed off, but the abrupt sound of gunfire startled him awake. Just then, the driver slammed on the brakes and the motorcycle dipped. Ike was flung out of the taxi and landed in a soggy trench along the side of the road. Ike lay there until the shooting stopped. After that experience, Ike began renting small cars to get around Saigon and Bien Hoa on his MPC errands.

Ike used the MPCs to purchase money orders in American dollars. After two days of work, Ike would have bought as much as $25,000 worth of U.S. money orders from local merchants who did business with GIs that he sent to Bangkok via the U.S. military postal system. It was a precautionary move. If the authorities ever stopped him on his way back to Bangkok and searched him, Ike would not have to explain why he was carrying so many money orders. But he also carried eight to ten bogus IDs with him as well, and that could have created a problem.

Ike and Dan Burch, who became known as 'Saigon Red' in Bangkok and Vietnam, bought authentic military IDs from Sylvia Bailey, a hustler they got to know in Germany. Bailey made a deal with a U.S. soldier who was stationed on a military base at Aschaffenburg, a large town in northwest Bavaria, and who had access to military IDs. One day, the soldier peeked through a keyhole and saw a warrant officer dialing a combination on a safe. When the warrant officer opened the safe, the soldier saw a stack of military IDs and ration cards. After hours, the soldier would sneak into the room, open the safe and take some of the IDs and ration cards. He sold them to Bailey, who paid for them with hashish she bought from a Jamaican dealer named Max, in exchange for some of the stolen ration cards. Max used the ration cards to buy gasoline. Burch paid Bailey about $20 for each stolen ID card and purchased as many as 20 at a time. Eventually, Mr. Yeung took Ike to Hong Kong, where they bought the special paper the U.S. military used to make their IDs, and Ike began to manufacture the fake IDs himself.

The amazing thing about the MPC scam—you could not get busted or go to jail. 'Two guys came to Bangkok from Spain.' Burch explained. 'I didn't know them, but they began going back and forth between Bangkok and Saigon and dealing in MPCs. They were not careful and carried some really bad looking fake IDs. They went to a post office in Saigon to exchange the MPCs for money orders one day, and the postal clerk became suspicious when he saw their military IDs and called the military police. They were arrested. One of them had a friend or relative who worked on one of the San Francisco newspapers. A reporter from the newspaper wrote a story about how "Americans were starving in Vietnamese jails." There was a lot of anti-war sentiment in the

U.S., so Uncle Sam pressured the Vietnamese government to release all Americans in Vietnamese jails. After that, we couldn't get busted. The U.S. and Vietnamese authorities were both too scared to do anything.'

In 1967, the Overseas Weekly, an alternative military newspaper, did an exposé of the MPC scam and identified Atkinson, Burch, Jackson and Johnson as 'The Bangkok Four.' Even with all the negative exposure, nothing happened to the Bangkok Four. It was business as usual and none of them had to pay anybody off to stay in the country.

LIKE IKE, BURCH was making thousands of dollars, but while Ike seemed content to play life by ear, Dan had a plan. 'I thought I had arrived,' Burch recalled. 'That's why I was in such a rush going back and forth between Bangkok and Saigon. Before too long, I had close to $100,000 stashed away in a Swiss bank. My goal was to salt away a quarter of a million dollars, buy an annuity, and then draw a monthly stipend. I would have it made for the rest of my life. But my trouble over MPCs with Jack ended my dream. I knew I couldn't make as much money gambling as I could have with MPCs, so I turned to drug trafficking, which made me a potential felon and exposed me to a life of crime.'

During his first trip to Saigon after arriving with Ike from Madrid, Burch was not impressed with how Jack had responded to a friend in need. He, Jack, Ike and Johnson had gone to the Plaza Hotel's mezzanine where they got into a craps game with some GIs and contractors. Ike lost all his money and asked Jack to loan him $300 so he could get back into the game. Jack said he didn't have any money, but Ike knew Jack was carrying some money orders and asked him what happened to them. 'I sent them to the U.S.,' Jack said. About two hours later, Jack had lost all his money in the craps game, but he reached into his back pocket and pulled out a $100 money order. Losing that amount, he reached again and pulled out another $100 money order. In all, Jack pulled out 12 one hundred dollar money orders and lost them all.

It was in the wee hours of the morning, and since all four brothers were cleaned out, they returned to Ike's hotel room. Ike was livid. He swore at Jack and demanded: 'Why did you lie to me about the money, man?' All Jack could do was look sheepish and say; 'I don't know, man. I don't know.'

Yet, Burch did not foresee any problems with Jack even when mild-mannered John Roy, the white brother who had migrated from Germany, called a meeting of the brothers who were in Bangkok at the time. Roy was staying with Ike and Dan, who lived together on Sukhumvit Road when they first came to Bangkok. At this point, Ike had returned to Goldsboro, North Carolina, for an extended visit. Atha and the kids had initially followed Ike to Bangkok, but as was the case in Germany, Atha did not like living overseas and quickly returned home. Ike, who was on a financial roll with the MPC scam, nevertheless had taken a break and returned home to keep his marriage together.

'I can still see the scene as if it was today,' Burch recalled. 'Roy, Johnson, George Pratt (an ex-GI, now retired, who had recently come to Thailand from Germany) and I were inside the house. The front door was open and Jack was sitting on the steps. He could look into the house and see Roy talking to us. Roy said: 'I've called you guys together to tell you I'm going back to Spain because Thailand isn't big enough for me and (pointing to Jack) him. Jack is a low-down son-of-a-bitch and he's not worth two dead flies. I'd rather see an ashtray at a card game than Jack. Jack doesn't want to see anybody with anything. If he sees you with two cents, he's going to try to figure out a way of getting it from you. Then even if he gets it, Jack's such a fool, he'll blow it and then try to get some more money from you. Jack is no good!'

'We could see Jack sitting with his head down, not saying anything. I said to myself: "Jack's not like that." At the time I respected Jack. Then John Roy said: "I'm leaving this country because it's not big enough for Herman Jackson and me. What good is it to stay in Thailand when, whatever you have, Jack is going to try to get it away from you. I like you guys, but I don't want to be around that bastard any longer!"'

John Roy did leave Bangkok. His plan was to save $100,000 and return to New Orleans and buy a car lot. Ike and Burch never did see Roy again, but as far as they know, he fulfilled his dream. Roy's tirade shocked the brothers, and they wondered what had gotten into him. Burch was early into his relationship with Jack, but eventually he would view Roy as a prophet. Little by little, Jack's actions would chip away at his best-laid plans.

One time, for instance, Burch, Johnson, Ike and some of the brothers were at Shorty's Place, a bar in Da Nang, Vietnam, owned by a man whom Jack had known from his service in the Triple Nickel. Jackson fancied himself a master chess player and challenged Burch to a game of chess. He went ballistic when Burch beat him easily. Jack angrily swept the chess pieces off the board, and they went flying in all directions. 'I started laughing,' Burch recalled. 'At the time, I didn't think Jack would take it out on me.' But troubled by Jack's changing relationship with him, Burch had begun observing Jack more closely when he was in the company of other military veterans and noted the deference with which he treated them. Burch eventually concluded that Jack did not respect him and was jealous of him because he was nearly two decades younger and had served only two years in the military service, yet was doing well in Thailand.

On another occasion, Burch met a GI named Jackson who had taken the Embassy Flight to Bangkok. Jackson was on his way to Saigon, but decided to lay over. Burch invited Jackson to stay at his house until he was ready to resume his trip. Jackson was tired from his trip, so after getting him settled, Burch headed for La Fee's to check out the scene. 'I picked up a nice-looking Thai girl and took her back to the house for some fun. After we finished, I took her back to the bar. When I returned to the house, Jackson (the traveling GI) was there waiting for me. He looked puzzled.

'Man, something strange happened to me tonight,' he said,

I asked: 'Like what?'

'He said. "I had the sheets up over me and I was sleeping good. I heard somebody comin' up the steps. I didn't move because I thought it was you. Then all of a sudden this guy jerked the sheets off of me. It scared the shit out of me! I said: 'What the hell is going on?'"

'It was Jack. He apologized to Jackson and told him that a man fitting my description had left the bar with one of his girlfriends. Jack didn't catch me, but I know he held it against me.'

And he held a grudge against anybody else close to Burch. 'Jack was even jealous of Claudia, my girlfriend who had joined me from Spain,' Burch said. 'Jack told Pratt Benthall that Claudia was buying too many clothes, and that she was even learning how to speak Thai. Jack thought he was "Mr. Thailand," and he didn't want anybody to be more familiar with the country than he was.' Jack eventually banned Burch and Claudia from La Fee's, no explanation given.

BUT LIFE WAS good for Dan Burch, so he ignored the slight and focused on the MPC scam. On one of his MPC trips to Bangkok, Burch was standing in line ready to exchange dollars for MPCs with an Indian exchange merchant. Ahead of him was a retired first sergeant named Guieppo, whom Burch had not seen in some time. He noticed that instead of giving the merchant dollars, Guieppo was writing out a check. 'It hit me,' Burch recalled. 'I realized I didn't have to go back and forth between Bangkok and Saigon, hauling U.S. money with me. The Indian exchange merchants were trusting souls, if you did regular business with them. I could stay in Saigon, write checks and let the money accumulate. That is what I did. I returned to Bangkok and put everything in order and came back to Saigon. But then Jack messed everything up.'

Rather than use the tried-and-true U.S. military post office in Saigon to ship money orders back to Thailand, Burch decided to give Jimmy Smedley, who had moved from Germany to Bangkok and who was also in Saigon hustling MPCs at the time, $40,000 in money orders to bring back to Bangkok for him. When Jack learned who had Burch's money orders, he sweet-talked the easy going Smedley into giving the money orders to him to hold for Burch. Realizing how much money Burch was sending from Saigon, Jack went to the Bangkok post office and explained that Burch had moved, and Burch wanted him to pick up his mail. When Burch returned from Saigon and went to the post office to pick up his mail, he was told: 'Your friend got your mail for you.' Once the clerk described the friend, Burch wondered: What the hell was going on? Then he got nervous. In the mail that Jack picked up was $40,000 in money orders. All Jack had to do to cash them was to forge Burch's name.

Thoroughly pissed, Burch confronted Jack. 'Why did you take my money orders?'

Mr. Thailand had an explanation. '(Ellis) Sutton has your money, man. When he came to Bangkok recently, he came by my house and stole a lot of money from me.'

'Where is he?' Burch demanded.

'Well, he's gone back to the U.S. God knows where.' Jack replied

Later, Burch caught up with Sutton, who confirmed that, yes, he did get some money from Jack when he was in Bangkok, but he did not steal it. Jack owed him the money.

Burch was now convinced that Jack was up to no good and out to destroy him. He would have to watch his back.

A couple of months later, Burch found out that Jack had sent $38,000 of Burch's money orders to his sister in California. The U.S. Customs officials in Hawaii, however, had apparently randomly selected Jack's package to inspect, and when opening it, they found the money orders. Jack's sister denied that she had anything to do with the package, so Customs confiscated the money orders. 'Jack was never prosecuted,' Burch explained. 'I don't think he ever got the money orders back, but I can't be certain. I didn't know what to do. The other $40,000 was still missing. I should have killed Jack. I thought about it, but I needed to stay in Thailand.'

CHAPTER 4

Switching Gears

HERMAN 'JACK' JACKSON always wanted to own a bar, and he got his wish when Luchai (Chai) Ruviwat sold him a part interest in La Fee's. Business boomed, and by 1967, the bar had become a must visit for the many American black GIs flocking to Bangkok on R & R at the height of the Vietnam War. The Vietnam War was much different for blacks than the one their forefathers had served in during World War II. Blacks were fully integrated into the Armed Forces now, and no one questioned their fighting ability. They made up 9.8 percent of the U.S. military force in Vietnam, but close to 20 percent of the combat troops and 25 percent of such crack army units as the paratroopers. And despite the racism prevailing in America, blacks were as patriotic as ever. The vast majority of black soldiers were low-ranking enlisted men, but the black enlistment rate in the U.S. military was three times greater than for whites.

The Bangkok entertainment scene reflected the tense racial situation in America and Vietnam at the time. Whites and blacks tended to hang out at bars whose clientele was drawn predominantly from their own race. 'The bars were strictly segregated by music,' recalled Pete Davis, a retired black DEA agent who came to Bangkok in 1971 to work. 'You would have country music in one bar and soul music in another. If you were black and wanted to go into a country music bar, even the girls would give you attitude. They would look at you as if to say—what are you doing here?'

The segregation could lead to racial tension, especially over Thai women. 'Many Thais considered any Thai woman who went with an American GI, black or white, to be a whore,' said Steve Jarrell, a former U.S. airman stationed at Utapao Air Force Base at Sattahip in the late 1960s and early 1970s. 'But those same Thai women who went with white GIs held their noses up when they saw Thai girls with black GIs. The vice versa was also true. So the Thai women were as segregated as the American GIs.'

But few bars in Bangkok catered exclusively to black GIs. Soul Sister was a big place with a live band and a coffee shop upstairs. The Whiskey Jazz also had two floors but it was small. La Fee's had become one of the more popular places, but it too sometimes gave patrons the feeling of being packed in a sardine can. Jack and Chai recognized a business opportunity, and they renovated a building on Petchaburi Road and opened it as a bar in June 1967. To massage Jack's ego, the bar was called Jack's American Star Bar. Both Ike and Jimmy Smedley became partners, with each of the four partners investing about $8,000 in the venture. Ike became a silent partner and Jimmy Smedley worked as the manager, a good fit despite Smedley's fondness for alcohol, because everybody seemed to like the retired U.S. military man who always wore a nice smile.

Peter Finucane, a journalist with the Bangkok Post newspaper since 1967, remembers Smedley as a congenial man with a shoulder twitch and a pocked-marked face adorned with a permanent smile and lots of laugh lines. 'Jimmy would sit at the bar facing the door so he could see everybody coming in,' Finucane recalled. 'He always had a drink in his hand, and nobody could figure out what kind it was. He wouldn't tell any one. It was like a classified military secret.'

Finucane and John McBeth, a friend and fellow journalist, were two of the few Whites who frequented the bar. 'Sometimes we would get a little aggravation and a few stares,' McBeth explained 'But Jimmy would always take care of us and seat us at the bar. He kind of presided over things at Jack's.' Smedley told everyone he met that the opening of Jack's American Star Bar had given him a niche in life. No way would he ever go back to Saigon and exchange dollars for MPCs.

While Smedley played genial host, Luchai kept an eye out for potential trouble and hired the girls. It was a requirement to include a local Thai partner in a business arrangement. The Thai partner, as was the case with Chai, would also have the local contacts and could serve as a buffer in case the partners had any problems with the authorities. Mr. Yeung and another Thai named Mr. Udong took care of the bar's legal matters.

For Ike, the investment and money he made from Jack's was pocket change, because he was still going full blast with the profitable MPC scam. Yet being a business partner gave him a legitimate reason—a front, if you will—for being in Bangkok. Ike would not have to worry about being summarily kicked out of Thailand.

Patrons of Jack's American Star Bar would enter through a heavy creaking front door that had a large red tinsel star on the right. On the bar's ground floor was a dance area where Thai girls, some of them sporting elaborate afros, danced with black male patrons to the funky sounds of such popular tunes as 'Funky Chicken,' 'Rubber Legs' and 'Mechanical Man.' Anybody could stand up and sing, if they had the desire or the nerve. 'One of the funniest things I saw at Jack's was a small Thai man who weighed about 90 pounds, singing James Brown's "Hot Pants,"' Davis recalled 'He'd screech: "Hot Pants!" and then shout: "Yeow!", trying to imitate Brown.'

On the second floor was a restaurant with the best soul food east of Harlem. A patron could feast on barbeque ribs, pork chops, pig's tails, feet and ears, chitterlings, fried chicken, black-eyed peas, grits and collared greens until the wee hours of the morning. Smedley would boast: 'We sell everything on the pig from the tail to the ears.'

The partners would stock the liquor supply with booze purchased from the local U.S. Army PX. With Ike, Jack and Smedley being retired military, they could buy it cheaply and in quantity and avoid the steep tax the Thais put on booze. They bought cigarettes and food items cheaply from the PX as well. The bar had no problem recruiting pretty young Thai girls or getting them to become part of an internal spy network that reported on what the GIs patrons were saying.

Finding girlfriends was easy for Ike or his buddies, most of whom liked to play the field. Ike's wife Atha had come to Bangkok with the kids for while, but, as was the case with Germany, she did not like Thailand and returned home quickly. Ike never liked to mess around with a lot of women, so he settled into relationships with two pretty Thai women, one who worked in the American commissary and another who worked at Jack's American Star Bar.

Terry Nardi and Steve Jerrell were two white airmen who worked in the field maintenance service at Utapao Air Force Base and organized 'Salt and Pepper,' a six-member band that played during their off duty hours and included two black airmen. In late 1969 and early 1970, Salt and Pepper played every second weekend for six-months at Jack's Star Bar. 'The band got along fine in Jack's because we had a good appreciation of black music,' explained Terry Nardi, Salt and Pepper's founder. 'We played the songs of such musicians as Wilson Picket and Otis Redding—the music the crowd wanted to hear—and once we started, the crowd really liked us.'

Daniel Burch was not invited to join the Jack's American Star Bar partnership, so he opened his own bar. Burch and his girlfriend Claudia rented some space at the First Hotel on Petchaburi Road away from the strip and called it Chez Moi. Seating about 60 patrons, Chez Moi started off well, but after about seven months the bar began losing money. 'Back then, the Thais viewed Americans who opened businesses in (Thailand) as cash cows,' Burch explained. 'I was still doing the MPC thing, so I hired a Thai manager and a Thai bartender to take care of the bar for us. It was a bad mistake. They robbed us blind. By the time we figured it out, it wasn't worth the hassle. So we decided to close the bar down.'

Robert Johnson continued to run Johnny's Place until the summer of 1970 when tragedy struck. Johnson's Corsican girlfriend Millie had a fiery temper, and they constantly argued, especially over Johnson's mounting gambling debts. Johnson had begun gambling with some Chinese in a strange game he knew little about. Millie discovered that jewelry and other valuables were missing from their house. After arriving in Bangkok, the couple had a baby boy, and he wore an expensive gold necklace. One night, without telling Millie, Johnson took the necklace to gamble with the Chinese. He lost the gold chain. When Millie found out, she went nuts and in a fit of rage slit the three-year old baby's throat.

The Thai authorities charged Millie with murder and threw her in jail, but Johnson, with Mr. Yeung's help, got her released on bond, possibly bribing some Thai officials. Johnson got her an American passport and a U.S. WAC (Women Army Corp) ID, and then Robert and Millie took the Laos route to Paris, France, where he had met her. 'Johnson cut Millie loose,' Burch recalled. 'He felt the obligation to get her out of a Thai jail and back to Europe, but the death of their baby ended their relationship.'

IN JUNE 1968, Burch was reportedly deported from Thailand to Laos, but the details of that report are in dispute. According to a DEA intelligence report, a joint investigation by the Thai police and the U.S. Army Criminal Intelligence Division (CID) disclosed that Robert Johnson, Herman Jackson, Pratt Benthall and Daniel Burch were dealing in false military IDs stolen from a military facility in Germany. The military police had subsequently apprehended Smedley at the main PX compound in Bangkok in possession of false ID and ration cards, and Johnson was also implicated. The report, however, noted that while orders to deport Johnson and Smedley had been prepared, they were never served.

'None of that information adds up,' Burch said. 'First, the authorities were always confusing Pratt Benthall and George Pratt, so the wrong guy is identified in the report. I never saw Pratt Benthall in Thailand. Jimmy Smedley was retired military; he would have no need for ration cards.'

As for his deportation, Burch explained it this way: 'Unless you had a permanent visa to stay in Thailand, you had to go out of the country every 90 days and get your passport stamped. I was legally in Thailand within the 90-day period, so they had no reason to lock me up and deport me. There were several other Americans I know in Thailand without permanent visas, but they were not thrown out. I was working on getting a permanent resident visa to stay, but Jack said to let Mr. Yeung and Mr. Udong, his lawyers, handle it. The lawyers got Ike and Smedley their resident visas, but they kept stalling me. Jack would say: "Don't worry, we will be taking care of it."' But they never did.'

Robert Johnson and George Pratt came to see Burch while he was in prison awaiting deportation. Burch explained: 'The Thai prison had a wire fence with an open mesh around it, and a visitor could come right up to a prisoner and talk to them. Johnson told me: "Man, I hate to see a sucker (Jack) get down on somebody like this. "Pratt called Jack 'a rotten son-of-a-bitch" and blamed him for getting me thrown out of the country.'

According to the DEA intelligence report, an informant told Thai police that Burch and Benthall were involved in smuggling gold and currency between Vientiane, Laos, and Jack's American Star Bar. But Burch said that did not make sense either. 'I went back to Germany and didn't stay in Laos,' Burch said 'Besides, why would I deal with Jack's American Star Bar after what Jack did to me?'

Today, Ike is baffled by the bitter Jackson-Burch relationship. 'I knew Jack and Dan didn't like each other, but I didn't know all that was going on. Jack was Jack. I accepted him for what he was. I don't think he ever tried to screw me. If Jack was jealous of me, he never showed it. Jack knew I could make him money.'

EARLY ONE MORNING in the fall of 1968, Ike paid a visit to Jack at his Bangkok home. Jack had asked Ike to come over to discuss something important. Jack brought Ike to the patio and told him to look at the front page of the newspaper while he took care of some things in the house. Ike read an article that reported on a widespread heroin epidemic in the U.S. He had not been to the U.S. for some time, and he was interested to read that blacks were consuming a large part of the illegal drugs.

'Glad you could come by.' Jack said to Ike when he rejoined him on the patio. 'How are you doing?'

'Fine, my friend. How about yourself ?' Ike replied.

Jack nodded and said: 'Did you take a look at the paper?'

'Yeah. That's really something about the heroin problem back home.'

'I'm glad you looked at it. I don't think I've ever told you anything about Nitaya's family. Do you know anything about them?'

Nitaya was Jack's latest Thai girlfriend, but she would become the love of his life. Ike recalled the first time he saw her in a kimono at his house when she and Jack stayed overnight at Ike's place. With her slender figure, long, silky black hair, dark eyes and doll-like face, Ike thought she was the prettiest creature he had seen in Bangkok

'What?' Ike said, caught off guard by the strange question. 'No, I don't. Why did you ask that question?'

'Because it has a lot to with what you just read. Nitaya's family is about the biggest opium grower in Thailand. They know how to process opium into heroin, and they can do it for a couple of thousand dollars a kilo. Do you know how much a kilo of heroin can get in the U.S.?'

Ike shook his head. 'How much?'

'From $100,000 to $150,000.'

Ike tried to comprehend the staggering numbers.

Then Jack called Nitaya to come to the patio. Jack asked her to describe what her family had been doing for decades.

Ike listened intently. 'This is really something, Jack, but what does it have to do with me?'

Jack pulled his chair closer to Ike. 'You think you're making money with MPCs? Think of what you can make with that stuff. You're the man who can make it happen. You got contacts in the military and all over the place.'

'I don't know anything about drugs; I don't even use them,' Ike argued. 'It's not the kind of thing I want to be a part of.'

Jack kept on Ike, reminding him of the millions of dollars they could make. Ike thought about the MPC scam. He was making a lot of money, but was tired of the weekly trips to Saigon. Besides, it was getting dangerous. The enemy was stepping up its attack on American troops, and Saigon was becoming like Fortress Vietnam. He thought about the riches the new venture offered, and the excitement of starting a new scam. The money from the MPC exchange was still rolling in, but the scam had become too easy. He was getting kind of bored. He looked at Jack, his partner, who had never steered him wrong. 'Okay, man,' Ike said, reaching across the table to shake Jack's hand. 'Let's do it!'

Ike knew enough about the military transportation system to know that Jack's plan could work. He could recruit plenty of brothers who were not afraid to take chances.

NITAYA TOLD IKE about her relatives who had the heroin connection and lived in the Golden Triangle. While in Bangkok, Ike had heard about the famous Golden Triangle where opium was grown and heroin, manufactured. The Golden Triangle refers to a 350,000 square kilometer area that included the mountains of three Asian countries (Laos, Myanmar and Thailand) and to a lesser extent, Yunnan province in China. The region is covered by forest and is inhabited by a tribal, clannish population, estimated at 300,000 people, who live in about 300 villages. It is an area of little government control where the principal means of transportation is the backpack, an elephant or a mule.

The Golden Triangle's rise to prominence in the international drug trade came soon after World War II ended. At the time, the region was producing less than ten tons of opium a year. But that all changed when the communists led by Mao Tse Tung conquered China in 1949 and clamped down on opium production, spurring the Golden Triangle to increase production. That began to happen when the Nationalist Chinese (the Kuomintang or KMT) fled for the safety of the Shan states of Burma, which are part of the Golden Triangle.

From there, the CIA-supported KMT prepared for an invasion of Red China, but their military operation was a failure. The KMT settled into their new home and began expanding and monopolizing the opium trade in the Shan states. According to historian Alfred McCoy in his book *The Politics of Heroin in Southeast Asia*: 'The KMT shipped the opium harvests to northern Thailand where they were sold to General Phao Siyanan, a Thai policeman who was a CIA client. The CIA had promoted the Phao-KMT partnership to provide a secure area for the KMT, but this alliance soon became a critical factor in the growth of Southeast Asia's narcotics trade.'

The KMT remained in Burma until about 1961 when Taiwan cut off economic aid and the Burmese army drove the KMT out of existence. Many of them married into the local populace. The opium trade was the largest cash crop in the region. By this time, opium production had grown by almost 500 percent, from less than 10 tons in the years after World War II to an estimated 300 to 400 tons by 1962. Opium was now an integral part of the northern Thailand economy. The Bangkok Office of the National Narcotics Control Board estimated that 260 villages in the northern provinces of Payao, Chiang Mai, Chiang Rai and Mae Hong Son were involved and relied economically on the opium trade. But stopping the growth of the opium trade became a formidable challenge for Thai authorities. For instance, the frontier in Chiang Mai province alone that required guarding was about 1,500 kilometers long.

Beginning in the early 1960s, first the KMT and then later the war lords of the Golden Triangle, most notably Khun Sa, who with his powerful multi-thousand strong Shan United Army, was trying to create a separate Shan nation, established heroin refineries in the Golden Triangle to support their war efforts. Heroin had come a long way since Alder Wright, an English chemist, first synthesized the narcotic drug in 1874, naming it diacetylmorphine. In 1898 Bayer Chemical Company renamed diacetylmorphine "heroin" and introduced it to the public as cure for morphine addiction.

Subsequently, heroin had a Doctor Jeckle and Mr. Hyde-type history. First it was hailed as a wonder drug that could relieve such ailments as pain, diarrhea and coughing spasms. The American Medical Association even endorsed heroin as a safe treatment for respiratory ailments, but the medical establishment came to realize that heroin was at least as addictive as morphine (in fact, heroin is about 25 times more powerful than morphine). By 1924, the U.S. outlawed the drug. In the following decades, the world continued to recognize the dangers of heroin; by 1963, it was used medically in only five countries and manufactured legally in only three. By then, however, heroin had replaced morphine and opium as the illegal drug of choice on the street.

Ethnic Chiu Chao gangsters, who can trace their origins to nearby Swatow on China's south coast, got involved with the Golden Triangle heroin trade, and they brought chemists from Hong Kong to work in their heroin refineries. Until the Hong Kong chemists became involved, a number 3 heroin, a light tan colored powder, with a mere 3 to 6 percent purity was the best heroin that the drug traffickers could manufacture. But, by the time Ike and Jack started their heroin ring, the Golden Triangle refineries were starting to produce number 4, China White heroin that could reach nearly 99 percent purity. The opium addicts of Southeast Asia were the principal users of the lower grade number 3 heroin, usually smoking it. But American GIs in Vietnam began using the injectable number 4 heroin, and the spread of the drug soon reached epidemic proportions. In September 1970, an Army Engineer Battalion in the Mekong Delta of Vietnam surveyed 3,103 U.S. soldiers and found 11.9

percent had used heroin since their arrival in Vietnam. Two years later, the White House Office for Drug Abuse Prevention interviewed 900 enlisted men who had returned from Vietnam in September 1971, the peak of the heroin epidemic among U.S. soldiers in Vietnam, and found that 44 percent had tried opiates while in Vietnam and 20 percent reported themselves as being addicted.

On July 5 1971, a *Time* magazine article titled '*The Heroin Plague: What Can Be Done?*' revealed that since 1969 the number of heroin addicts in the U.S. had risen from 200,000 to 300,000. 'New heroin users are turning up every week in the suburban high schools, on factory lines and in the legions of the drug culture that once spurned smack as they spurned napalm,' Time reported.

Timing-wise, Ike and Jack were about to enter the international heroin trade at the most opportune moment. Nitaya's main family contact, whose services the two partners would use most often in the formative years of their operation to buy hundreds of kilos of heroin for the U.S., was simply known as Papa San, a shadowy figure whom Ike only met twice. Ike believes Papa San was Nitaya's uncle, and he lived in Bangkok on a small street off New Road. The DEA later learned that Papa San had two contacts that helped him make the heroin buys from the Golden Triangle. One was an unidentified Chinese male who lived about four miles from the alligator farm on the outskirts of Bangkok. The other, identified simply as Jim, was the manager of a tailor shop in Chai Pons on New Petchaburi Road. Jim would furnish any amount of heroin so long as half the money was paid up front.

Ike never did learn Papa San's real name, but it didn't really matter. He had the type of heroin the market wanted. As Ike explained, 'China White is the best grade of heroin. In New York, one could dilute and cut pure China White using diluents, such as quinine or mannite, to produce heroin of six to ten percent purity that was safe to inject. It was the smack that junkies craved for.'

Nitaya's family was the main connection for the Atkinson drug ring's heroin, but Ike used a variety of other sources when available, if they could deliver the quantities and offered fair terms. Their purchase price averaged $4,000 per kilo of pure heroin. The couriers were only paid about $3,000 per trip. In the U.S., the kilo would be cut with diluents into four kilograms of 25 percent pure heroin, fetching $25,000 each, or a $100,000 for every $7,000 investment. Retail sales of heroin, after it was further diluted for safe injection (5-6 percent purity) was sold on the street for $10 per gram, building in a significant profit margin for retailers as well. However, retailers take a much greater risk of exposure to law enforcement action and 'rip-offs.' Atkinson only sold his heroin at the wholesale level.

Ike and Jack rented a house in Bangkok that extended over a klong. 'We had a trap door in one of the bedrooms where we stashed the heroin,' Ike recalled. 'When we got going, I would buy as much as $100,000 worth of heroin at a time. We would pack the kilos there. The house was never left unguarded.'

In 1969, the DEA received information that Luchai Ruviwat and a member of the Thai government were working together as heroin suppliers. Chai, however, would not become a prominent supplier until after 1972 when Jack got in trouble with the law.

Another supply source was identified as a cabbie nicknamed 'Jimmy,' who worked outside the Asoke Building on Soi 21 in Bangkok. A DEA informant reported that when he was talking with Jimmy, he had learned the cabbie had supplied heroin to the Atkinson-Jackson ring on several occasions. Jack would give the taxi driver half the money prior to delivery and the other half after delivery. In 1971, a U.S. Army Criminal Intelligence

Division (CID) investigation reported that a businessman named Tosdi Iankiosanntis was allegedly involved with the Atkinson-Jackson ring. Jack had been observed at the Motor Coach Travel Service in Bangkok, Tosdi's legal business front. Carrying a suitcase full of money, Jack was reportedly meeting to negotiate the purchase of heroin.

One informant described for the DEA what he knew about the ring's operation. He stated that on one occasion Jackson, by fronting his money for about 15 days, purchased 15 kilos of heroin through the family sources of his wife, Nataya. At this time, Atkinson and Jack were paying about $2,250 per kilo, but the quality of heroin was not more than 75 percent pure. The heroin was packaged in one-pound quantities. First it was wrapped in strong transparent paper, the kind used for drawing blueprints, then put in a plastic bag, which was placed inside a brown cardboard box. The box was further wrapped in brown paper and then again in plastic. The informant stated that Jack had bought between 28 and 30 boxes of heroin from those sources.

Dealing with various dealers could cause some headaches. One DEA informant claimed that Jack had bought a murder contract on a source of supply whose name was believed to be Ought Sapsong, because he had 'cheated' Jackson out of $3,400. Sapsong allegedly disappeared with Jackson's money after offering to sell him heroin cheaper than what he had been paying. But many law enforcement officials marvel at how violence-free the drug ring was, considering the level at which it operated. Ike never carried a gun and was never implicated in any murders connected to the drug trade. Sergeant Smack, however, knew how to use a gun, if need be. After all, he was ex-army.

THE PLAN OF operation was as follows: Jack would handle the supply, and when Ike was not in Bangkok, Jack would also see to it that the heroin was properly packaged for shipment to the U.S. It would be up to Ike to figure out how to get the drugs into the U.S. Atkinson would move back to Goldsboro and await the arrival of the heroin. He would then set up sales to drug distributors eager to purchase the high-grade heroin.

In taking numerous military hops since his retirement in 1963, Ike was familiar with how Customs officials operated. Only once had he seen MPs bringing out a specially trained K-9 unit to sniff luggage. In that incident, one of the dogs went towards a young serviceman. It looked to Ike as if the man had been smoking weed earlier, and the dog caught the scent. 'I've got nothing,' the nervous serviceman blurted out. The MPs took him to a nearby bathroom where Ike could hear the man insisting that he had no drugs with him. After strip-searching the detained serviceman and finding nothing, the MPs took him out of the bathroom and searched his luggage. Again, they found nothing. On his many trips back and forth between Bangkok and the U.S., Ike never did see anyone arrested for a drug violation.

Later, as their drug operation grew and expanded, Jack would recruit couriers in Jack's American Star Bar. But in the beginning, plenty of brothers were willing to smuggle a few kilos of heroin to the U.S. They didn't even have to be actual members of the military. Military uniforms were easy to come by, as were medals, stripes and badges. Travel orders or leave papers could be counterfeited to perfection, and Ike knew how to make fake military IDs. The false orders would often identify emergencies as a reason for the leave, which gave the bearer high priority status for travel. The DEA later identified some of the couriers that it believed were using false papers: Herman Gaillard (Peter Rabbit), Ernest Jackson, Jr., Curtis Reid, Gregory Purnell,

Norman Wendell Young, Thomas Hart, Thomas Southerland and Larry Drake Atkinson (Ike's nephew). Ike identified his first couriers as Peter Rabbit, Thomas Southerland, Eddie Wooten, and Howard Scott, an associate from the Washington, DC area.

FOR THE FIRST smuggling trip in early August 1968, Ike chose a route that took him from Bangkok to the continental U.S. via Anchorage, Alaska. It was a regular military route, and when the plane landed in Anchorage, it invariably arrived at night. All the Customs officials would ever do was question the arriving passengers, asking them if they had anything to declare. Eventually, the Atkinson-Jackson drug ring used every conceivable method in their courier smuggling system, including film canisters and individuals wearing leg casts, but on the test run, Ike kept it simple. He just packed four kilos of heroin and eight pounds of "Thai stick," at the time the best marijuana on the planet, in a duffle bag and locked it. Ike was taking the marijuana to his brother Dallas' close friend who lived in the Baltimore area and had asked Ike to bring him some. The plan, if it could be called that, was to throw the duffle bag in the corner of the C-141, and if the authorities wanted to check it, Ike could say that the duffle bag was not his. The trip involved some risk, but it was a lot like shooting dice. As a courier, Ike could roll snake eyes (the losing combination when the dice are rolled), so to speak, but the situation was weighted in his favor, given the laxness in military security in those days.

With Ike was Thomas Southerland, dressed in military uniform and carrying official looking papers, who came to Bangkok from Wilmington to make some money. The test run proceeded like a charm, and Ike and Southerland had no problem getting through. Ike marveled at how easy the operation had been, given the long trip and many landings. Now it was time to get down to business and put a plan into operation.

The next trip occurred later in August 1968, and involved a courier that Ike recruited. The courier got through just as easily as Ike and Southerland did. The next trip, also successful, occurred shortly afterwards and involved smuggling about five to six kilos of heroin. The courier on this trip looked like a real patriot. He was carrying propaganda leaflets for the Special Warfare Center. The third trip after the test run occurred prior to 17 December 1968, and consisted of a shipment of seven or eight kilos of heroin that Eddie Wooten smuggled into the U.S. in a duffle bag. On the next trip, Ike had his couriers use six duffle bags, three of which contained heroin and three without. The military aircraft was scheduled to arrive in Elmendorf, Alaska, where, if no cargo was off-loaded, the couriers knew there would be no Customs clearance other than an official boarding the plane and asking the passengers which duffle bags belonged to them, and maybe making a cursory search. If a search was made, then the duffle bags without the heroin would be declared as theirs. As with the previous trips, the heroin was successfully smuggled into the continental U.S. and onto the on-going flight to McGuire Air Force Base, located in south central New Jersey, about 15 miles from Trenton.

AFTER BEING DEPORTED from Bangkok in June 1968, Daniel Burch went back to West Germany where he stayed several months before returning to the U.S. Burch traveled to New Jersey to look up Pratt Benthall, an old friend of Ike's. Burch and Benthall were two inveterate gamblers, and they got into a heavy craps game in which Burch took $11,000 from Benthall. 'It was not hard taking money from Pratt,' Burch recalled. 'He liked cocaine and that occupied his attention. He'd carry little vials around with him that contained cocaine.'

Burch then returned to his hometown of Akron, Ohio, to think about his future now that, thanks to old 'buddy' Jack, the dream of using the MPC system to build a nest egg had become a house of cards. Burch heard that Ike had followed through on establishing a Bangkok-based heroin smuggling network, and he decided to go to Goldsboro to see if this new venture was something that might interest him. He was surprised to learn that Ike was using duffle bags to smuggle the contraband. 'Duffle bags are too risky,' Burch told Ike. 'What if a Customs agent looks inside. Why don't you use AWOL bags?' Burch showed Ike how a false bottom could be sewn into an AWOL bag where the heroin could be hidden and showed him how to pack the heroin and then stitch the bags with a crochet needle so it looked as if the re-stitching was sewn in the factory. Later, Ike would buy the AWOL bags from the American PX in Bangkok, five or six at a time, for about $15 or $16 each.

Ike asked Burch to come back to Thailand and oversee the job of sewing and fitting the AWOL bags, but Burch declined. Still, the job took some skill, so Ike asked Burch to teach the procedure to Rudolph Jennings, a boyhood friend from Goldsboro, who was eager to go to Bangkok. Jennings became an expert at the job; no Rudolph stitched bag being carried by a courier was ever confiscated because the authorities suspected that it contained heroin.

BURCH NOW DECIDED to enter the drug trade with eyes wide open. 'People around Akron didn't have quality dope, so when I started to traffic Ike's China White to the city, it became very popular. My plan was to make enough money so I could get out of drug dealing by 1975.'

Burch was still determined to get his 'MPC' money back from Jack. He had sent his girlfriend, Claudia, to Goldsboro with a tape-recorded message for Jack: 'I want the money you stole from me.' But Jack did not respond. While in New Jersey, breaking Benthall in the craps game, Benthall had told Burch that he had seen Jack with a suitcase full of money, but he did not know where he was now. After teaching Jennings how to stitch AWOL bags, Burch returned to Akron. A few weeks later, he heard that Jack was back in Goldsboro. Burch, packing a gun and accompanied by two friends, headed to Goldsboro in search of Jack and his money.

In Goldsboro, they eventually found Jack parked on Neuse Circle about to pay Ike a visit. Burch sat in the back seat of his car, his gun ready, not really knowing what he would do. When Jack started to get out his car, Burch told one of his friends in the front seat to call out to Jack: 'Yo, Jack, come over here. Sanchez from Fort Bragg wants to ask you some question about Thailand.' Sanchez was a mutual friend of both Jack and Burch. Jack turned around, smiled, and started to walk towards Burch's car. When Jack got close to the driver's side of Burch's car, Burch jumped out and in a threatening voice, said: 'Come on Jack, we are going for a ride.'

Startled, Jack's gray eyes got big, and he had the look of panic on his face. Seeing that Burch held a gun, Jack pushed the door toward him and took off a like an Olympic 100-meter sprint champion. Burch and his two friends watched Mr. Thailand scamper away. Realizing that Jack believed he was running for his life, the three friends burst out laughing. Not too long afterward, Jack began to pay Burch the money he owed him. Life among the band of brothers was starting to return to normal.

CHAPTER 5

The Investigation Begins

DANIEL BURCH BECAME a regular customer of the Atkinson-Jackson drug ring, and by the early 1970s the DEA had identified him as one of Ohio's biggest drug dealers. The DEA learned that he had traveled several times to Bangkok to make heroin buys. A Burch associate told the DEA that she, along with two other women, met with Burch at the Taft Hotel in New York City to develop a plan to smuggle heroin from Bangkok. In June 1972, Burch, using the alias, 'Daniels,' together with a male associate and the three women, traveled to Bangkok to make a heroin buy. Using U.S. Army uniforms, false military orders and a combination of military and commercial travel, the ring smuggled the heroin to the U.S. via Europe.

On 16 November 1973, Burch, after arriving at the port of New York City aboard the Queen Elizabeth II, had his first run-in with the law over drugs. U.S. Customs arrested him for possession of hashish. 'When I got off the boat, I had a smoking pipe on me,' Burch recalled. 'It was not even a hash pipe, but it tested slightly positive for hashish. Customs decided it wasn't enough dope to detain me, so they let me go. I went through Customs and down the steps to a warehouse to get my green Cadillac. I had spent a couple of months in Europe traveling all over in that car. Some DEA agents got wind of a passenger who had a pipe on him that tested positive for hashish. Two agents came down to the warehouse and interrogated me.

The agents wanted to take me back through Customs, but a Customs official was watching the interrogation and told them they could not do it. They argued; the DEA agents got mad and arrested me. I was put in lock up overnight. The next morning, I got out on bond and found a lawyer. He couldn't understand why I was arrested and got the case dropped. The incident never affected me but, truthfully, one of the women I was with in Europe had used the pipe to smoke some hashish.'

BY THIS TIME Burch was one of the major buyers of heroin supplied by the Atkinson-Jackson drug ring. Ike dealt strictly with black dealers, and he had no contact with La Cosa Nostra which had dominated the U.S. heroin trade since the end of World War II. 'I considered myself a Lone Ranger,' Ike recalled. 'I was the source of all my action. Many people in Southeast Asia had the capability to smuggle heroin to the U.S., but none had my connections. When I was on U.S. turf, I never had any problem with the Mob trying to muscle in on my action.'

Initially, La Cosa Nostra used Italian refineries to manufacture heroin but when the Italian government cracked down, the Mafia and Corsican gangsters established a new trafficking route known infamously as the French Connection. Morphine base was smuggled from Turkey to the Marseilles area where it was refined into heroin and then shipped to the United States via Sicily and Montreal. According to the President's Commission on Organized Crime, the French Connection gave La Cosa Nostra a monopoly on the U.S. heroin trade from the late 1940s to the late 1960s, allowing the Mob to control an estimated 95 percent of the heroin being smuggled into the U.S.

But by the early 1970s, U.S. President Richard Nixon had launched his 'War on Drugs.' The U.S. began pressuring key countries involved in the international heroin trade, and law enforcement began having greater success against the French Connection. By 1973, Turkey, supported by $35.7 million in U.S. aid, had eradicated all illicit opium production in the country, and the French government had closed most of the country's heroin refineries. Within months, the street price of heroin in the New York City area tripled and the purity dropped by half, both indicators of a serious heroin shortage.

Still, this development had unintended consequences. The 'success' against the French Connection did nothing more than create the market conditions that boosted the expansion of the illicit heroin supply elsewhere and made Southeast Asia a much more important players in the international drug trade. During the 1970s, Southeast Asian heroin from the Golden Triangle rose from single digits to between 25 to 30 percent of the total heroin supply in the U.S.

GIVEN THE TURBULENCE and uncertainty in the international heroin trade, the Atkinson-Jackson ring was able to find more than enough contacts eager to buy their high-grade China White heroin, and Goldsboro, North Carolina, emerged as an unlikely major center for heroin trafficking. By the early 1970s, automobiles with out-of-state license plates began arriving in the rural hamlet. Given his networking skills, Ike had established contacts in New York City, Baltimore, Philadelphia, Pittsburgh, Washington, DC, and many other major cities along the eastern seaboard. Using Travis Air Force Base in the San Francisco area, the Atkinson-Jackson network expanded to California, truly making Ike Atkinson a kingpin.

Initially, once the couriers smuggled the heroin into the U.S., Ike would give it to his nephew Buster Jack, who would take the heroin to a farmhouse near Goldsboro where it was kept with a friend whom Ike trusted. As the money from the sale of dope accumulated, it would also be stashed at the farmhouse. Ike eventually stopped using Buster Jack after finding out that he was stealing from the stash. Ike would now deliver the loads to the farm himself. Only Ike and Herman Jackson knew where the stash was located, but Jackson told a girlfriend, a rash move that would eventually cause Ike problems.

IKE SUPPLIED MANY of the major black drug traffickers of the day, including such enterprising gangsters as his pal from Germany, Eddie Wooten, who operated out of Okinawa and in the Washington DC area; Martin Trowery of Pittsburgh, Pennsylvania; William 'Dog' Turner, another major dealer from the DC area; New Jersey based Frank Lucas, who, in his golden years, would achieve fame as Hollywood's version of the so-called 'American Gangster;' Ellis Sutton, Ike's old acquaintance from his GI days in Germany in the late 1950s and early 60s; and Zack Robinson and the legendary Frank Matthews of New York City, two of the biggest dealers.

In the early 1970s, DEA intelligence identified Dog Turner as the top narcotics dealer in the Washington, DC area. He conducted part of his operation out his apartment located on upper 16th Street Northwest in DC and was suspected of trafficking significant quantities of heroin between DC and Pittsburgh. Turner first appeared on the DEA's Southeast Asia radar screen in January 1970 when the DEA determine that he traveled to Bangkok to buy heroin directly from the Atkinson-Jackson ring. Arriving in Bangkok with two associates, Turner headed to Jack's American Star Bar where he learned from James Goodwin, a bar bouncer, that both Atkinson and Jackson were in the U.S. Still, according to information the DEA received, Goodwin was able to help Turner buy about four kilograms of heroin.

An informant told the DEA that the Peace of Mind Wig Shop and a basement club at 10th and U Streets Northwest

DC were the Turner organization's major distribution centers. Turner's luck ran out in 1975 however, when he was convicted on a Federal charge of income tax invasion and began serving a six-year sentence in Lewisburg Federal Penitentiary. In that same year, 'Dog' also was indicted on a Federal conspiracy charge in the Southern District of New York. 'In my drug-dealing days, I knew of "Dog" as a big-time drug dealer, but I did not know him personally,' Ike recalled. 'I met him later in Petersburg (Federal Penitentiary) and we became friends.'

Wooten used Okinawa as a heroin transshipment point because of reports that the Okinawa government was not overly concerned with the smuggling of illicit drugs internationally, so long as it did no harm to Okinawa. Given Okinawa's ineffective immigration and Customs controls and the large number of flights arriving and leaving the territory, it was tough to monitor drug trafficking in Okinawa.

Ike did not know Frank Matthews, the so-called 'Black Caesar' of the New York City drug scene, or Zack Robinson, who owned a bar around 56th Street and 7th Avenue in the Big Apple called 'The Turntable.' But they were two of the biggest drug dealers in the emerging period of the big black drug kingpin. Robinson worked with Matthews, who became a legend after he disappeared in 1974 with a reported $15 million, never to be seen again. Born in 1944 in Durham, North Carolina, Frank Matthews arrived in New York City, barely out of his teens, settling in Brooklyn and then moving to New Jersey where he established himself as a major drug dealer. By the early 1970s, Matthews was handling multi-ton shipments in at least 21 states. His major supply likely came from Europe via Venezuela, but he was willing to buy heroin from any source, provided it was a quality product. 'I don't believe Matthews bought heroin directly from Atkinson,' said Don Ashton, a retired DEA agent who headed the administration's Wilmington, North Carolina office in the mid-1970s. 'More likely, it was people who worked with Matthews who did. But it shows how fluid the drug trade became after the breakup of the French Connection.'

In early September 1974, Ike met with Martin Trowery and his associate Richard Golden at Ike's Bangkok residence to arrange the purchase of heroin. On September 11th, Trowery and Golden arrived from Bangkok at the San Francisco International Airport. Golden made it through U.S. Customs, but Trowery, for an unknown reason, aroused suspicion and was detained. Customs officials arrested Trowery when they found about one kilogram of heroin hidden in the false bottoms of his two black AWOL bags. About a half-hour later, Customs arrested Golden when he returned to the Customs area to inquire about Trowery's whereabouts. Officials also found a kilogram of heroin in one of Golden's two AWOL bags.

'I can't recall where I met Marty (Trowery), but we became buddies,' Ike recalled. 'He was about two or three inches taller than me but had my build. I had a guy named Jesse Paul who would go to Pittsburgh and deliver heroin to him. Once I knew Marty was okay, I told him he could come to Bangkok and pick his dope up, if he wanted. He came to Bangkok once and returned to the U.S. with no problems. The second time, he brought a white guy (Golden) with him, but they were arrested in San Francisco. Liz, Marty's sister, came to Goldsboro to tell me her brother got busted. I helped Marty and his friend pack the bags, but I don't know what had happened to them in San Francisco. It was a real surprise.'

Ellis Sutton used his connection with Ike to supply heroin to buyers in eastern North Carolina. He traveled frequently to Bangkok to gamble. Ike and many of the brothers became drug dealers, but the passion for gambling that dominated the early history of their association still seared. A poker game, in which Ike participated when in Bangkok, took place practically every weekend at Smedley's house in Bangkok. It began on a Saturday, early in the afternoon, continued into the night and on into Sunday.

On one trip, Herman Jackson accused Sutton of stealing $27,000 ($8,000 in currency and the rest in money orders) from Jack's American Star Bar. As we read earlier, Jack also blamed Sutton for stealing Burch's money, which Smedley had given Jack for safekeeping. In any case, the money that disappeared from Jack's American Star Bar was to have been used to bribe a Thai colonel who, in 1969, headed the Thailand Narcotics Bureau. Still, Jack had the nerve to sign a complaint against Sutton with the Thai police. If Sutton ever came back to Thailand, the police would arrest him.

This incident, needless to say, strained the Jackson-Sutton relationship, but business trumped emotion, and the two drug traffickers continued to see each other, even working together on occasion. Once when Sutton was getting ready to visit Bangkok, Jack asked him to take some money back to Thailand for him. Why Jack would do so, given Sutton's untrustworthiness, is unknown. But while Sutton was in Thailand, Jack received word from Thomas Hart, an associate from eastern North Carolina, that Sutton was an informant. Furious, Jackson contacted his half brother, Andrew Price, who was in Bangkok, and told him to notify the Thai colonel on their payroll of Sutton's presence in Thailand. Too late—the police missed Sutton by a couple of days; he was already back in the good old U.S.A.

'Ellis was something else,' Ike explained. 'The truth is, I always liked him and he was welcome in my house. We heard rumors about him that he was probably passing on information to the authorities. So I knew we had to watch him. He tried to get me busted once, but then he got me out of it. So he must have liked me.'

Frank Lucas, who worked directly with Ike, became Ike's most controversial associate. The controversy, however, did not boil over until decades later. When they first met is not certain, but it was probably at least five or six years after Ike became a drug trafficker. In the grapevine of the drug trade, Ike had heard of Lucas, and Ike's nephew Larry, the son of Dallas and Juanita Atkinson, who was a friend of Lucas, had tried to get them together for some time. Frank Lucas was based in Teaneck, New Jersey, and had a drug dealing organization dubbed the 'Country Boys' that became known for its violence.

'I was at my sister Pearl's house in New York when my nephew Larry came by,' Ike recalled. 'Larry said Frank Lucas wanted to see me. Could I meet with him? I knew he lived in New Jersey and that is where I thought Larry was going to take me. But we ended up going to this small apartment in New York City. Frank was holed up there, afraid to go home. He owed the Italians (La Cosa Nostra) some money and feared they might try to kill him. I thought it was kind of funny—this guy, who was supposed to be a big drug dealer, holed up in this tiny room. Larry said Frank needed a loan, so I gave him $25,000

It would not be the last time Frank would hit me for money.' Lucas would also 'borrow' many elements of Ike Atkinson's story, which Hollywood later incorporated into the movie 'American Gangster.' The movie tried to make Lucas the embodiment of the 1970s black gangster.

THE ATKINSON-JACKSON drug ring grew rapidly, but its success in moving increasingly larger quantities of heroin internationally meant that, eventually, it would catch the attention of law enforcement. In the 1950s, with the French Connection still dominating the international drug trade, the DEA, then known as the Federal Bureau of Narcotics (FBN) and between 1968 and 1973 as the Bureau of Narcotics and Dangerous

Drugs (BNDD), did not have a single agent in Southeast Asia. Not until 1963 did the FBN open an office in Bangkok. In the 1960s, U.S. Customs also had a presence in Southeast Asia, including Thailand, but according to a January 1973 report of a survey team that the Committee on Foreign Relations, U.S. House of Representatives sponsored, Customs had to establish its own intelligence collection capacity in Southeast Asia because the 'BNDD is not likely to work on behalf of Customs.' Consequently, Customs began sending its own intelligence agents overseas. The BNDD complained to the survey team that it 'did not receive a regular flow of intelligence from Customs.' The lack of coordination and cooperation between the BNDD and Customs and the need for better intelligence cooperation on drug trafficking operations helped lead to the creation of the DEA on July 1 1973. The new Federal agency combined Customs agents who had been working drugs with the BNDD agents. Relocated from the Treasury to the Justice Department, the DEA became the sole agency responsible for coordinating all of the Federal government's anti-narcotics law enforcement activities.

By this time, reports prepared by the DEA's Strategic Intelligence Office were warning that Southeast Asia Golden Triangle could replace Turkey as the U.S. primary source of heroin supply. President Richard Nixon agreed, and his Administration increased the number of agents assigned in Southeast Asia and the amount money spent annually to aid local narcotics police.

Since the U.S. Government's resources were limited, priorities had to be established. The Atkinson-Jackson ring and the other heroin smuggling organizations that operated out of Southeast Asia using the U.S. military system were not the highest among them. Instead, the high-profile Chang Chi-fu aka Khun Sa, the legendary Burmese warlord who established heroin refineries in the Golden Triangle to support of his separatist movement was the number one priority.

Born in 1934 to a Chinese father and Burmese mother, Khun Sa entered the drug trade in 1963 when the Burmese government allied with him to fight its enemies. Within a year, however, Khun Sa parted company with the Burmese government and established an independent kingdom in the northern reaches of Burma, near the border with China. In 1969 the Burmese government captured Khun Sa but freed him in 1973 after the warlord's second-in-command kidnapped two Russian doctors and negotiated successfully for Khun Sa's release.

THE U.S. BEST anti-narcotics strategy in Southeast Asia had a formidable obstacle to overcome if the new strategy was to work—the corruption that permeated the Thai military and legal system, particularly law enforcement. 'What is called "corruption" in Thailand dates back hundreds of years to when the ancient Thai Kings would dispatch individuals to serve as government officials in their Provinces,' explained Chuck Lutz, a retired DEA agent who served in Bangkok in the mid 1970s. 'There were no salaries because the citizens were expected to provide subsistence to government officials. The tradition continued, even though a civil service was created. The meager salaries forced the Thai civil servants to keep their hands out just to survive. It evolved to where those who could pay the most had the greatest influence; and civil servants expected to be bribed. This created a situation in which the wealthy controlled the government. Only since the mid-1990's has a middle class emerged in Thailand, with an economy that is beginning to pay living wages, although by all accounts the civil service lags behind.'

From the late 1950s, the Thai military controlled the narcotics trade from the rural Golden Triangle to metropolitan Bangkok, the gateway of international drug markets. In 1972, investigative journalist Jack Anderson published a blistering article in The Washington Post titled: 'Drug smugglers corrupt Thai officials.' CIA, State Department and Justice Department officials told Anderson that more and more heroin was pouring from Burma into Thailand destined for international markets with the aide of corrupted government officials, which, supposedly, was one of America's closest allies. Anderson charged, amid strong Thai government denials, that international dope smugglers had even corrupted government officials in Thailand.

Even the collapse of the country's military dictatorship in the so-called 'Democratic Revolution' of October 1973 did nothing to change the situation. Moreover, the corruption generated by the military's control of the country's narcotics trade permeated Thailand's ruling class and government service. In May 1971, the report of the Special U.S. Congressional Study Commission noted that 'in Thailand, a former diplomat and member of one of the most respected Thai families is reputed to be one of the key figures in the opium, morphine base and heroin operations in the country and throughout Southeast Asia.'

An embarrassing parade of high-ranking Thai military and law enforcement officials were relieved of their duties because of corruption of one sort or another. On September 30 1971, for instance, the Director General of the Thailand's National Police, retired ostensibly because of his age. But one U.S. official in Bangkok assured the Survey Team that the Director General was 'corrupt' and forced out, but that there was no evidence that he was involved in narcotics trafficking. Another U.S. official in Washington, DC, however, told the survey team that the Director General was involved in narcotics, and that was why he 'retired.' Then in October 1972, the Deputy Commander of the Crime Suppression Division of Thailand's National Police was fired because of his involvement in narcotics trafficking.

The corruption even permeated everyday Thai life. Haney Howell, who, beginning in 1971, worked as a reporter out of CBS Television's Bangkok office, recalled his trips to Bangkok after assignments in Bangladesh, Laos and other South and Southeast Asian countries. 'We would arrive in Bangkok with our television gear and our pockets packed with hundreds of dollars. If we had to leave our equipment in the airport, we would pay this guy $100, another guy another $100, and so on. The system of corruption worked so well that it was almost transparent. It was just part of doing business in Thailand.'

Retired DEA agent Brian Raftery, who joined the Administration's Bangkok office in 1973 and transferred out in June 1975, recalled what it was like investigating drug traffickers in Thailand. In successfully completing one investigation, Raftery thought he had put away Min Han Paio, a major opium smuggler, for a long time. 'An informant told me that he was going to meet with Min Han Paio. I said: "You can't be talking about Paio; he's in prison.." The informant said: "Paio's not in prison; I just had lunch with him." I said: "What?" So I went and staked out Paio's girlfriend's place to see if he would show. Sure enough, after a couple of days, here comes Paio walking down the street, laughing and joking, going to see his girlfriend. Walking about 20 feet behind Paio was a guy in a prison guard uniform. I said to myself; "What's going on?" I investigated and found out what was happening in the prison. They had two prisoner checks, one early in the morning and the other late at night. Paio paid off the warden and the guard to let him out of prison during the day. I took some photos of Paio and the prison guard in the street that somehow showed up in the Bangkok Post newspaper. Paio got locked down in prison and the warden was re-assigned to the jungle outposts in northern Thailand.'

On February 6 1975, while in custody in North Carolina, Ike revealed in an interview with Joe Dean, then an Assistant U.S. Attorney for North Carolina, that he had contact and dealings with a retired Thai colonel and an associate who was 'Nationalist Chinese.' According to what Ike told investigators, if he needed 50 or 60 kilos he would call the corrupt colonel and place the order. It would take four or five days to deliver. The colonel would pick up the chemicals in Bangkok necessary for producing heroin in Bangkok and take them to the laboratory. On one occasion, Ike had seen the chemicals that the colonel picked up. They had to pass several military checkpoints, but there was no security. The guards had been paid off.

Given the corruption, DEA agents had to search out cops in Thai law enforcement agencies that they could trust. In the words of Brian Raftery, DEA agents had to 'carve their own niche.' 'When I came to Bangkok, one of our guys was working at the Metropolitan Narcotics Unit, but nobody was working at a place called the Crime Suppression Unit,' Raftery recalled. 'They spoke nothing but Thai in the Suppression Unit, so my Thai got pretty good. But I did find a couple guys there with whom I could work.'

The DEA arranged with Thai law enforcement what Chuck Lutz called a 'marriage of convenience.' 'We would make the cases for our Thai counterparts,' Lutz revealed. 'We had the trust of the informants; the Thai police didn't because of the corruption. Our Thai colleagues did not want to know everything that was going on, which was understandable. If an investigation was compromised, they knew that they would get blamed for the leak. So they were very content to wait until we had the information. We wouldn't tell them until the last possible moment that, for example, in such and such a house, they could find 30 kilos of heroin. They would then go to the house and serve the search warrant. If nothing was found, they could not be accused of tipping the bad guys off. We were both happy with the arrangement.'

Paul Brown, a retired DEA agent who was assigned to the Bangkok office from 1970 to 1976, said that the corruption in law enforcement went beyond the police. 'Yes, it was tough to find an honest Thai cop to work with in those days, but if the police weren't bought off, we worried about whether the bad guys would get to the judge. We cracked a couple of heroin labs. People got arrested, but then the court cut them loose. It was extremely frustrating.'

The DEA worked hard to encourage the competent and honest anti-narcotics elements within the Thai police. According to historian Alfred McCoy in his book, *The Politics of Heroin in Southeast Asia*, 'In launching any sizeable anti-narcotics operation, the DEA had to coordinate with the Thai police and was forced, in effect, to outbid the traffickers for their services. While the (criminal) syndicates could offer money, the DEA rewarded its cooperative counterparts with cash bonuses for seizures, free trips to the FBI Academy in Washington and new military hardware for their units.'

Lutz agreed with McCoy about the challenge that the power of the criminal syndicates posed, but he added that McCoy's assessment is not entirely accurate. 'The DEA never sent Thai Police to the FBI Academy,' Lutz explained. 'We had our own National Training Institute with separate DEA basic and in-service training, state and local police training and international training components. We either sent our counterparts to an international training school in Washington, DC, or had them attend in-country training courses taught by DEA training teams that traveled overseas. And we provided them with police, not military equipment.'

GIVEN THAILAND'S SITUATION, it was understandable that, as late as 1974, the DEA office in Bangkok had little current intelligence on the Atkinson-Jackson drug ring and had made little progress in busting it. In January 1974, Chuck Lutz, a young agent from Philadelphia who had joined the BNDD in October 1970, was assigned to the DEA's Bangkok Regional Office. In early 1975, Paul Brown, his supervisor, called him into his office. Lutz recalled the meeting: 'Paul said to me: "I hate to do this to you, Chuck, but we just had an agent transferred to the U.S., and we have to re-assign his cases. I'm going to give you the Ike Atkinson case." I had never heard of Ike Atkinson. So I went back to the file room and found at least a drawer-and-a-half on the Atkinson investigation. It was unbelievable! The investigation went back in time nearly a decade and included information about Ike when he was in Germany. I spent a week reading and trying to learn about the case. There were DEA reports, Customs reports and U.S. Army Criminal Investigation Division (CID) reports. But the thing that stood out—no informants. They are vital in infiltrating a criminal organization. Even in today's technical environment, informants are essential. If you get a court order for a wire tap, for instance, an informant can help stimulate conversations between crooks and tell you what their intentions are.'

The files showed that as early as June 1968, two undercover agents for the BNDD, working under the guise of being Army deserters, started hanging out in Jack's American Star Bar. They reported to their superiors that deserters and AWOL soldiers were being helped at the bar and provided with phony IDs and counterfeit ration cards for use in black market activities. According to the undercover agents, they were hidden from military police patrols during routine checks of the bar. They also reported that the bar was a cover for preparing false travel orders to be used for conducting illegal activities throughout

Southeast Asia and the U.S. Despite these reports, no raids of Jack's Star Bar ever happened, nor was anybody from the bar ever arrested for such activities.

Ike Atkinson questions the accuracy of the intelligence. 'Never during my time in Bangkok did I ever meet any deserters,' Ike said. 'I didn't have time to mess with them. If they were in the bar when I came to Bangkok, they certainly didn't tell me they were deserters, nor did they ask me for my help. None of my partners ever talked about no (sic) deserters.'

BNDD and Customs set up a task force that targeted the Atkinson-Jackson drug ring in the early 1970s. Months were spent interviewing informers, conducting surveillance on individuals associated with the ring, making undercover buys and building intelligence. As part of the investigation, the DEA sent John Pope, a black agent, to Jack's American Star Bar to play pool, mingle and try to pick up useful information. 'Pope did that for a couple of months, but nothing really happened,' said Paul Brown, a retired BNDD/DEA agent who worked in Thailand at the time. 'The people in the bar got suspicious and they wanted to know who he was.'

The BNDD even filmed the comings and goings at Jack's American Star Bar in the early 70s. In 1976, John McBeth, a reporter for The Bangkok Post, went to the U.S. Embassy for a briefing with DEA officials. McBeth was surprised to learn that the DEA agent doing the briefing recognized him, even though they had never met before. McBeth recalled: 'The agent said to me: "We used to watch you have a drink with Smedley and wondered why you were a part of it." The BNDD had set up surveillance across the street from the bar, and they were using infrared cameras to take photos of customers from Jack's American Star Bar. Being a lone white man, I must have stuck out like a sore thumb. It was a shock to think the BNDD actually thought I might be working with the Atkinson ring.'

Despite the time and effort, the Customs-BNDD Task Force made little progress, and it was disbanded in 1972.

AS THE MONTHS rolled into years, the ring continued to encounter little security in the long pipeline that moved the heroin from Bangkok through the U.S. military transportation system to domestic military bases. Yet, as successful as the drug ring was in using couriers, Ike always looked for new and better ways to move the contraband. After all, using couriers still involved the risk of human foible. What if, despite the best planning, one of the couriers made a careless or stupid mistake, got busted, and began singing like a canary. He could blow the entire operation. Ike worried about that. As his drug ring expanded, the risk of failure would increase, and for a gambler who always strived to put the odds in his favor, that possibility was unacceptable. Ike noticed that some of his couriers were getting over confident, even cocky. One day, Ike was furious to learn that during one smuggling trip, some of his couriers had actually started a craps game in the bathroom of the airport at the military air base in Okinawa. Talk about drawing attention to yourselves!

AT ONE OF the poker games at Ike's house in 1969, Ike met Robert Ernest Patterson, an administrative specialist at the U.S. Air Force Post Office in Bangkok. Ike liked Patterson from the start. The postal clerk played cards like a pro and carried himself as a military man should. Tall and lean, with short-cropped hair, Patterson was well groomed, and Ike noticed that each day he wore a fresh, immaculately pressed shirt and pants. When Ike went to the military post office, he watched Patterson and was impressed with his work ethic. Patterson looked like the type of brother one could count on.

Ike never was comfortable with the way he had to move heroin and money between Bangkok and the U.S.—personally carrying it in AWOL bags or else having to depend on somebody else to carry it—inherent with the element of human risk. One day, while Ike was at the post office, seeing Patterson at work, the idea hit him like a revelation from above. Why not send the heroin and money through the postal system? After asking Patterson some questions and doing a little research, Ike learned that the military's postal system was as lax security-wise as its transportation system. The postal clerks frequently failed to follow prescribed regulations in accepting material for posting, and once the mail arrived in the U.S., postal officials failed to give the mail cursory inspection.

It did not take much coaxing for Ike to persuade Patterson to become the point man in Ike's new scheme for smuggling drugs and money. Patterson's job was simple: make sure that packages Ike gave him were sent via one of the three weekly flights from Bangkok to Seymour Johnson Air Force base in Ike's hometown of Goldsboro. Ike would go the mailroom at Seymour Johnson AFB and pick up his packages containing the drugs. Ike, in turn, would send packages containing money back to Bangkok to buy more drugs or to pay people for services rendered. When those packages arrived at Bangkok, Patterson would handle them as well. For his efforts, Patterson would get $1,000 per delivery.

Soon, with Ike flying frequently between Bangkok and Goldsboro, the new smuggling scheme was operating and running as smoothly as the courier system. Ike, however, never got used to how the dependable well-groomed Patterson would deliver the packages to him. Ike's new partner in crime would strap on a helmet, tie down the package of money to the back of his motorcycle and then drive through the chaotic and often bewildering traffic of Bangkok. When Ike was in

Bangkok, Patterson would arrive at Ike's door and hand him the package with a friendly greeting and nary a wrinkle in his clothes. It was truly a mission accomplished.

Jack let out a soft laugh and said: 'They arrested me, but I broke out of jail.'

Ike burst out laughing. 'Are you serious? Didn't they handcuff you?'

No, I walked away,' Jack revealed.

'Walked away?' Ike said incredulously. 'How did you that?'

'Can you believe this?' Jack said. 'The Man was too busy trying to rip off our dope and money to worry about me. Those were some dirty cops!'

'Okay, buddy,' Ike said. 'We can talk about it when you come to Goldsboro. Take a bus and I'll pick you up.'

Peter Rabbit's mother had left Goldsboro to visit her sister. Ike told his friend that Jack was on the run and needed a place to hide. Jack had his safe house.

IKE WAS ON the run, having been part of the smuggling attempt, but he realized that to keep running was not his best interest. Once Jack was safe in his hiding place, Ike and Jack discussed the situation. They agreed Ike would turn himself in, but Jack would remain the drug-dealing partner who stayed out in the cold. On March 19 1969, Ike surrendered to local law enforcement and was incarcerated in the county jail in Wilson, North Carolina. The North Carolina authorities had notified BNDD Dennis Hart, Patch's 31-year old partner, that they had Ike Atkinson in custody. Hart came down to talk to Ike. The two agents were a sharp contrast in appearance. Patch was slim and wore a moustache and black cowboy hat. Hart was stocky and looked a little rumpled in appearance. They had both worked for the St. Louis Police Department and had plenty of law enforcement experience. But to Ike, Hart and Patch looked more like Fatty and Skinny than professional narcotics agents.

Later in court, Patch, who had been with the BNDD since 1968, admitted that he was one of the BNDD's 'old school agents.'

Prosecutor: You told us you had courses in breaking and entering. Patch: Yes, sir.

Prosecutor: And wiretapping?

Patch: Yes, sir.

Prosecutor: Were you one of the agents who felt justified in breaking the law to nab dope pushers?

Patch: To a degree, yes, sir.

Prosecutor: Did you engage in some other practices that aren't written into our Constitution?

Patch: Yes, sir.

Prosecutor: Like posing as a defense lawyer to get a confession?

Patch: Yes sir.

Prosecutor: Have you ever done that?

Patch: Yes, sir.

Prosecutor: Is that called the lawyer's trick?

Patch: Yes, sir.

Jack's claim that the narcotics agents had ripped off some of the dope was credible, given the corruption that had permeated the Federal Bureau of Narcotics (FBN) New York Office in the 1960s. In December 1968, just two months before the bust at Pearl and Matthew Parks' residence, the same year the Bureau of Narcotics and Dangerous Drugs (BNDD) was created to replace the FBN. The New York Times reported that 32 former FBN agents from the New York office had resigned since the FBN launched an investigation in August 1967. U.S. Attorney General Ramsey Clark told the press that the investigation had uncovered 'significant corruption' that involved 'illegally selling and buying drugs, retaining contraband for personal use and sale, taking money allocated for informants and failing to enforce the law.' As part of the investigation, the Internal Revenue Service (IRS) scrutinized the tax returns of the former FBN agent suspects. In some instances, the dirty agents acted as if they were working as mobsters. The authorities, for example, arrested two agents in 1967 and indicted them in August 1968 on the charge of conspiracy to use thousands of dollars in seized genuine and counterfeit bills to buy narcotics for re-sale on the illegal market.

At the county jail, Hart took Ike into a room where they could have some privacy. Hart flashed his credentials and explained to Ike that he was the BNDD's chief agent in Ike's case. He then opened his briefcase, took out photos of Jack and Ike's brother, Edward, and said: 'We know everything that has taken place. Where is Herman Jackson?'

'I know where Jackson is,' Ike said coolly. 'He wants to surrender.'

'That's fine; let's arrange it,' Hart replied, slightly taken aback by Ike's straight forward answer.

On March 21 1969, two days after his arrest, Ike posted a $25,000 cash bond, and at three or four in the afternoon, Ike took Patch and two other agents to his house on Neuse Circle. Waiting for them was Herman Jackson.

After Jack's release on bail, Ike and Jack made frequent trips to New York City to confer with their lawyer Howard Diller, a former FBN agent and a former Assistant Counselor to the Commissioner of Narcotics in Washington, DC. 'My sister Pearl learned that Howard Diller had done a good job of representing somebody she knew well and recommended him,' Ike recalled. 'Howard had a nasal New York tone of voice and an abrupt big city manner, but I was crazy about him. I knew that when he gave us advice it was the best we could get. Jack and I ended up paying Howard $100,000 apiece to represent us in the 1969 case. The case made Howard Diller. He was able to leave his firm and start his own law practice on Broadway Avenue.'

ON JULY 30 1969, a Federal grand jury indicted Ike and Jack, as well as Pearl Parks, Mathew Parks, Edward Atkinson and Pratt Benthall on drug trafficking charges. Benthall was still on the loose, and a bench warrant was issued in the Eastern District of New York for his arrest. In August, the U.S. Attorney's Office dropped the charges against Linda Atkinson, Rodney Raiford, David Horton and Jane Burton. Ike pled guilty to unlawfully distributing 2.2 grams of heroin. Judge George Rosling sentenced him to ten years in prison and fined him $2,500. Ike's legal counsel immediately appealed the case.

IT LOOKED AS if Ike would be going away to the Big House for a long time, but the case was far from over. On August 22, Hart met with Ike at a restaurant on Broadway Avenue in New York City. Ike sat down first in a chair that was facing the door, but Hart asked Ike to exchange seats. Then Hart patted Ike down.

'You know there are some rumors about missing heroin from the detention center,' Hart said. 'Ike, have you talked to any other agents about it?'

Ike remembered what Jack had told him about the agents at the detention center who were too busy messing with their dope to worry about Jack. 'No, sir,' Ike said. 'You are the only agent I've talked with in private. I've talked to some other agents, but only in your presence.'

Hart shook his head like a parent scolding a child. 'I wish I could trust you fully, Ike. My confidence in you has not gone up more than 5 percent since the last time we talked at that county jail (in Wilson).'

'I have not talked to anybody else,' Ike insisted.

When the conversation ended, Ike and Hart walked in silence around the corner to Church Street. As they were about to cross the street, Hart suddenly stopped and turned to Ike. 'How would you like to go free in your case?' Hart asked.

Stunned, Ike blurted: 'You got to be kidding, Mr. Hart.'

'No, I'm not kidding. What would you say if I told you everybody could walk in the case? Your sister could get back the car the police impounded, and Jack would get his money back.'

Excited at the prospects, Ike smiled and shook his head. 'Man, that would be just fine.'

Hart was silent for a moment, and then he grabbed Ike's arm tightly. 'We could do business if you can come up with $50,000.'

Ike knew there had to be a catch but raising $50,000 would be no problem. 'Let me see what I can do, Mr. Hart,' Ike said.

Hart concluded the meeting with a stern warning: 'You will be in hot water, Ike, if you mention this matter to anyone. Understand?'

Ike assured the agent that he would tell just Jack and brother Edward and nobody else about the $50,000 'fee' for doing business. Hart had no problem with that.

During the next several weeks, Hart called Ike to check on his progress in raising the money, Ike told him that he and Jack had their portion of the money, but his brother Edward, whom Ike asked to contribute, had reservations about the deal. Edward doubted that Hart had the power to take care of the case so that everybody charged could walk.

On October 8, Ike had the first of several meetings with Hart at the Drop-In Inn on Clove Road in Staten Island. Hart thought Ike would bring the money, but Ike disappointed him again. They continued to talk on the phone, sometimes twice a day. Hart was showing remarkable patience, but he kept sounding like a broken record. 'You're running late, Ike. You better get the money.'

On November 3, Ike was in a New York court, attending one of several hearings at which Howard Diller, his lawyer, was trying to suppress evidence in the case before it went to trial. When the court recessed, Ike and Hart met in the latrine. The broken record asked: 'Do you have the money?'

'Yes, I have it in my hotel room,' Ike said.

'Bring it to the Drop-In (Inn),' Hart ordered. But Ike failed to show again. The next day at the courthouse, Hart asked Ike why he didn't show up with the money. 'I was sleepy,' Ike said. Again Hart told Ike to show up at the Drop-In Inn with the money. Hart was exhibiting remarkable patience; his aggressive demands for the money were free of overt threats of violence. Still, Ike knew Hart was a dangerous individual.

Ike showed up, but again, without the money. This time Hart came with Patch. Hart told Ike to get in his car and follow them. They drove about ten miles before stopping at a white brick building on a West Side pier. Ike didn't know where he was, but he was certain that the agent would not do something stupid and try to physically force him to turn over the money.

Hart and Patch walked over to Ike's car and told Ike to get out. Patch began searching the car. After a few minutes, he turned to Hart and yelled: 'I may have something here.' Hart ordered Ike to put his hands on the building and stay put while they examined what Patch had found.

'Did you bug the car?' Hart snapped.

'I don't know what you're talking about,' Ike said.

A device stuck in the car's lighter is what had caught Patch's attention, but after examining it more closely, the agents concluded it was not a bugging device.

Frustrated by Ike's stonewalling, Hart yelled at Ike: 'We're tired of the runaround. You got the money in the hotel room?'

Ike looked at red-faced Hart and said: 'Right.'

'Then we are going to get it now!'

'Can't you wait until tomorrow night to pick it up,' Ike had the temerity to ask.

Fatty and Skinny looked at each other in disbelief. Hart yelled: 'Hell, no! We will get it now!'

The three men in their two cars drove back to the Americana Hotel where Ike and Jack were sharing a room. While Patch and Hart waited in the car, Ike went to his room to get the money.

Jack was lying in bed, relaxing. Ike explained what happened and said he was going to give the agents the money. 'Do what you think is best,' Jack advised.

Ike went back outside and gave the agents $20,000.

'Get the rest of the money as fast as you can,' Patch ordered. 'I'll be calling you.' Hart informed Ike that the amount of money he and Jack owed the two agents was now $60,000, not $50,000.

ON NOVEMBER 7, Ike was in court again. Hart was there, too, and he told Ike: 'I'm working for you. Go see the lawyer about the tax charge. I think you're going to like it.' To Ike's surprise, he learned that the court had dropped the very serious trafficking in heroin charges, which had the heavy mandatory penalties, in exchange for Ike and Jack agreeing to plead guilty to the lesser charge of failing to pay a duty on heroin imported into the US—the tax charge to which Hart had alluded.

The deal did sound fishy when reported by the press, but prosecutor Denis Dillon, who had served as the Assistant U.S. District Attorney for the Eastern District since 1966, maintained that Hart had never actively intervened in the negotiations that produced the plea bargain.

More importantly, though, the case against Ike and Jack already had a serious problem. 'Clemons was a key witness in the case,' recalled prosecutor Dillon. 'I told Dennis Hart that I was putting Ike and his people before the grand jury, and I needed to put Clemons before the grand jury as well because he was the key witness. Hart said: "Oh, really?" He seemed a little surprised and said: "I can't produce Clemons right now, but I can produce him for the trial." I said: "That's okay. When we get a date for the trial, you got to produce the informant." He said: "Okay, let me find him." Hart called back in a couple of days and said: "I can't find him but give me a few days and I will." Another couple of days went by and Hart called again: "It's going to be tough to have Clemons testify. We found him with two bullet holes in his head." I said to Hart: "That's kind of redundant. One bullet would have been enough."' Hart said: "I guess we can't go forward with the case." I said: "Yeah, we can." Hart sounded surprised, but he didn't object.'

On October 27, Bobby Clemons was found dead in the back seat of a Buick parked in Brooklyn beneath the Verrazano-Narrows Bridge. Clemons had two bullets in his head and another four in his neck; he had been dead for at least four days. Two NYPD detectives assigned to the Clemons murder investigation came by Dillon's office. 'I told them that Hart told me Clemons had taken two bullets to the head. One of the detectives said that only the murderer could have known how many bullets were in Clemons head. A lot of mystery surrounded Clemons death, but we never suspected Atkinson and Jackson of killing him. The NYPD had Patch and Hart as the prime suspects.'

UNBEKNOWNST TO HART, Ike was fed up with the Fatty and Skinny show and wasn't going to take it anymore. 'During the suppression hearings, Ike had come up to me in the courtroom,' Dillon recalled. 'Ike said: "Mr. Dillon, we are guilty. I'm not denying that, but Patch and Hart are telling you a story. It hasn't happened the way they said it did." Yeah, yeah, I thought. I was listening to Hart, but I began to have my doubts about him and his investigation.' Being suspicious of Hart and Patch and curious about what happened to Ike's and Jack's money and dope, the authorities came to Goldsboro to talk to Ike about it. At first, Ike was reluctant to tell the Feds anything, but finally he did.

In early December, John Thompson, a BNDD agent who had been with the Feds since 1955, made several trips to Goldsboro to interview Atkinson and Jackson and to find out what they knew about Patch and Hart. Ike told the BNDD agent all about the shakedown.

After the plea bargain, Hart continued to call Ike and press him for the money. In early December, Ellis Sutton was staying at Ike's house, and he suggested that Ike tape record his conversation with Hart. On December 19, Hart called while Ike was in bed with the flu. They had agreed to use the term "information" to refer to money whenever they talked on the phone. The tape recorder was on. Hart told Ike: 'You can't come up with too many more fucking excuses. You ought to have run out of them by now.' They agreed to meet on December 23, but Ike was still not feeling well and he failed to show.

Ike and the BNDD worked out a strategy to bust Hart and Patch. By this time, Hart was no longer a BNDD agent. On December 5, he quit after two-and-a-half years of service, and moved to Springfield, Illinois, where he became an agent for the Alcohol and Tax Division of the Internal Revenue Service(IRS).

But Hart still wanted the rest of the $60,000, and to collect it, he arranged a meeting with Ike for December 26.

The BNDD gave Ike about $500 in $1 and $5 bills and wrapped the money in a package to make it look like a substantial amount. The plan—the BNDD would arrest Hart once he picked up the money. Hopefully, Patch would be with him.

Hart did call Ike on December 26. 'Look, I'll tell you what I want you to do,' Hart explained. 'You got all the information, right?'

'Don't do no rush job,' Ike protested.

'Well, yeah, a rush job. I'll tell you what to do. You get all the information, right?'

'Yeah,' Ike replied.

'Okay you hop in the car there, one of those three or four cars sitting out in front of your house. You take a right. You know where the Pure (Oil) truck stop is down there?'

'You mean (the one) right here in Goldsboro?' Ike asked.

'Yes. In about five minutes.'

'God almighty!'

'I just drove here from New York,' Hart retorted.

'Well, you are going to have to hold where you is (sic),' Ike said. 'I gotta go pick it up. It won't take about a minute.'

'Where you gotta go?' Hart asked.

'I got to get it where I got it. It's in town.'

'Okay, how long are you going to be?'

'Ummm, maybe ten or 15 minutes,' Ike advised.

'I'll tell you what,' Hart said. 'Why don't you come here and I'll follow you. You know, that way, I won't have to come back here or wait.'

'That won't put you where my stash is, will it?' Ike asked. 'Nah, no,' Hart replied.

'I'll be down in about five minutes,' Hart said.

Hart came with Patch and they did meet Ike at the Pure Oil truck stop, where the BNDD agents had the rendezvous under surveillance. Patch and Hart were busted and indicted on three counts of bribery and one of conspiracy. Patch was fired from the BNDD after rejecting an offer to resign.

It looked as if the prosecution had a slam duck case, but Patch and Hart hired F. Lee Bailey, one of the country's best criminal lawyers. Born in 1933, in Waltham, Massachusetts, Bailey was just 38 years old, but already he had made a legal name for himself defending such high-profile defendants as Sam Sheppard and the Boston Strangler. In 1954, Sam Sheppard was found guilty of murdering his wife, Marilyn. Hired by Sam's brother, Stephen, Bailey successfully argued before the U.S. Supreme Court that Sheppard had been denied due process. Bailey won a retrial and Sheppard was found not guilty. The Boston Strangler was Albert DeSalvo, and Bailey tried to argue an insanity defense for him, but he was found guilty. Later, Bailey would also defend Patty Hearst and be part of the defense team for O.J. Simpson.

Ike and Jack were two of the 12 witnesses who testified for the prosecution, which was headed by Marvin R. Loewy, an attorney for the organized crime and racketeering section of the U.S. Department of Justice. In cross examination, Bailey got Ike to admit that he was a drug dealer who was smuggling heroin into the U.S. from Thailand, so the jurors would have to weigh the veracity of his testimony against that of two former law enforcement officers. The defense had 10 witnesses, including Patch and Hart, who testified that Ike's and Jack's version of events had been fabricated in order to obtain a light sentence on the tax violation charges. Although Ike and Jack had pleaded guilty to the tax violation, they still awaited sentencing.

Hart and Patch were tried twice, and twice Bailey managed to get the judge to declare a mistrial. In the first trial in

November 1970, Federal judge Orrin G. Judd refused to accept the jury's verdict of guilty after a poll of jurors revealed that two of their members were unconvinced of the defendant's guilt. Bailey had polled the jury of seven women and five men after the foreman qualified the judge's guilty verdict with a plea of clemency at the close of the seven-day trial. Bailey's questioning then disclosed that two jurors, a man and a woman, had doubts about the defendants' guilt, but they agreed to go 'along' with the other jurists provided that the verdict included the recommendation for clemency.

When the court questioned the woman juror about her decision, she said: 'After I said "no", they get together and explain to me again— not really, (they) forced me, made me say "clemency"'.

Bailey then asked: 'And those other people explained to you their views and so forth to try to persuade you to find them (Patch and Hart) guilty?'

'They didn't exactly do this,' the juror revealed.

Bailey pressed: 'Were you, in fact, persuaded to change your vote because they all agreed to recommend clemency?'

'That's right,' the juror acknowledged.

Bailey asked: 'If they told you the man would go to jail for years and years, would you have voted guilty?'

The juror said: 'I would have said 'not guilty.'

The judge declared a second mistrial in March 1971 when Ike, under intense pressure from Bailey's questioning, blurted out that he had submitted to a lie detector test. 'Ike was an inexperienced witness, and Bailey managed to maneuver him into revealing he had taken a lie detector test,' Dillon recalled. 'Bailey then asked the judge to admit the test results into court. Lie detector tests are not very reliable, but the case really started to go downhill from there.'

Judge Judd subsequently ruled that the defense could introduce into the court proceedings the polygraph tests that the witness (Ike) had failed to pass. This was the mistrial that broke the back of the government's case. On December 7 1971, on a motion by Loewy, Judge Mark A. Constantino dismissed without comment the charges against Patch and Hart. The Federal government had concluded there was no 'realistic possibility' of convicting the two former agents in the pending third trial. Prosecutors knew it would take more than the testimony of two admitted drug traffickers from Thailand to convict two former law enforcement officials from New York City.

'The case got really screwed up,' Dillon conceded. 'I did my best to rescue it, but in the end the only thing we could do was ask the court to dismiss all charges against Hart and Patch.' And the murder of Bobby Clemons was never solved. Ironically, while Hart and Patch walked, Ike was in jail and waiting to see if the Appeals Court would overturn his ten-year sentence and $2,500 fine.

CHAPTER 7

The Denver Connection

IKE STILL HAD to spend about eight months in jail at the United State penitentiary in Atlanta for the tax charge. Upon release, he did not miss a beat of his life on the edge. After making sure everything was okay at home in Goldsboro, Ike took a military hop to Bangkok to get his drug trafficking operation back on track. 'Prison life was not as bad as I thought it would be,' Ike recalled. 'I adjusted well, made friends and bided my time. Once I got out, I had no intention of joining the straight life. I continued to do the same thing.'

Life on the edge, though, would not be the same. Thanks to Ike's problems in New York City, law enforcement agencies had now exposed his drug ring, and it would be much more challenging for him and his partner Herman 'Jack' Jackson to continue their drug smuggling operation without the constant threat of arrest. Still, Ike did not feel that he had to change his modus operandi, since he saw no evidence that the authorities were keeping a close eye on him. When in Bangkok and moving around the city, Ike did take precautions to ensure he was not being tailed. Periodically, he would drive along and then suddenly pull off to the side of the road to see what cars went by and what cars may have stopped behind him. Ike cannot recall one instance where he knew for sure he was being followed. Nor did he ever feel for certain that his residences in Bangkok or Goldsboro were under police surveillance in those years, although he was not completely sure that the authorities were not spying on him. On one occasion in Bangkok, Ike saw a Thai man and a white man sitting in a car outside his home, looking kind of suspicious. But as Ike perceived the situation: You cannot get ahead in life if you begin to see danger in every suspicious looking car.

Jack was now well known to U.S. and Thai law enforcement and even U.S. legislators, who publicly decried the surging tide of heroin pouring into the U.S. from Thailand. One 1971 study prepared by the U.S. Foreign Relations Committee put a law enforcement bull's eye on Jack's back, identifying him by name, summarizing his alleged role in the Thai drug trade and concluding that 'BNDD agents in Bangkok are of the opinion that Jackson is probably paying a Thai legislator in Bangkok.'

In May 1971, Jack Anderson, the noted investigative journalist and nationwide columnist, wrote an article about how Jackson was busy importing drugs from Thailand into the United States while out on bond for the 1969 New York drug case that evolved into a corruption case involving Dennis Hart and Richard Patch. Following up on Anderson's report, a broadcast-media news team from the U.S. trekked to Bangkok to interview Jack about Anderson's claim. Unruffled by the attention, Jack sounded like a diplomat deflecting a tough question, denying he had ever been in the narcotics trafficking business. Actually, Jack had to make this disclaimer because he was re-stating what he had said to defense lawyer F. Lee Bailey under oath in the Hart and Patch corruption trial, which was still ongoing.

A good question for the broadcast news team to ask Jack would have been: 'Are you an informant as well as a drug trafficker, Mr. Jackson?' On the stand under oath at the Hart-Patch trial, Jack denied being a snitch when the aggressive Bailey pointedly put that question to him.

Jack: (I'm) not a stool pigeon. I said I would tell the government my part of this thing, to cooperate with the government.

Bailey: Weren't you going to turn in some people in the same business you were in, in exchange for something?

Jack: No, sir.

Bailey: Oh?

Jackson: No, sir.

Bailey: Did you give the government any information along the way?

Jack: I gave them some information about different things.

Bailey: You gave them names, didn't you?

Jack: A couple of names they already had.

Bailey: Of people you had already done business with?

Jack: No.

Bailey: Names of people in the heroin racket? Is that who the names were? How many names?

Jack: A couple.

Bailey: In connection with what offences?

Jack: With a—they asked me did I know these two particular men. I told them yes.

Bailey: Okay, and then you gave them some information?

Jack: I gave them some information to help the government stop the flow of drugs out of Thailand and into the (U.S.) country.

DEA and Customs intelligence reports indicate that Jack officially became an informant in the spring or early summer of 1968, well before the bust at the Queens, New York, residence of Pearl Parks, Ike's sister, although the true extent of the snitching is not known. All BNDD agents who were stationed in Bangkok in the period from 1968 to 1970 and who might know something about it are dead. But according to one U.S.

Customs intelligence report: 'Jackson agreed to initiate cases against (Robert) Johnson and Philip Michael Galley (at the time, Johnson's partner in drug trafficking) and to set up buys for Federal agents for them. Jackson indicated he could obtain information about Johnson from his brother in Thailand, Andrew Price, and on July 10 1969, Jackson advised Federal agents that his brother had indicated the drug dealers, Johnson and Galley, were in Bangkok, Thailand.'

It was uncertain, though, what motivated Jack to cooperate with the Feds. Certainly, to get a lighter prison sentence for the tax case would have headed the list of reasons. Further, it was no secret to the band of brothers that Jack and Robert Johnson did not get along; in fact, they loathed each other. Jack probably had the same issue with the charismatic Johnson that he had with Daniel Burch—namely, Jack could not see somebody—anybody—getting ahead of him in life. Jack could have been trying to do to Johnson what he was suspected of doing to Burch: Get Johnson in trouble with the law and out of the picture in Thailand. Or maybe Jack was trying to string The Man along. Jack did go to the Embassy in Bangkok and report to the BNDD, which had its office there. The BNDD intelligence reports indicate that certainly happened. But the BNDD also noted that 'Jackson's information never proved reliable enough to result in the seizure of a heroin shipment that could lead to the arrest of Johnson.' In a 1976 report, the BNDD complained that Jackson never did pass on 'any information of value.'

BY THE SUMMER of 1971, the Atkinson-Jackson ring was operating not just in the eastern U.S., but also in California. To set up the California connection, Ike arranged a drug deal with David Lee Brooks, a former serviceman who came to Bangkok in 1969. 'When I met Brooks, he was about 25 years old,' Ike recalled. 'He was good looking and the girls in our bar were always fighting over him. Jack hired Brooks to work at our club and take care of the stage during performances. He was good at it. I liked him and everybody in my family loved him.'

Ike trusted Brooks, so he had no problem collaborating with him on a drug deal when the opportunity presented itself. That happened for Ike, unfortunately, in early September 1971, when two drug dealers named Robert Lee Jenkins and John Jerry Williams unknowingly discussed over the phone the sale of heroin with a BNDD undercover agent, John Sutton. On about September 6 Williams and Eli Homer Hamilton, an associate, met with Monica Burkley in Bakersfield, California, to make the deal happen. On the same day, Williams and Burkley took a flight from Los Angeles to Atlanta and on to Florence, North Carolina, where they met with Brooks, who brought them to a hotel in Goldsboro. It was Ike's good fortune that Brooks introduced him to Williams and not to Burkley. The authorities believed Ike gave Williams a quantity of heroin on September 9 1971, which Williams taped to Burkley's body. Williams and Burkley moved the heroin by plane from Atlanta to Bakersfield, California, via Los Angeles. The next day, Williams removed the heroin from Burkley's body and proceeded to cut it into smaller packets. The same day, Williams and Jenkins delivered the heroin to special agent Sutton and they were busted.

Ike, Brooks and the others were charged with conspiracy to violate the narcotics laws. The California court set a $50,000 cash bond for Ike and for Brooks. At the arraignment and pleas hearing on December 27 1971, both Ike and Brooks pleaded not guilty. The court set the trial for April 18 1972, in Bakersfield.

Ike traveled to Bakersfield for the trial and stayed at the home of Joseph Coley, a boyhood friend who had served in the Navy. The situation did not look good for Ike. He knew

Brooks would not talk, but he sensed that the evidence was strong against him. The authorities were confident that they finally had the case that would put the man they had nicknamed Sergeant Smack away for a long time. A big part of the Feds' case was the testimony of Monica Burkley, who, before the trial, identified Ike from photos as being the individual who delivered one kilo of heroin to Williams at a motel in Goldsboro. When Burkley took the stand on April 18 1972, however, she changed her story. While identifying Brooks as the man who picked her and Williams up at the Raleigh-Durham Airport on September 7 1971, she could not identify Ike. According to Ike, he was lucky because Burkley told the truth on the stand. They had never met, but her word—if she had lied —would have been enough to convict him.

The trial lasted just one day. The jury found Ike not guilty and on April 18 1972, the court dismissed the charges. But the next day Brooks was found guilty of conspiracy to distribute and sell drugs and was sentenced to seven years in prison. Ike arranged for Brook's Thai wife and their children to be brought to the U.S. where they stayed at Ike's house while Brooks served his sentence. Ike had dodged another legal bullet, but the close call did not change anything. 'Once I beat the charge, I went back to Bangkok and it was business as usual,' Ike recalled.

FOR JACK HOWEVER, another run-in with the law had a different outcome. Indeed, it was a criminal career-shattering event, which, ironically, would involve an individual approaching Jack with a plan to smuggle drugs, rather than Jack initiating the drug smuggling venture. The operation would eventually have a course-altering effect on the Atkinson-Jackson drug ring.

During the spring of 1971, Sylvester Searles and Johnny Trice were sergeants in the U.S. military assigned to the U-Tapao Air Base in Thailand. Still in his early 20s, Searles was a five-year veteran who had worked as a keypunch operator and a records shipment clerk before becoming an aircraft cargo specialist, which essentially meant he loaded and unloaded pallets of cargo and recorded the shipments. The 6' 2" Searles, a Jersey City, New Jersey native, had a speech impediment and, at times, many times, it was difficult to understand him. So it was inevitable that someone would stick him with the nickname of 'Mumbles.' That understandably explained Searles reticent nature and why he normally stuck to himself. Law enforcement officials, who later interrogated him, described Mumbles as extremely insecure and not the type of guy you would normally want to stick your neck out with on a big heroin buy.

Searles was a dreamer of things illicit. Watching goods coming and going through U-Tapao, he often thought how easy it would be to smuggle things back to America as cargo aboard military aircraft. He thought about it often because he always seemed to be broke, or at least he claimed to be.

The shorter Trice was energetic and gregarious and seemed to make friends easily. He, too, had thought about the military transport system and how easy it would be to smuggle things to the U.S. But while Trice and Searles had criminal thoughts, neither man had ever been in trouble with the law.

The two servicemen could not be described as friends, but occasionally they would talk when they bumped into each other; they lived in the same barracks at the U-Tapao Air Force Base. One day in April 1971, when both men were off from work, they began a casual conversation in front of a Coke machine in the barracks. It was a meeting of the minds, for they eventually chatted about how goods could be shipped to the U.S. to make some money. Mumbles agreed with Trice when he said: 'You can send packages through the Air Force. I guess you could get rich that way.'

They discussed smuggling specific items, including stereos and marijuana, and agreed that, if the opportunity presented itself, they would try to smuggle something into the U.S. They promised to keep in touch. That same evening, Trice bumped into Master Sergeant Gerald Gainous at the barracks. Trice had known Gainous since 1967 when both men were stationed at Travis Air Force Base. With 19 years of service, the 37-year old Gainous had spent his entire adult life in the military. Sources remember Gainous as being articulate and clean-cut looking, with short hair and a strong military bearing. Hollywood handsome, Gainous had a smooth manner that made him worthy of his nickname—'Slick.' With a wife and three children, he appeared to be a solid family man, but he had met Ike in the 1970s and became friends with him, Jack and many other members of the Atkinson-Jackson drug ring. In being associated with the ring, Gainous was always on the lookout for new ways that the drug ring could smuggle heroin into the U.S.

Trice told Gainous about his conversation with Searles. Gainous agreed that it would be 'nice' to figure out a way to smuggle 'goods' into the U.S. using military aircraft, but he did not elaborate. A few nights later, Gainous came by Trice's residence and asked him if he had seen Searles again. Trice said 'no,' then Gainous invited Trice to Bangkok to meet 'The Main Man' at Jack's American Star Bar. Trice, of course, heard of the bar—every Black serviceman who had been to Bangkok knew about the legendary watering hole—but he wondered who 'The Main Man' was. He is William Herman Jackson, Gainous explained. Searles remembered Jack from a few years before when he was serving in Bangkok at the Don Muang Air Base in Bangkok. He was surprised to learn that Jack owned the bar.

At the meeting at Jack's American Star Bar, Trice did most of the talking while Jack listened. Trice explained his idea for using

U-Tapao as a base for smuggling items out of Thailand and into the U.S. He was a shipping clerk, Trice explained, and knew how the system worked. Trice had given Jack some interesting information, and Jack said he would be in touch with him.

Trice left the meeting with 'The Main Man' excited; returning to U-Tapao, he found Searles and told him all about it. They agreed their plans could amount to something. A few weeks later, when Searles spotted Jackson in the U-Tapao terminal, he got up his nerve and approached 'The Main Man.' 'I got a way to ship something to the U.S.,' Searles confided. 'I am broke and have no money.' Jack looked around, and then with a slightly perturbed expression, told the eager young man: 'Be cool. I will see you later.'

MEANWHILE TRICE HAD left Thailand on May 29. He was on leave and his next posting would be Tinker Air Force Base in the suburb of Midwest City, Oklahoma. A major military base, Tinker is the home of the Air Force Materiel Command Oklahoma City Air Logistics Center, which is the worldwide manager for a wide range of aircraft, engines, missiles, software and avionics and other accessories and components. Today, Tinker has more than 26,000 military and civilian employees and is the largest single-site employer in Oklahoma. The installation covers approximately nine square miles and has 760 buildings with a combined floor space of over 15,200,000 square feet.

After spending four days in California, Trice went home to Chicago to visit his mother. Not long after, Trice got a call from Gainous, who was now stationed at Seymour Johnson Air Force Base in Goldsboro. As a member of the Strategic Air Command, he had a top security clearance which, later he told a court, gave him access to a number of 'privileges.'

Gainous was a great contact for the Atkinson-Jackson drug ring, giving it a virtual spy within the military system.

'A guy named Sylvester Searles is talking with Herman Jackson,'

Gainous told Trice: 'Is that the same guy?'

I believe so,' Trice said.

'Yeah, good,' Gainous replied. 'I will write and give him your address and let him know where you are going to be. When will you be stationed at Tinker?'

'I believe I'm leaving on the 29th of June,' Trice said.

Gainous called Trice again and learned that he had got an extension on his leave and would not be departing for Tinker Air Force Base until July 6. Once Trice settled into his new posting in Oklahoma, Gainous paid him a visit to see if he was still on board with the smuggling operation. Gainous told Trice to write a letter to Searles and give him his contact information and details about shipping goods to Tinker. After Gainous left, Trice wrote two letters to Searles, sending one and throwing the other in the wastebasket. He was having big doubts about participating in the smuggling operation. Smuggling stereos and maybe a little marijuana was one thing, but heroin? He had never been in trouble with the law. Was the money really worth the risk of a long jail sentence?

IN EARLY AUGUST 1971 Searles was working in the freight section at the U-Tapao base when a tall black male he did not know came up to him. In a low voice, the stranger said: 'Somebody wants to see you outside.' Mumbles told his supervisor that he was taking a break and then followed the man to a car parked in front of the warehouse. Sitting inside the car was Jack.

'How is it going?' Jack said with a friendly smile.

'All right,' the man of few words answered.

Then in a deliberate tone Jack said: 'Is everything still okay?'
'Sure,' Searles said.

Jack pulled out a letter and handed it to Searles. The letter
was from Johnny Trice. Searles read the letter. It contained
directions on how to ship a box to Tinker Air Force Base.

Searles was floored. How did Jack know Trice? He had
never mentioned Trice's name to Jack. Searles and Jack had a
discussion about the instructions. Searles assured Jack that he
understood them. They agreed to meet the next night at Jack's
American Star Bar.

When Searles arrived at the bar, he went immediately to the
men's room. Jackson came in and handed Searles a key to a
room in the hotel located behind the bar. 'Go there and wait,'
Jack instructed. On the way to the hotel, Searles felt alive;
something big was finally going to happen, and he soon would
be making some real money. During the meeting, Searles, in
his eagerness, tried to impress Jack, telling him about the time
a man offered him $100 to ship some morphine to Vietnam.
'That's peanuts,' Jackson scoffed. 'I want to ship something worth
more than gold—seven kilos of heroin.' Using his hands, Jack
showed Searles what size box it would take to ship that amount
of contraband. He would get $15,000 upon the operation's
successful completion, Jack informed Searles.

Jack wanted a test shipment done first to see if the operation
could work. In the test run, they would pack the box with
trash and garbage. Searles agreed but said he would need some
money to pay his Thai associates who were helping him with
the operation. Further, Searles said, he would only work with
Jack or Andrew Price, Jackson's brother, whom he knew well.

'It (the heroin) must be packed airtight so the drug dogs
won't sniff it at U-Tapao,' Searles advised.

Jack agreed. 'It will packed air-tight and dogs won't sniff
it.'

Searles and Jack returned to the bar where Jack gave Searles $20 and told him to come back the next night and talk to Andrew Price about getting the rest of the money. The next night, Searles arrived at the bar about 8:30p.m. and sat at a table in the dance hall. Price came over and joined him. Intelligent looking, Price was tall and angular and his easy-going manner made him well liked in the Atkinson-Jackson circle of brothers.

'How is it going?' Searles asked. 'Alright' Price said.

'Did your brother tell you everything?' Searles asked.

Price said, yes, and then he slipped Searles some money. Price went out and came back with some more money, amounting to about $300 in Thai currency.

In September 1971, Searles went to Jack's Bangkok home to pick up the box that would be used for the test package. He then took the box with him to the Don Muang Air Force Base, packed some trash and old rags in it, and made arrangements for a co-worker to ship it from Bangkok to Travis Air Force Base via U-Tapao. Searles also completed some forms required for the shipment. The ring was now ready to make its first run. Searles notified Price as soon as the box left U-Tapao. A few days later, it arrived at Tinker Air Force Base; now Trice would have to pick it up.

Jack waited for word from Trice that the test run had worked. And he waited and waited but heard nothing. So he sent Gainous to Midwest City in Oklahoma to see Trice and find out what happened. Trice had just got off work and was lying down, trying to take a nap, when he heard a car pull up in the driveway. The doorbell rang three times and then Trice heard a knock at the door. He got up and peeked out the window. It was Gainous. Trice hesitated. Should he open the door? He had made up his mind. No way was he going to get involved in heroin smuggling. Still he answered the door. Gainous paid off the cabbie and came in.

Gainous got to the point. 'What's the problem? Where is the package?'

'Man, I'm working at night,' Trice complained. 'It's hard to see when anything is coming to the base.'

'You need to get on the ball,' Gainous advised Trice. 'You're not playing with kids, you know. You have people where you work. You can ask them to help you look for the package.' Then Gainous sweetened his demand. 'Any way, we will give you about $15,000, you know, because you are taking a pretty big chance doing it.'

BUT TRICE NEVER picked up the package, throwing a monkey wrench into the operation. Price told Searles. 'Everything is frozen. Do nothing more until we can arrange another test shipment.' Once again Price and Searles had numerous meetings and once again Searles prepared the shipping documents. In late November 1971, the ring made another test run and shipped a second package of garbage, this time to Lowry Air Force Base.

The Atkinson-Jackson drug ring had contacts at the base who were ready to help it with the smuggling operation. Located in the Colorado cities of Denver and Aurora, Lowry Air Force Base was heavily involved in the training of the U.S. Army Air force Training Command in World War II. From 1954 to 1958, Lowry was the temporary home of the U.S. Air Force Academy until its construction was completed at Colorado Springs. In 1967, the base became home to the 3320th Returning Group, which re-trained eligible court-marshaled men for re-entry into normal active duty ranks.

Searles saw to it that the shipment of garbage left Thailand for the U.S. When the shipment arrived at Lowry, no one would pick it up. That was the plan. If the package remained unclaimed for a period of time, officials at the base would have to open it, but garbage was all they would find. Jack's spy would report back whether the plan had worked. Now it would be time to send the real thing.

In preparation, Searles gave Price one of the special boxes used for shipping packages through the military transport system; in turn, Price gave Searles a completed set of shipping documents that Searles would use as a model for their shipment of heroin. The two men met several times. At least one meeting was held at Jack's house in Bangkok. Searles asked Price to provide him with a typewriter so that he would not have to type the documents using a typewriter from U-Tapao. It would be a smart move in case anything went wrong. Unfortunately for the drug ring, Price gave Searles a typewriter that he had used to type labels for a shipment of heroin sent in April 1971 to Fort Monmouth, an installation of the Department of the Army in Monmouth County, New Jersey. Customs officials intercepted the package, which was addressed to a fictitious unit at the Supply Support Services Building, 116 (03) at Fort Monmouth, and opened it because the necessary forms that should have been attached to the package were missing, and they thought the forms might have been inadvertently packed inside.

'The typewriter proved to be a crucial piece of evidence,' explained Paul Cooper, who, at the time, was the Assistant U.S. Attorney in Denver. 'We compared the type from the typewriter used to prepare the forms to the Fort Monmouth seizure with the type on the label used for the package of heroin shipped by the drug ring to Denver. They matched.'

Seales had to hand-write one document because the type would not fit on the shipping label. The box was packed with the heroin and Price gave it to Searles, who brought it to Don

Muang Air Force Base in Bangkok, to be put into the military transportation system. But there was one problem. Mumbles did not have the authority to put the box on the plane. All he could really do was complete the forms and give them and the package to someone who had the authority. This is what Mumbles did with the first two shipments, unbeknownst to Jack and his associates.

'Searles was in a bind, so he approached a White kid on the tarmac and offered to pay him $500 if he would put the box on the plane for him,' explained Mike Schwartz, a retired Customs agent who worked the Denver connection case. 'Of course, the kid got suspicious. He took the money and box and went to the U.S. Air Force security and told them what had happened. Air Force security opened the box, found the heroin inside and contacted Customs.'

The authorities decided to set up a sting. First, they allowed the box to go to its final U.S. destination, Lowry Air Force Base, as if nothing had happened. On January 4 1972, Searles monitored the shipment at U-Tapao, as it made its way from Bangkok and onto a flight to Travis Air Force Base.

Once the box cleared Customs at Travis on January 4 it was opened again and the contents given to a chemist who tested the white powder inside and found that it was on average about 85 percent pure heroin. Some of the contraband tested as high as 100 percent. The box's contents, which contained 20 individual packages, were estimated to weigh 17.3 pounds and to be worth between $8 and $10 million.

'Every official document in the case said that there were 17.3 pounds of heroin,' Schwartz recalled. 'But I weighed the 20 packages before they were sent to the lab, and they weighed a little over 21 pounds. So what happened? When the shipment was seized at Travis, the Customs agents were in such a hurry to move it that they weighed one package and multiplied that weight by 20 and came up with 17.3 pounds. So sitting on my desk were about four pounds of heroin no one knew existed. It took me about a minute to make a supplemental seizure report for the 'missing' heroin.'

The U.S. Customs officials had the box delivered to its vault in Denver, where they re-packaged it with 20, 10-gram samples of heroin and filled the remainder of the plastic bags with soap powder. Florescent powder was sprayed on the inside of the box and two electronic beepers placed inside. One beeper would activate when the package moved; the other when it was opened. The agents then re-sealed the box and took it to the Railroad Express Agency that on January 7 1972, delivered the box to Lowry Air Force Base, Hangar Number 2, Building 402.

Outside the building, Customs agents listened with electronic gear, monitoring the beepers. They guarded all exits. In the hangar, perched in a crow's nest, an agent peered down from the ceiling of the cavernous building. He had a clear line of vision to the floor and to the bin where the box containing the heroin was placed. To the authorities, the operation was a lock. Even Houdini would not be able to escape. In a few hours, maybe a few days, they would bust members of one of the world's largest international heroin smuggling rings.

ANYWAY, THAT WAS the plan. About 4 p.m., Paul Cooper got a phone call at the Federal courthouse where he was prosecuting another case. Cooper had been with the Denver District Attorney's Office before he became an Assistant U.S. Attorney in 1971, one of 1,300 such federal prosecutors in the country. He was assigned to the Bangkok heroin case and was looking forward to prosecuting it. The caller told Cooper to come to the Lowry Air Force Base immediately. Cooper dashed out of the courthouse, jumped into his car and sped to Lowry.

'I really thought we had made the bust,' Cooper recalled. 'But when I got there, I was told that agent watching the bin from the ceiling had fallen asleep and didn't see who picked up the package. The beeper went off and the package had moved, but nobody knew where it was or if someone had gotten it out of the hangar. We closed the base down and searched every vehicle leaving it, but the box with the heroin samples just vanished. Air Force intelligence told us that they had a couple of suspects: two sergeants who lived off base who had access to the hangar.'

It was 'blush time' for law enforcement in Denver. U.S. Customs would not talk about what had happened, and they stopped answering press inquiries. A Rocky Mountain News report complained: 'Reporters' questions must be put in writing and sent to the Custom's regional office in Houston. It takes months to get a reply.'

The authorities were eventually able to arrest two suspects: Sergeant Charles E. Jones, 24, of Natchez, Mississippi, and Airman Michael Massie, 18, of New York City, both of whom were stationed at Lowry. When the hands and clothing of the two servicemen were put under a black light, the authorities found that they tested positive for the florescent powder. It looked like the good guys had gotten their men but as a U.S. Customs report explained: 'Subsequent laboratory analysis of their clothing and scrapings from their hands resulted only in an opinion from an expert that it was probable the parties had been inside the box. No positive connection was possible. The complaint against those two parties was subsequently dismissed.'

But the authorities moved quickly to bust others in the criminal operation. On January 14 they arrested Searles. It did not take too much work before Searles was mumbling up a storm about his co-conspirators. 'We arrested Searles to make it look as if he was still part of the ring,' Cooper explained. 'It was for his own protection because he agreed to cooperate.'

On the way from Bangkok to Denver, the plane carrying Searles stopped at Guam, where he could be arraigned in a U.S. Federal court, since Guam, a U.S. possession, was U.S. territory. He was put in a holding cell with two other prisoners. Shortly after the authorities took Searles out of the cell, his cell mates ate some food that had been brought to the cell. The food had been poisoned, and the cell mates who ate it got sick and almost died. 'That was a remarkable development,' Cooper recalled. 'Was there a connection to the Denver case? We never did find out. But Searles made it to Denver and was put into protective custody at a youth center located in the suburbs. By that time Searles was really nervous and more inarticulate than ever.'

Searles revealed to the authorities how a retired army sergeant named William Herman Jackson, his brother Andrew Price and Air Force sergeant Gerald Gainous had conspired to smuggle high-purity heroin into the U.S. He also revealed his involvement with Johnny Trice. On January 19 1972, Customs agents went to Tinker Air Force Base and interviewed Trice. He turned over the letter that he had not sent to Searles but had trashed. Taken before a Federal grand jury in Oklahoma City, Trice talked about his numerous contacts with Gainous and about the call Gainous had made on January 16 advising him of Searles's arrest and telling him to stay cool. 'Go ahead and admit you know me but say that you know nothing about any trafficking conspiracy,' Gainous instructed Trice.

On the night of January 20, surveillance on Jackson's trailer in Goldsboro revealed that Gainous met Jackson at about 10.15 pm and remained with Jackson in the trailer for about five minutes. Later, at the trial, the prosecution played up these events, but Jackson's defense attorney argued: what was the big deal? What did it really reveal about the alleged conspiracy? 'We were trying to show that the conspiracy was based in Goldsboro where Jack had a residence,' Cooper explained. A search of Jackson's trailer found no hard evidence, other than corroborating evidence of his telephone bills showing numerous long distance telephone calls to Bangkok to phone numbers used by Jackson and Andrew Price.

In Thailand, a search warrant was executed at Jackson's Bangkok home, the place where Price was living at the time. The authorities found Searles's phone number, the shipping information used for the shipment of the real thing (the heroin) to Lowry Air Force Base and other information tying Price to the case.

WHILE JACK WAS incarcerated in a Wayne County, North Carolina, jail, the best policy for him, given the gravity of the charges against him, would have been to keep a low profile and his mouth shut. But the jail was overcrowded, and the authorities gave Jackson a cell mate, Richard Thomas Pigford, a small, thin, bug-eyed petty criminal, whom one law enforcement source described as being 'weasel-looking and weasel-acting.' Despite the serious situation, Jack could not stop scheming or recruiting for the Atkinson-Jackson drug ring. Jackson told Pigford that he could make some money by going to Bangkok and bringing back some heroin worth $2,000 there, but which Jack could sell for at least $20,000 in the U.S. Jack would send a female recruit with Pigford because, Jack figured, couples were less suspicious. The female would then smuggle the heroin to the U.S. in a special girdle. 'You can get in touch with the "Fat Man" (Ike Atkinson),' Jack also suggested. 'He's at the Statler Hilton Hotel in New York City and will have some heroin with him when he returns to North Carolina.'

As the cell mates idled away their time, Jack kept confiding. 'I'm going to beat the case,' Jackson told Pigford. 'The agents won't find the box, and so they're not going to get their evidence in court.' Jack said that the guys charged with picking up the box (Jones and Massie) were just common thieves and didn't have anything to do with the operation. Jack bragged: 'We have people from all over the place working for us. Our intelligence is almost as good as the government's. That's why I'm not talking to the Fat Man while I'm here in jail.' Jack said that Ike would take care of Gainous's family while he was in jail.

Jack talked about a murder in 1969 about which the authorities were trying to get Gainous to talk. 'Gainous doesn't know about it,' Jack confided. 'I know who did it, but I'm protecting Slick by not letting him know about it.'

All of this information was passed on to the authorities; Pigford had turned snitch, trying to get a lighter sentence. Pigford testified before a grand jury on February 10, the same day Searles had testified, but he refused to take the stand against Jackson at the trial, fearing the long reach of the Atkinson-Jackson drug ring. He had come to believe Jack's boast that he had spies everywhere, and Pigford had heard about the heroin shipment that disappeared right under the nose of the law. No amount of cajoling or threats from the prosecutors could get Pigford to change his mind. Pigford even threatened to testify falsely if he was put on the stand. Ironically, Pigford was eventually sent to Leavenworth Federal Penitentiary where Jack was incarcerated after his conviction. Pigford was petrified and wrote Paul Cooper a letter requesting a transfer. His request was denied. In a letter to Pigford, Cooper reminded Pigford that he had contacted Jackson's lawyer and had 'offered to testify to facts which were not true, in order to help Mr. Jackson and Mr. Price, his co-defendant.'

ON FEBRUARY 11, 1972, a Federal grand jury indicted Herman Jackson and 33 other people in the Denver drug connection case, the biggest one Denver had ever seen. The trial began on May 22, 1972, but one day later a juror revealed that some of the jurors discussed the case before the presentation of any evidence. So Judge Olin Hatfield Chilson declared a mistrial and reconvened the trial on May 24. Jack could not testify in his own defense because he had acknowledged on the stand in the Hart-Patch trial that he trafficked in drugs in Thailand. 'If he had taken the stand he couldn't have contradicted what our witnesses said about him,' Cooper explained. 'It made it easier for us to get a conviction.'

Two days later the jury reached its verdict. Jack, Gainous, Price and Searles were all found guilty. Jackson received a 30-year sentence and was fined $50,000. Andrew Price received 15 years and Gainous, 10 years. Searles had already received an 18-month prison sentence after testifying against Jack and Gainous. And Johnny Trice? 'He was never charged since he had backed out of the operation,' Schwartz revealed. 'He was lucky the prosecutor didn't push it. Technically, he could have been charged.'

TODAY, PAUL COOPER considers the Atkinson-Jackson drug ring the 'Most unusual criminal organization he ever encountered in his long legal career,' recalling, 'I talked with Jackson and Atkinson. They were both cordial. They operated like sophisticated businessmen who were extremely good at what they did. During the trial, Atkinson came by my office to see about making a deal to help get Jackson out of prison. I don't know what he was going to offer because I wasn't interested. We knew we could send Jackson away for a long time. The DEA told me that Atkinson's visit was a good sign that we had really hurt his drug ring.'

About four or five months after the trial, Cooper put Jack before a grand jury. 'I asked him what happened to the heroin in the hangar,' Cooper recalled. 'He looked at me and wouldn't answer. I threatened him: "I'll hold you in contempt." Jackson laughed and said: "What are you going to do? Put me in jail." A couple of the grand jury members couldn't help laughing. I think I even smiled.'

The missing shipment was never found and the authorities still have no clue what happened to it. Today, Ike is tight-lipped about the matter, declining to talk because the people who helped with the 'disappearance' of the heroin are still alive. 'The Feds weren't as smart as they thought they were,' Ike explained. 'Our main man at Lowry Air Force Base was tipped off that the Feds were on to Jack's shipment. Our people said that somebody was working on the lighting inside the hangar where our heroin was supposed to go. My man could tell that the Feds were fixing the hangar for surveillance. So he had to get the box before it went into the hangar. We got the box out, but there was just a small amount of heroin in it. That's all I'll say.'

Cooper would have loved to have made Ike part of the conspiracy, but Ike actually knew nothing about the details of the smuggling operation. 'I didn't give Jack any money for it, and I didn't know who was involved with him,' Ike recalled. 'It was a risky operation. We had never gone that route before, and Jack didn't really know some of the key people he was working with. But it wasn't a bad idea because it involved a new way to ship our dope. We worked together, but we didn't need each other's approval for individual projects.

CHAPTER 8

The Nail in the Coffin

WHEN IKE ATKINSON came to visit Federal Prosecutor Paul Cooper in Denver looking to work out a deal to help his partner, William Herman Jackson, Cooper had already heard the rumor that had been rippling through the law enforcement community. In December 1972, the authorities had diverted a military plane, scheduled to arrive at Dover Air Force Base, to Andrews Air Force Base in Maryland. The plane carried Ike Atkinson and Thomas Southerland carrying bogus military papers, as well as 64 other passengers and the cadavers of two servicemen killed in Vietnam, which, the authorities suspected, contained heroin. The authorities did not find any heroin in the cadavers, but they believed Ike and Southerland did have the contraband on the plane and somehow had removed it from the cadavers while the plane had a 16 to 24 hour layover at Hickam Air Force Base in Honolulu before proceeding to Travis and then to Andrews, having been diverted from its original destination of Dover AFB. The traffickers were able to get the contraband off the plane because there was minimal security. Or at least that is the scenario the authorities presented to the press to explain why no heroin was found at Andrews.

'The rumor didn't surprise me,' Cooper recalled. 'I believed it could have happened. The Atkinson-Jackson organization was one of the most innovative drug rings in history. I knew from prosecuting the Denver case that Atkinson and Jackson had many exotic ways of getting dope into the country. I figured using cadavers was just another way they were doing it.'

Fueled by the sensational news reports surrounding the incident at Andrews and the desire to uncover the shocking scheme that allegedly used the dead bodies of brave American soldiers to smuggle narcotics into the U.S., many other journalists and other law enforcement officials came to believe the reports. 'Oh yeah, I remember those reports about drug-laden dead bodies,' recalled Haney Howell, who worked for CBS News in the early 1970s and was based in Bangkok. 'It happened; CBS did a story about it. The traffickers were well connected and they were moving large quantities of heroin using cadavers and coffins.'

One retired U.S. Air Force colonel recalled a meeting he attended at the FBI's J. Edgar Hoover building in Washington, DC, after the incident at Andrews became public. The theme of the meeting—'Is the Military Airlift Command (MAC) the largest heroin smuggling organization in operation?' 'I first heard about the (Andrews Air Force Base) case at that meeting and that is why I knew it did, in fact, happen,' the colonel explained. 'The answer that came out of the meeting was "No". MAC was not directly involved with drug trafficking. It was decided that drug cases, like the Andrews one, were rare.'

Michael Marr, the Assistant U.S. Attorney for the District of Maryland, who was involved with the investigation of the Andrews incident and later prosecuted Southerland, recalled getting a briefing from the BNDD agents assigned to the case. 'We were surprised that we didn't find any heroin when we searched the plane,' Marr recalled. 'Later, we came to believe that they (the Atkinson-Jackson ring) had removed the heroin in Hawaii.' Marr characterizes his explanation of what happened to the heroin as a 'reasoned assessment,' explaining that 'when false documents are involved in a case but no contraband is found, it heightens your awareness and raises the question: Why are the suspects carrying false documents?'

Several leading publications and press agencies, including *Time* magazine, *The Washington Post*, the *Associated Press*, *United Press International* and the U.S. Armed Forces *Stars and Stripes* newspaper published unquestioning press reports about the Andrews incident. Without conducting a serious investigation, *Time* magazine concluded that, while authorities did not find any drugs, 'they did discover that one of the two bodies that had undergone autopsy earlier had recently been re-stitched.' The Pacific edition of the *Stars and Stripes* reported that anonymous officials said, 'The heroin is believed to have been sewn inside the bodies of servicemen and in the lining of their caskets in plastic packages from 5 to 25 kilos (31 to 51 pounds).' No explanation was given or any follow up story ever written to explain how this could have possibly happened or if, indeed, it could have happened at all. A July 7 1973 *Washington Post* report suggested that the arrests of those responsible for the cadaver connection were 'imminent.' But that never happened; no arrests were made; and no retraction or follow up story was ever published.

Even William 'Dog' Turner, whom Ike did not meet until his incarceration in the late 1980s at Petersburg Federal Penitentiary, was dragged into the conspiracy. When he was convicted of income tax evasion in 1975, the Associated Press reported that Turner was a man who 'Federal authorities said took part in smuggling heroin in the bodies of Vietnam War dead.'

Over the years since December 11 1972, the date the C-141 was detained at Andrews Air Force Base, sloppy media reporting and conspiracy theorists kept the cadaver-heroin connection story alive. When Ike was tried and convicted in 1976, the press reports mentioned teakwood furniture but not cadavers and coffins as smuggling methods used by Ike to traffic heroin. Former Assistant Attorney Joe Dean, who prosecuted the 1975 Federal case against Ike and several of his associates in North Carolina and Thailand, said that he did not bring up the caver-heroin connection at the trial because there was no evidence it ever existed and to present it would have hurt the prosecution's case.

But in 1987, when Ike was arrested again for heroin smuggling and doing time in Otisville Federal Penitentiary, the rumor appeared as fact. Ike became the man who, according to a *Washington Post* press report, was responsible for 'masterminding a heroin importation ring that shipped the drugs from Southeast Asia to the United States in dead servicemen's bodies.'

Since the December 1972 incident at Andrews Air Force Base, the so-called 'cadaver-heroin connection' has become the grist of conspiracy theories. After all, what could be more shocking, more criminally innovative and more disgusting than having heroin smuggled via coffins and in the bodies of soldiers who gave their lives for their country? It is remarkable that Hollywood has not made a horror movie called 'The Cadaver Connection,' incorporating a ghoulish plot with ghoulish characters.

In 1977, noted investigative journalist Brian Ross did a report for NBC Television about 'The Black Mafia' in which he presented a mystery man who claimed to be a part of the cadaver-heroin connection. Then in the 1980s, the Atkinson-Jackson drug ring was connected to the sensational Jeffrey McDonald murder case in North Carolina in which McDonald, an Army medical army doctor stationed at Fort Bragg, was convicted of murdering his wife and two children. The connection is based on the recollections of a deceased police informant named Helen Stoekley who claimed to have belonged to a cult.

Two retired DEA agents have claimed with authority that the cadaver-heroin connection did, without a doubt, exist. One of them, Dan Addario, has written how he uncovered heroin in the bodies of a dead GI in a Bangkok hospital in the fall of 1974. Mike Levine, the other DEA agent, who has found some fame as an author and radio show host in New York City, claims that the usual suspect, the CIA (Central Intelligence Agency), was involved with smuggling heroin in cadavers via Thailand. And in 2004, a man named Bob Kirkconnell claimed in an e-mail to a conspiracy web site that he had first-hand knowledge of the legendary flight that was diverted to Andrews Air Force Base in 1972, or was it 1973?

Like all conspiracy theories, the cadaver-heroin smuggling story has had a viral life of its own. But did it really exist? What truth is there to the story? Let's go where no journalist has gone before and actually investigate the details of the alleged conspiracy and what it would have taken to make it work.

AS WE READ in the prologue, after Thomas 'Sonny' Southerland was arrested at Andrews Air Force Base, he was brought to trial for impersonating a military non commissioned officer. Convinced that the cadavers on the plane carried heroin, the authorities grilled Southerland for hours. 'They put me in a room and kept asking me all kinds of questions, trying to break me,' Southerland recalled. 'They threatened me by saying I was going to spend 150 years in jail. I told them that I didn't have anything to do with no (sic) coffins. They didn't believe me. They kept hammering away. They wanted me to tell them what we (Ike and Sonny) did with the dope.'

After Southerland pleaded guilty to charges of impersonating a military officer, the alleged cadaver-heroin connection played a role in Southerland's sentencing. 'We presented the evidence (in court) about what we knew of the heroin and the cadavers, and the judge was impressed because of the use of military aircraft and the horrendous way the drugs were being smuggled,' Marr explained. 'The judge gave Southerland the maximum sentence: four five-year sentences, to be served consecutively.'

Marr still believes that, in the words of *Time* magazine, 'One of the two bodies that had undergone autopsies had recently been re-stitched.' But was it? What really happened when the authorities detained the plane and examined the two bodies?

IN 1971 AND 1972, Howard Wright was the Senior Research Agent in the U.S. Customs office at Wilmington, North Carolina. He was investigating the Atkinson-Jackson drug ring and heard several rumors about how it was using cadavers to smuggle heroin from Vietnam. 'I remember going to Goldsboro to check out a funeral home that was supposed to be a part of the alleged conspiracy,' Wright recalled. 'But I didn't find anything. We had to investigate the rumors, of course, but none of them ever panned out.'

On a cold December night in 1972, officials at U.S. Customs headquarters in Washington, DC ordered Wright to come to Andrews Air Force Base for an important meeting. 'When I got to Andrews, a pathologist was already present, and he was examining the two cadavers that had been on the plane,' Wright recalled. 'Looking at the stitching on the cadavers, you could tell that they had been autopsied. I was there when they opened the bodies and looked inside; we didn't find any heroin and the pathologist sewed the bodies back up. Nobody at that meeting said anything about how one of the bodies had already been re-stitched. We looked at the coffins as well—picked them up, checked their linings. We even tore the linings open to see if there was any heroin behind them. Nothing about those cadavers or the coffins was out of the normal.'

Wright was not your ordinary observer. He was a licensed mortician who had graduated from a mortuary college in Nashville and knew what he was looking at. He did not see any evidence that either of the bodies had been re-stitched. 'The re-stitching would have had to have been exactly right not to notice it, but that's a difficult thing to do even for a trained pathologist. There was no evidence that the bodies had been tampered with. I didn't notice anything unusual about the cadavers.'

THE NIXON ADMINISTRATION was upset by the possibility that drug traffickers were using the military system and the bodies of dead GIs from the Vietnam War to smuggle heroin into the U.S., and it put pressure on Ellsworth Bunker, the U.S. Ambassador to South Vietnam, to have an investigation conducted into the Andrews incident at his end. Two U.S. Customs agents based in Saigon were sent to the mortuary in Tan Son Nhut Air Force Base near Saigon to check out the story.

Initially, the Tan Son Knut facility was the only mortuary that the U.S. Army used to process the remains of its servicemen killed in Vietnam. The number of fatalities, however, continued to climb, and, by 1967, the Army realized that Tan Son Nhut was inadequate to carry the entire load. So on June 20 1967, a smaller mortuary was opened at the Da Nang Air Base in the northern part of South Vietnam. The Da Nang mortuary remained open until early 1972 when the U.S. withdrawal from the northern provinces of Vietnam began and the responsibilities and personnel of the Da Nang mortuary were transferred to the Tan Son Nhut facility. By early 1973, increased Viet Cong activity in the Saigon area, together with the drawing down of U.S. forces from Vietnam, led to the closing of the Tan Son Nhut mortuary and its move to Thailand.

'We interviewed several people and took a good look at the (Tan Son Nhut) mortuary,' explained one of the investigating Customs agents. 'About 20 people were working there, and they were obviously puzzled by the cadaver-heroin connection rumor. In our report to the ambassador, we concluded that it couldn't have happened, given the amount of people who would have been involved. Thinking back to our investigation and what we found, the alleged conspiracy really didn't make any sense.'

The U.S. Army's Criminal Investigation Division (CID) conducted its own investigation. In December 1972, Lebert Baxter was on leave vacationing in the U.S. from his dual position as both Base Commander and Head of the Personal Effects Department of the Tan Son Nhut Mortuary. It was Baxter's second tour of duty at the mortuary. He had served previously from January to December 1969 as operations officer, meaning he was responsible for overseeing the processing and identification all remains of dead U.S. servicemen in Vietnam. Baxter's leave was well deserved. He had been working twelve-hours days, seven days a week, and slept in his office at the mortuary. The job was his life. Until the call from his superiors, Baxter did not recall any rumors about cadavers and heroin during his two tours. 'My men and I were too busy to pay attention to any rumors,' Baxter said.

He had already enjoyed ten of his thirty days of leave when he got the call a few days after Christmas from the Mortuary Affairs head office in Washington, DC. 'I was told: "You've got a problem at Tan Son Nhut,"' Baxter recalled. 'We don't know what happened and we don't believe it, but the only way to clear it up is to have an investigation.' When I returned to Tan Son Nhut on about December 29 or 30 (1972), the situation was quite tense. It was a serious charge that reflected badly on everybody at the mortuary. We realized, though, that the only way to clear it up was to have an investigation. But it was like having to go to court to prove you are innocent because a lot of fuss had been made.'

The CID investigative team spent six weeks at Tan Son Nhut and did an exhaustive investigation. Working around the clock, the investigators talked to everyone possible. 'The investigators might show up at the mortuary at two in the morning, five in the afternoon or nine in the evening,' Baxter recalled. 'They were spot checking, doing a thorough job. They literally looked under every rock.'

Investigative teams were also sent to Okinawa and Kyoto, Japan; Honolulu, Hawaii; Clark Air Force Base in the Philippines; the army fort in Oakland, California; and Dover Air Force Base in Delaware —that is, any location that could possibly be part of a cadaver-heroin smuggling connection. After its investigation, the CID produced a 350-page report that concluded there was no conspiracy to transport heroin via coffins and/or cadavers. To make it work, the report noted, the criminals would have needed at least 250 co-conspirators, given the logistics and the smuggling route that stretched from the outskirts of Saigon to the cities and small towns of America.

'Think about it,' Baxter said. 'With so many people needing to be involved, it would have been impossible for everybody to keep their mouth shut. Somebody would have made a mistake. Somebody would have gotten drunk in a bar and said something. Somebody would have spilled the beans to the wrong person. Yet, there is absolutely no evidence that anybody ever used cadavers to ship heroin.'

In the early 1970s, Al Dawson was working in Vietnam as a journalist for the United Press International (UPI), when he got wind of the rumor about the cadaver-heroin connection. Dawson thought he might win the Pulitzer Prize if he could prove the story true. 'I investigated but never wrote a word because the story turned out to be just a rumor,' Dawson recalled. 'It never happened. It's like the Lock Ness monster story. It makes for great reading, even if it's not true. In my selfish way, I wish the story was true. I would have been on the front-page of every newspaper in the world. But today I'm convinced beyond a doubt that it never happened.'

This author's investigation has not found one instance where someone has been arrested, let alone convicted, for participating in the cadaver-heroin connection. Given what I know about drug trafficking, it is reasonable to assume that some drug trafficker may have tried to use cadavers. After all, they have tried every conceivable smuggling method, from body cavities of living persons to shaving cream cans, and from concrete posts to tanks containing tropical fish. But if it was done on the scale suggested by the sensational media reports, there would be some record or document that provides concrete information about the conspiracy. Yet, there is absolutely no documentation.

HOW WERE THE personal remains of dead servicemen collected and processed, brought to the Vietnam morgues, transferred to the mortuary facilities on the U.S. mainland and turned over to the next of kin of the dead servicemen for burial? It is necessary to examine the system to understand how difficult it would be for drug traffickers to have used such a process for their criminal objectives.

The speedy transportation network in the Vietnam War Zone was a key element of the evacuation process. In most cases, the U.S. army used helicopters to evacuate and deliver the remains from the battlefield to the collection point. Within

24 hours, they would be airlifted from the collection points to the Tan Son Nhut or the Da Nang mortuaries. Refrigeration was available at the collection points and at the two mortuaries, which helped slow down the decomposition of the remains considerably, although problems did arise in some remote areas where refrigeration was not available.

'At the mortuaries, everything was done to ensure the accurate identification of the remains before they were processed and placed in what we call a "transfer case,"' explained Doug Howard, Deputy Director, U.S. Army Mortuary Affairs Center in Fort Lee, Virginia, who worked at the Tan Son Knut mortuary in the late 1960s and early 1970s. 'Coffin is not a word that is in the mortuary affairs vocabulary.' The transfer cases were made of aluminum, not wood, and were light-weight and easy to handle.

The transfer case with the remains would be taken to the airport at Tan Son Nhut or to the one at Da Nang, placed aboard an airplane and flown back to the U.S. mainland. It took 12 to 15 hours from the time the remains arrived at the mortuary until they were placed aboard the plane. Anybody who tried to put heroin in the cadavers needed to do so during this stage. Both Howard and Baxter, however, point out that the mortuaries had a high level of security. 'Preventing an unauthorized person from entering one of the mortuaries in Vietnam was not a problem,' Howard noted. 'The mortuaries had very controlled environments. If you didn't have a reason to be there, you could not enter. The Vietnam mortuaries were not open for visitation.'

After the CID completed its 'Andrews' investigation, the U.S. Army implemented a set of new procedures at the mortuaries that made the process even more secure. Most importantly, before the investigation, the remains were moved from the mortuary to the airport without any accompanying security.

After the investigation, however, the mortuary personnel were required to call the CID that then sent military police to the mortuary. After observing the mortuary staff put the remains in the transfer cases, the CID would attach a security seal to the transfer case so it could not be opened without alerting the authorities. The remains were then escorted to the airport, where they were loaded on the plane and shipped to the U.S. mainland.

Even if we allow that it could have been possible prior to the new procedures, the cadaver-heroin connection conspiracy would have needed a special kind of person to deal with the remains of war; after all, the GIs who died did not normally do so peacefully in their beds at night. Many of the cadavers were mangled, blown up and often barely recognizable. To preserve the remains, formaldehyde was often sprinkled around the inside of the cadaver and the smell of the formaldehyde could be overwhelming. Actually, said Howard, the pungency is a good thing since formaldehyde is a carcinogen and therefore highly toxic. 'The pungency will drive you away from the dangers associated with the inhalation of formaldehyde. Even if you could do it, you have to be crazy to try and put heroin in a cadaver because you are asking for serious health problems.'

And even if we grant that such drug traffickers, if they ever existed, were nothing better than risk-taking animals, such an elaborate process would beg the question: How could those involved in the smuggling network in Vietnam communicate with their associates in the U.S. or Thailand, and who would be on the receiving end of the heroin?

Baxter pointed out: 'All phone calls from South Vietnam to the U.S. and to other parts of the world, including Thailand, were monitored. The authorities would likely have intercepted at least some of the calls that the drug traffickers made. So if they were aware of this security issue and did not make any phone calls, how could they alert their associates in the U.S. and let them know the shipment was coming?' In other words, how would the right hand know what the left hand was doing, and vice versa?

Moreover, with all the cadavers from Vietnam arriving stateside at Dover Air Force Base and to Oakland Army Base in Oakland, California, how could they coordinate this chain of delivery? Remember, too, that the Atkinson-Jackson drug ring, which was suspected of being behind the cadaver-heroin connection, was based in Bangkok, Thailand, not Vietnam.

AS THE VIETNAM War drew to a close, the military mortuaries closed: Da Nang in February in 1972 and Tan Son Nhut in March 1973. The staff and equipment of the mortuaries were consolidated in Thailand. On January 23 1973, the military established the U.S. Army Central Identification Laboratory at Camp Samae San, Thailand. Its purpose—to look, search for, recover and identify servicemen lost as a result of the Vietnam War.

The last U.S. troops withdrew from Vietnam on March 29 1973, the result of the signing of the January 29 1972 Peace Accords. On January 27 1973, William B. Nolde officially became the last American soldier to die in Vietnam. There is some controversy surrounding the last death of the Vietnam War. Forty-one US servicemen were killed and forty-one servicemen were wounded during the Mayaguez Incident in Cambodia between May 12 and 15, 1975, which happened a month and a half after the fall of Saigon. Army PFC Jon O. Nacy died on 8 November 1975 and is arguably the last American to be killed as a result of the Vietnam War. But Cambodia has nothing to do with the claims of the cadaver-heroin connection conspiracy supporters. The fact is —after William B. Nolde's death on January 27 1973, there were no more U.S. casualties—absolutely none—in Vietnam, the result of the Vietnam War, which could have allowed the cadaver-heroin connection to continue, if such a connection did indeed exist.

THE REMAINS OF U.S. servicemen killed in Vietnam prior to 1971 were shipped to one of two mortuaries in the U.S. The remains of servicemen whose families resided east of the Mississippi were sent to the mortuary at the Dover Air Force Base in Delaware, while the remains of those who resided west of the Mississippi were sent to the mortuary at the Oakland Army base, California.

ONCE THE REMAINS arrived at Oakland or Dover, the staff opened the transfer cases, gave the human remains an identification number, moved them to the preparation facility where they were taken out of the pouch encasing them, dressed the cadavers, applied cosmetics and then placed the remains in a casket. Each of the remains was assigned an escort, usually a member of the military, who stayed with the deceased until he or she reached the autopsy area. Once processing was completed, base officials then made arrangements for the shipment of the remains overland or by air to funeral homes that the next of kin had selected.

Since 1960, all air shipments of the deceased to their hometowns have used commercial airlines or if their hometown was within 400 miles from Dover, a hearse was contracted from a local Dover area funeral homes. One can see how many people would have to have been involved to continue smuggling the heroin to its destination, wherever it was supposed to be.

Also, many families of the deceased opted for cremation of the remains so family members would also have to have been in cahoots with members of the drug ring to allow any contraband placed in the cadavers to be removed prior to cremation and not burned to a crisp. As Howard put it, 'To make the conspiracy work, there would have to have been collusion from beginning to end.' Still no record exists that can identify anybody who was ever arrested or convicted for participation in a cadaver-heroin connection.

YET, IN DEFIANCE of common sense and despite the lack of credible evidence, the rumors continue to persist, sometimes fueled by informants who realized the authorities would listen to a good story if they were fed one. Some agents who worked the Atkinson-Jackson drug ring investigation believe that informants tried to take advantage of law enforcement's interest in the cadaver-heroin connection by creating rumors about it. 'That's how the cadaver story got bigger and bigger,' said retired Customs agent Wright. 'All it takes is an informant to tell a story to an agent.'

According to DEA intelligence reports, an informant in Goldsboro 'tipped off' the authorities to the flight that was diverted to Andrews. Southerland has no doubt who that informant was. 'It was Sutton,' Southerland said. 'He was a big snitch. Everybody knew it. He really spread a lot of lies.'

A once-restricted transcript of an interview conducted by an un-identified agent with Ellis Sutton illustrates this point. The transcript of the interview is undated, but it appears to have been conducted soon after the December 1972 incident at Andrews Air Force Base. The agent was asking Sutton what he knew about drug trafficking in North Carolina when the interrogation touched on cadavers and heroin and the flight with two cadavers that landed at Andrews Air Base.

Agent: What do you know about this Sullivan (Thomas Southerland) deal?

Sutton: What do I know specifically about it?

Agent: Yeah.

Sutton: About the dead body?

Agent: Well the whole thing is what we are after.

Sutton: They have been planning that. I can tell you another way what (sic) they were planning to do. But I can't say specifically about this dope 'cause I was in jail then at the time. I don't know no (sic) more than the information that I got. And—I intend—if I'm put in the right place, I can get you some more.

Agent: Well, what were they planning?

Sutton: What—the dead body?

Agent: Uh-huh.

Sutton: See they propositioned the funeral home man that the bodies come to. And I don't know where them (sic) bodies were going. They had a man down there in Georgia. You know we talked about that once before—No, that was you (sic) I talked to about it. In Atlanta? The undertaker down there?

Agent: They knew an undertaker, but there's nothing about any movement in the—

Sutton: Right. But that's the plan they were getting. They was (sic) making the plan. But you can't never (sic) ship to somebody. You can't ever get it there until somebody is going to his funeral home. He had to get it.

Agent: Now, we're talking about back in '69.

Sutton: Right.

Agent: But now you're—

Sutton: But now you're talking about here. But these bodies were supposed—I'm just trying to think whether somebody told me these bodies were supposed to go to a funeral home. They were supposed to go—I'm not sure—to New Bern, North Carolina, if I'm not—I'm not sure. That's where this was supposed to be.

Agent: Which is "this"?

Sutton: This drug was supposed to be shipped in dead bodies to him, to his funeral home in New Bern, North Carolina.

Agent: Who is "him?"

Sutton: I don't know his name.

Agent: Have you ever heard it before?

Sutton: It's a funeral home I hear—I haven't heard it. Yeah, they told me the funeral home man's name, told me his name, but he's a father and son and he's in jail now. I think they said, or on bond or something.

Agent: How old is he?

Sutton: I can't say that? Said they put him under big bond. Said he didn't have no (sic) trouble with it.

Agent: If I called some names, would you—

Sutton: Probably would remember his name?

Agent: Roberts?

Sutton: No.

Agent: Doug?

Sutton: No.

Agent: Henderson?

Sutton: No. Call another one and let's see.

Agent: Darwin?

Sutton: Uh—

Agent: Moore?

Sutton: No, not Moore. It's either Henderson or the other one you called. Either one of them. He's—he got caught doing something, they say. But he ain't had no trouble getting out of jail either.

Agent: Well, what did you hear about it being a funeral home in New Bern?

Sutton: I heard that since I been in Raleigh here that he was supposed to be in the business.

Agent: Who (sic) did you hear it from?

Sutton: From some of the inmates from drug cases that (sic) deal in drugs down in New Bern.

Agent: Well, let me see if I understand you right. That there was drugs—Are you saying that there were drugs on the aircraft that Ike and those (who) were on (it) and that they were supposed to have gone to New Bern?

Sutton: The drugs was (sic) coming into New Bern, but somehow these people got a lot of information or something, or somewhere down the road they got funny and they got off in Hawaii.

Agent: Wait a minute now. Let me start over. Are you saying that you heard that the bodies that were on the plane that was searched with Ike and Sullivan (Southerland) were destined for a funeral home in New Bern?

Sutton: In New Bern. Say he's been getting—he got something before.

Agent: I doubt that.

Sutton: Yeah. He says he got something before?

Agent: Did you check on that?

Sutton: It was checked on, but I don't recall where they were headed for.

Agent: No, they weren't headed for New Bern.

Sutton: I think they just manufactured that, essentially.

Agent: Do you know of any incident in which heroin was brought into the United States inside a body or inside a case.

Sutton: I can't say that, no.

Agent: Okay.

Sutton: I can't say that. This is a new thing, but Ike told me he had to ship different ways. But I can't say about the bodies when I probably getting no more than me about—

Agent: Right. It was in connection with a customer or receiving shipment, or something, but there's nothing at that time in your information that had anything to do with shipments involving caskets or bodies or anything.

Later in the interrogation, the conversation about heroin and cadavers continued.

Agent: Well, how long have you heard this kind of thing about different ways or bodies? How about that kind of stuff? How long have you been hearing rumors about that?

Sutton: I have been hearing rumors since Christmas.

Agent: Since Christmas of this year?

Sutton: Of this year.

Agent: Well, what about before that? Have you heard, to your recollection—I mean you mentioned a while ago about a funeral home in Atlanta, Georgia.

Sutton: That was earlier when—

Agent: But did you hear that heroin was being brought back in any bodies any time before December of this year?

Sutton: I heard something that there was some brought back to a funeral man. They didn't say it was shipped to a funeral man. They didn't say how, it was in the bodies or what. And this was supposed to have been in Atlanta. This man was supposed to—not his father—the young boy.

That ended the conversation about the coffins. As it progressed, it seemed to stretch the agent's credulity. It is this kind of nonsense upon which the cadaver-heroin connection has been built.

SINCE THE CADAVER-HEROIN connection rumor first surfaced in the late 1960s and early 1970s, a number of reports about it have appeared, some of them presented by individuals apparently trying to promote their agendas. In 1997, NBC television news aired an investigative report by respected journalist Brian Ross that described how black gangsters were rising to prominence in the U.S. and how some of them were in Southeast Asia shipping heroin to the U.S. It mentioned Ike Atkinson specifically. The report included a segment of an interview of no more than 30 seconds with a man named Harold Beauchamp. It did not identify the prison in which Beauchamp was incarcerated, but in the interview Beauchamp claimed that he was involved in smuggling heroin in coffins from Vietnam. Ross did not investigate Beauchamp's claim, but in 2007 the producers of a 'Gangland' segment that appeared on the History Channel used the Beauchamp interview to boost Frank Lucas's claim that he pioneered the cadaver-heroin connection. 'I have never heard of Beauchamp and nobody in my organization who is still living has heard of him,' Ike said. 'He had nothing to do with us.' As for my investigation, I was unable to find any information on Harold Beauchamp or anyone who knew him.

IN APRIL 2004 Bob Kirkconnell, who identified himself as a retired master sergeant, sent an e-mail to the conspiracy theory web site Wanttoknow.info. Kirkconnell claimed that in 1972 or 1973 he was involved in an investigation at the Kadena Air Base in Okinawa of heroin being smuggled into the U.S. using 'killed-in-action human remains' out of Vietnam and that it involved a master sergeant named Southerland and a major whose name Kirkconnell could not recall but that sounded a lot like Ike. According to Kirkconnell, the plane 'contained between 80 and 87 transfer cases (87 is the number I recall) containing remains killed in action, out of Vietnam.' Kirkconnell wrote that when Japanese Customs agents in Okinawa opened the transfer cases, they found that all the bodies had their internal organs removed. McConnell wrote that the master sergeant took off to Hawaii where he was apprehended.

Almost nothing about this report is accurate. Southerland was not posing as a master sergeant and Ike was not a major.

Southerland had never been in the U.S. military. Ike was a retired master sergeant. There were two not 87 corpses on board the plane that eventually landed at Andrews Air Force Base. Southerland was not apprehended in Hawaii and Ike did not disappear. No report ever appeared that claimed heroin was found on cadavers at Kadena Air Force Base. The plane flew to Hawaii and then to the U.S. mainland. This is the kind of misinformation that has fueled the cadaver-connection conspiracy theory.

THE FAMOUS JEFFREY McDonald murder case presented one of the most bizarre associations with the alleged cadaver-heroin conspiracy. On February 17 1970, MacDonald, then a captain and a medical doctor in the U.S. Army, was assigned to the Womack Army Hospital at Fort Bragg, North Carolina. It was the day that McDonald's wife and two young daughters were murdered. McDonald has spent more than 27 years in prison for the crime but has steadfastly insisted he is innocent. Many people believe McDonald, and several scenarios have been spun suggesting that McDonald was framed. One of the most sensational scenarios points to the existence of a satanic cult, which was supposedly based in the Fort Bragg area and involved with drugs. Police informant Helena Stoekley claimed to have been a member of the cult, and she is presented as a reliable witness who could prove McDonald innocent.

Stoekley claimed high-ranking Army officials, including two Fort Bragg generals, were involved in drug trafficking, along with members of the Army's CID and the Fayetteville (North Carolina) Police Department. Stoekley was aware of Ike's drug operation and she claimed that, because of corruption, his organization had a high level of protection. She also claimed that many members of Ike's network were involved in satanic cult activity and they had threatened her with death if she talked. According to proponents of this conspiracy theory, local drug dealers hated McDonald because he was pressing them while in his drug treatment program to name suppliers.

As the conspiracy is spun, Everette Beasley, who served on the Fayetteville Police Department from 1953 to 1973, gave a statement to now-retired FBI agent Ted Gunderson on May 5 1986, sixteen years after the murder, and nearly three years after Stoekley's death in January 1983. According to Beasley's statement, Stoekley made the familiar claim that heroin was being smuggled into the U.S. in the body cavities of dead soldiers being returned by air from Vietnam to the U.S.

Beasley's statement reads, in part: 'Helena told me after the McDonald murders that there were contacts in Vietnam who put the drugs in the GI bodies, in plastic bags after the autopsies were completed. The bodies were sewn up and shipped to Pope Air Base, Fort Bragg, (Seymour) Johnson Air Force Base and other bases which she (Stoekley) did not name.'

'When the bodies arrived in the U.S., they were met by a contact in the United States at one of the military bases, and, after the drugs were removed by this contact, the bodies were sent to their final destination. The person who met the bodies at the respective air bases knew which bodies to check, based on a pre-determined code. Although I believe Helena knew their identities, she never gave me this information. Helena told me that people who handled the assignments in Vietnam and those who met the planes in the United States were military personnel. She stated most of the drugs came from Thailand. Helena stated that the drugs and pickups were made at the base at Fort Bragg.'

This unverified informant testimony has passed as "evidence" of the cadaver-heroin connection conspiracy. In reality, the McDonald conspiracy as it relates to the cadaver-heroin connection conspiracy is not true. The cadavers were not shipped to Fort Bragg or any base other than the Dover Air Force Base or Oakland Army Base. And at Dover and Oakland, many people would have been needed to make this conspiracy work, but no contact person who would have had to meet the planes and to help move the bodies to 'their final destination' was ever identified or arrested. Moreover, what possible 'pre-determined code' would have worked, given the logistics of the alleged cadaver-heroin connection? How could the drugs come from Thailand if the bodies are being shipped directly from Vietnam?

No one has ever stepped forward to support Stoekley's claims. She died of liver failure in 1983, but not surprisingly, some conspiracy theorists even claim that her death is suspicious. As for Ike having anything to do with a satanic cult, does the man featured in this book sound like he would waste his life worshipping Satan? Besides, there is not one iota of evidence.

MICHAEL LEVINE, A retired DEA agent and author of *Deep Cover*, a scathing critique of U.S. drug policy, has tried to link the cadaver-heroin connection to the usual suspect—the Central Intelligence Agency (CIA). Levine claims that the CIA had a 'heroin factory' in Chiang Mai, Thailand, which the agency used to produce and then smuggle massive amounts of heroin into the U.S. in the bodies and body bags of GIs killed in Vietnam. Levine claims he has evidence of the scheme but says the U.S. Government killed his investigation. He is vague about the details of this sensational charge. When I telephoned Levine and asked him to be a source for this book, he said he was planning to write a book about the alleged cadaver-heroin conspiracy and declined to talk about it. Levine did not respond to my question: Why would the CIA use the cadavers of GIs in Vietnam in a complex scheme to smuggle heroin via Thailand?

After all, if the CIA is the so-called 'Invisible Government,' whatever has been said about the agency's competence or lack of it, doesn't the agency has the means and power to use much easier methods to smuggle heroin if they wanted to do that? Also, why would the CIA do it, where was the heroin going, and to whom was it sold?

Levine has an essay in the book, 'Into the Buzz Saw', which contains a footnote (USA versus Jackson et al) that does not include a date or any identifying information. It's obviously a reference to a court case. When I asked him what the date of the citation was and its significance, Levine said he did not know the date for sure but thought it was 1970 or '71. Levine claimed that one of the informants he handled, while working undercover in Bangkok, made a 'full statement' implicating William Herman Jackson in the trafficking of heroin in cadavers, and this 'explosive' information came out in that court case. Jackson was in court in 1970 and 1971, defending himself in the New York City heroin case and testifying in the Patch-Hart alleged corruption case. They were the only court cases in which Jackson was involved during those two years. A thorough perusal of the transcripts of those court cases found no mention of the cadaver-heroin conspiracy, a fact confirmed by Dennis Dillon, the New York City prosecutor in the Patch-Hart case.

BUT WHAT ABOUT Dan Addario, another retired DEA agent, the one who had been head of the DEA office in Bangkok from 1975 to 1978? Surely he should know the truth. Addario published an article titled 'Super Narc' in the 'Image' section of the September, 25, 1988 issue of the *San Francisco Examiner*. Warren Hinckle, a well-known San Francisco journalist and political radical, actually ghost wrote the article. Addario, too, is trying to get a book published, which will incorporate his sensational 'findings' about the cadaver-heroin connection. In the article, Addario claimed that in the autumn of 1974 he personally discovered heroin inside the chest cavity of an American GI's corpse in a military hospital in Bangkok. Its discovery would have potentially put him on the fast track to higher positions within the DEA. Yet, he did not share this information with the American Ambassador or the CIA station chief, claiming that, 'when it comes to stopping narcotics, they (the U.S. Government) often have other—and higher—priorities.'

Addario's article, unfortunately, has had a lot of impact. Two decades after it appeared in print, some sources remembered the article and assumed its assertions to be true. To check out the accuracy of Addario's article, I shared it with DEA agents and journalists who were in Bangkok in 1974. Retired DEA agent Chuck Lutz, who served under Addario during this period, summed up the prevailing sentiment that my sources unanimously shared about Addario's article. 'Dan appears to have written a fictionalized account of the Atkinson-Jackson case, while confusing some parts of the case, sensationalizing others, making some up, using great literary license and assigning pseudonyms for all but himself and General Pow Sarasin (who, by the way, was not Director General of the Thai Police at the time, but the head of the Police Narcotics Suppression Center).'

But if Addario meant to use pseudonyms, he certainly did not inform the readers of his intentions. Nowhere in the article does he indicate that he is using this literary device. And if he did, he had a strange way of doing it. For instance, Jack and Ike become Carl Jackson, not William Herman Jackson, and Milt Atkinson, not Leslie 'Ike' Atkinson.

Sources point out several other inconsistencies about Addario's article that support the conclusion it is a work of fiction. While there are too many to catalog in full, here are some of the major ones. In the fall of 1974, there were no Vietnam War dead. So who is the dead GI in the Bangkok morgue? There were still some GIs stationed in Thailand as late as the Fall of Saigon in 1975 who may have died from injuries unrelated to Vietnam, but none that Atkinson's drug ring or any other trafficker could reasonably have predicted. Journalists who were working in Bangkok in 1974 say that Addario's discovery in the hospital would have been a sensational story, making a major leak to the media inevitable. At the time, Bangkok was the main listening post in Southeast Asia for U.S. journalists and journalists from other countries, and it was one of the worse places in the world to keep a secret. Moreover, some DEA agents who worked with Addario at the time, those whom I was able to locate and interview, said they heard nothing about a cadaver that contained heroin in a Bangkok hospital. Also, Addario was the head of the Bangkok field office at that time, and, given his administrative position as Regional Director, he would in no way have been out in the street conducting an investigation.

THE ADDARIO ARTICLE perpetuates the myth of the cadaver-heroin connection; it is a story unsupported by evidence or even common sense. Bill Slaughter, a retired North Carolina State Bureau of Investigation (SBI) agent interrogated Jackson for hours and had the opportunity to ask him numerous times about the alleged cadaver-heroin conspiracy. 'Jackson adamantly denied having anything to do with it,' Slaughter recalled. 'He would get really upset when I brought it up. I could tell from my interviews with Jackson that he had nothing to do with any coffins or cadavers.'

Slaughter's assessment of the cadaver-heroin connection is the same as the opinion of every other law enforcement official who investigated the Atkinson-Jackson drug ring and was interviewed for this book. There is no evidence that the cadaver-heroin connection ever happened.

Ike is upset that false rumors have tied him to the bogus cadaver-heroin connection and wonders if people will ever be persuaded that he had nothing to do with it. 'Why would I do something so awful as move heroin in cadavers?' he asked. 'I had so many easier and more effective ways of moving my dope. Besides, whatever wrong I did, I was still proud of my (military) service, and I would have done nothing to harm the memory of our brave soldiers who died serving the country.'

Ike is right when he says that the cadaver-heroin connection is the biggest hoax in the history of the international drug trade. The hoax gives credible conspiracy theories a bad rap. The bottom line—despite the hype, the claims and the hundreds of articles discussing the conspiracy as if it happened, there is not one shred of evidence to confirm that it ever did. Case closed.

CHAPTER 9
American Gangster
Revisited

FRANK LUCAS, THE drug trafficker whom Hollywood has made famous as the *American Gangster*, has done more than any other individual to propagate the cadaver-heroin connection hoax. Along the way, Frank Lucas has not only distorted Ike Atkinson's story but has literally stolen parts of his life. Lucas has been able to do this because in 2000 he got lucky and emerged from obscurity when *New York* magazine, a major print publication, wrote a long article about him. The article made the old gangster appear to be the second coming of the black gangster from the 1970s 'blaxploitation' movie era. Written by Mark Jacobson and titled 'The Return of Superfly,' the article profiled Lucas's life story entirely from Lucas's point of view and allowed him to portray himself, in the words of Jacobson, as New York City's 'biggest, baddest heroin kingpin in the original O.G. in Chinchilla.'

'Superfly' made many boasts in the article: that he was the first Black drug dealer to become independent of La Cosa Nostra and that he was the black gangster who established the Asian heroin connection, which allowed him to sell 'Blue Magic', a special type of heroin that, he boasted, was the purest smack on the street. Lucas told *New York* magazine that Ike Atkinson was related to him because Ike married one of his cousins, which made him 'as good as family.' Lucas said he went to Bangkok and visited Jack's American Star Bar where he learned that 'Ike knew everyone over there, every Black guy in the Army, from the cooks on up.' As the *New York* magazine article progressed, Lucas's claims about his Asian experience got more outlandish. Lucas, supposedly independent of Ike, managed to transport heroin 'almost exclusively on military planes to the eastern seaboard bases.' 'Superfly' met a mysterious English-speaking, Rolls Royce-driving, Thai-Chinese man with the sobriquet of '007', a 'fucking Chinese James Bond 007,' who took Lucas to the Golden Triangle where, during his first trip, he purchased 32 kilos for $4,200 a kilo. On the way back, 'Superfly' and 007's men, 'Bruce Lee types,' according to Lucas, 'fought off bandits hiding in the trees.'

Lucas claimed to be so clever and bold that he was able to transport heroin via a plane used by Henry Kissinger, U.S. President Richard Nixon's Secretary of State. As 'Superfly' explained to Jacobson: 'I mean who the fuck is going to search Henry Kissinger's plane?'

But how did Lucas get his heroin back to the U.S.? It was 'Superfly's' most controversial claim, comprising a mere paragraph of the article, but it helped to parlay the former drug trafficker to notoriety as the man behind the so-called cadaver-heroin connection. Not only that, but Lucas also dragged Ike into his claim to infamy. According to Lucas's fabrication of history, Lucas and Ike Atkinson brought over a carpenter from North Carolina who made 28 copies of government coffins, whatever they are, and fixed them with false bottoms so each coffin could contain six to eight kilos of heroin. Lucas tells his New York Magazine biographer that the coffins had to be snug because 'you could not have shit (heroin) sliding around. Ike was very smart because he made sure (that) we used heavy guys coffins. He didn't put them in no skinny guy's.'

How big of a drug dealer does Lucas claim to be? According to 'Superfly', he could sell his 'Blue Magic' on 116th Street between Seventh and Eighth Avenue in the evening and by 9 pm all of it would be gone. Superfly would have a million bucks, which he then packed in his beat-up Chevy, which he called Nelly Belle, and then drive to his home in New Jersey.

THE *NEW YORK* magazine profile made for a hell of a read, but that should have been the extent of its impact. In another month or two, many of the magazine's readers, no doubt, would have had just a dim recollection of the article. But 'The Return of Superfly' caught the attention of some big wigs in Hollywood with imaginations as fertile as Superfly's. Universal Studios struck a lucrative deal with Lucas, Jacobson and Richie Roberts, the former New Jersey state detective then prosecutor who helped put Lucas in jail in 1976 and later became his friend. It was a big break for Lucas who, despite claiming to be a legend and the biggest, baddest drug trafficker in New York during the early 1970s, was reportedly on welfare.

Having a movie made about his life must have seemed like a dream even for a hard-bitten old drug dealer like Frank Lucas. Mega Hollywood star Denzel Washington portrayed him in the movie, which had international distribution and reportedly grossed more than $180 million. 'Superfly' got to wear his sunglasses, looking bad for interviews with mainstream media publications (*New York Post*, *New York Times*), hip hop magazines and web sites (for example, Hiphopremix.com, Hiphopdr.com and Allhiphop.com) and television networks (Black Entertainment Television, History Channel and Dateline NBC).

The *American Gangster* movie is based on Jacobson's article, but it stretched his story even more. For instance, it glossed over the fact that Lucas was a big-time informant who had to seek refuge in the Federal Witness Protection Program to avoid potential violent repercussions for snitching on his criminal colleagues.

At the movie's end, Hollywood had transformed him into a good snitch who turned in only corrupt law enforcement officials. In doing so, the movie presented a totally boldfaced lie at the end of the movie by stating that Frank Lucas's and Richie Roberts's 'collaboration led to the conviction of three-quarters of New York City's Drug Enforcement Agency.' The truth—not one law enforcement official was ever arrested because of the collaboration of Frank Lucas and Richie Roberts. 'Superfly' only snitched on his fellow gangsters.

What kind of informant was Frank Lucas? Jack Toal, a retired DEA agent had a chance to work with Lucas in the late 1970s after he decided to inform. 'He was good at giving up lower level people on the street,' Toal recalled. 'He did everything by phone and never left the prison. He was in prison at the MCC (Metropolitan Correction Center) in Lower Manhattan and was kept there for a long time. He was good. Here Frank was in the Witness Protection Program, but was able to convince people on the street that he would never give them up.'"

Ike appeared as a character in the movie—as Lucas's cousin Nate who is living in Bangkok. Nate is portrayed as a 'gofer' for Frank Lucas in the movie and improbably introduces Superfly to the Chinese general in the Golden Triangle who supplied him with heroin. I say improbably because no way would Ike—or any drug trafficker, for that matter—give up his heroin source. Neither would any big time dealer—and Lucas claims to have been one—risk life, limb and bankroll to go blindly into the wilds of the Golden Triangle and buy his heroin supply. Only in Hollywood!

As the plot of *American Gangster* unfolds, one could almost hear the wheels in the minds of the movie viewer grind. How is big, bad Superfly getting the heroin into the country? As the movie reached its climax, Richie Roberts, played by Russell Crowe, inspected a military plane carrying the corpses of dead

GIs from the Vietnam War that had landed at a Newark, New Jersey, airbase. Roberts opened a casket and the shocking truth—as Hollywood spins it—is revealed. Much to the horror of the audience, our hero has uncovered packets of heroin in the coffins of the dead GIs, exposing what we know as the cadaver- heroin connection.

IT'S A GOOD story, one that, as we have seen, a suppliant unblinking media has fueled. Since the *American Gangster* movie was released on November 2 2007, anybody surfing the Internet will find hundreds of articles about the cadaver-heroin connection. As of July 9 2008, when one entered 'cadaver connection Frank Lucas' into either the Yahoo and Google search engine, you got 12,700 and 30,500 hits respectively on the topic, even though, as we have read, the connection never happened. Similarly, when you plugged in 'cadaver connection Ike Atkinson' in the Google and Yahoo search engines, one got 605 and 502 hits respectively.

That a large part of Lucas's story is suspect is not something the corporate media in America wanted to hear, once they realized the money they could make from *American Gangster*. Media outlets like NBC Dateline, Black Entertainment Television and the History Channel bought and promoted Frank Lucas's story hook, line and sinker. Brad Davis, a producer for *Dateline* NBC, called me in September 2007 and asked if I wanted to be interviewed for a segment that would examine the criminal career and life story of Frank Lucas. The segment was to air a few days before November 2 2007, the date *American Gangster* opened in movie theaters across North America. I suggested four other sources to the Dateline producer, two former federal prosecutors and two former DEA agents, all of whom, like myself, were well-familiar with Lucas's story and his claims to criminal fame. I informed Davis that all my recommended sources had questions about various Lucas claims. But he assured me: 'That's all right. We want to get the true story of Frank Lucas.'

Davis sat us all down for two-hour plus interviews in which *Dateline* NBC got a close up look at Frank Lucas from our perspective and had the opportunity to examine some of his claims. But a few days before the program was to air, the producer called and informed me that none of us would appear on the show because the segment had been cut down to half an hour from the originally scheduled hour. The only people who appeared on the Dateline episode were the stars, Denzel Washington and Russel Crowe, with the real Frank Lucas, Richie Roberts and Mark Jacobson. They were the 'experts' who talked about Lucas's story and reinforced the official movie story line. The producer assured us that *Dateline* would do another, more in-depth program about Lucas at a later date. That never happened.

One must conclude that my *Dateline* experience was a classic example of the sorry state of the American media and how it no longer makes any effort to distinguish between news and entertainment. But that was just the beginning. In the following weeks, other media jumped on the bandwagon and showed itself to be cheerleaders for the film that Universal was claiming to be based on a true story. The History Channel did a program for its new *Gangland* series that did not seriously examine any of Lucas's claims and essentially parroted the official story line. That is understandable. After all, Universal owns the History Channel. Black Entertainment Television (BET) followed suit with a puff profile for its popular *American Gangster* series and was awarded with access that led to a special hour-long *'Making of America Gangster'* feature that followed the airing of its Lucas profile.

BET and the History Channel interviewed me for segments about Lucas that was to appear in their *American Gangster* and *Gangland* series respectively. During the two, two-hour interviews, I spent some time debunking the cadaver-heroin connection. I explained that Ike, who, by the way, was not Lucas's cousin, had nothing to do with it and how he, not Lucas, was the American drug trafficker who pioneered the Asian heroin connection. None of the information I provided in the interviews made it out of the cutting room.

Indeed, since Universal announced that it was making the *American Gangster* movie, the media had all but collaborated in the falsification of Lucas's story and the distortion of gangster history. The most egregious example is the media's laziness in investigating Lucas's link to the so-called cadaver-heroin connection. Unbelievably, no journalist checked out the authenticity of the conspiracy by asking Lucas tough, probing questions like: Who was involved in the drug smuggling scheme? How did the cadaver-heroin connection work? How were you able to implement such a complex scheme when you did not have any military experience?

Today, DEA agents who investigated Lucas and the Asian drug connection and whom I have interviewed dismiss the notion that Frank Lucas could engineer such an elaborate drug distribution network as defying common sense. For the cadaver-heroin connection to function, Lucas, who was never in the U.S. military and did not live in Asia, needed a reliable heroin connection in Thailand and then had to find a way to smuggle the heroin to Vietnam and the mortuary office at Tan Son Nhut where the bodies were sent home to the U.S. There, Lucas would have had to recruit and bribe members of the military to place the heroin inside the coffins or actual corpses. Next, he would have needed to corrupt the entire transportation system from the mortuary to the U.S. Once the bodies arrived in the U.S., more corrupt military personnel would be needed to remove the heroin from the bodies.

Could a drug trafficking system like this have functioned at the height of the Vietnam War? It would have been relatively easy for them to check it out. Instead, since Frank Lucas and the *American Gangster* movie revived interest in the cadaver-heroin connection, the media has been content with publishing hundreds of articles that have treated its existence as fact.

The Associated Press (AP) was one media source that initially followed in lock step with the conspiracy—that is, until it decided to investigate some of Lucas's claims more closely. The investigation was prompted by John McBeth, a veteran Asia-based journalist who reported from Thailand in the 1970s and was familiar with the conspiracy rumors. McBeth complained to the AP about the inaccuracy of a story published in November, 2007. To AP's credit, it did take a second look.

In its initial story, the AP concluded: 'To get the drugs back to the States, Lucas established the infamous "cadaver connection," hiding the heroin in the caskets of dead soldiers.' In the follow-up article that appeared in January 2008, Jake Coyle, AP Entertainment writer, wrote; 'The Harlem kingpin's infamous "Cadaver Connection"—a pipeline of top-grade Southeast Asia heroin smuggled in GI caskets—has always been at the center of his considerable and enduring mythology. But it turns out that the casket story is just that—a myth.' In this follow up article, Lucas back-tracked big time, conceding in an interview with Coyle that he may have used the cadaver-heroin connection only once.

Coyle explained to me why the media has gotten it so wrong on the *American Gangster* story: 'This mess happened partially because journalists have been relying on secondary sources removed from the actual events.' McBeth concluded that 'the cadaver heroin connection was basically an urban legend that developed a life of its own because the journalists who wrote that stuff did not give it the common sense test, possibly because they had no idea of the geography of Southeast Asia. It's quite simple: the bodies of dead servicemen came out of Saigon; the heroin supplied to Lucas came out of Thailand. So how could the heroin have gotten into the coffins?'

WHILE INCARCERATED IN Butner Federal Penitentiary, Ike got a copy of the *New York* magazine profile of Lucas and could not believe what he read about the coffins. 'The article was nothing but a pack of lies, and I don't know how any magazine could print such an article,' Ike recalled. He wrote lengthy letters to the editor of the *New York* magazine and to Mark Jacobson, the author, explaining his true relationship with Superfly and questioning Lucas's claims. The recipients never answered the letters, but the letters do provide keen insight into Lucas's story and his relationship with Ike. Later, when we began collaborating on this book, Ike expanded on that relationship.

His letter to the *New York* magazine editor began with an all-out blast at the content of the article. 'Not so fast my friends,' Ike wrote. 'Your column or story given to you by Lucas doesn't come close to the truth, and I feel the true story must be told.' Ike went on to explain: 'It never happened. In fact, Lucas spread disinformation about the Southeast Asia connection. Frank never brought any drugs into the U.S.'

In the letter, Ike went on to debunk a lot of myths regarding his relationship with Lucas. For instance, regarding Lucas's claim of a family relationship, Ike wrote: 'I am not now, nor have I ever been married to any of Frank Lucas's relatives.' His categorical denial is backed up by Ike's family members who, when interviewed by this author, said Lucas has no connection to their family.

AS WE HAVE seen, Ike Atkinson did not even meet Frank Lucas until about 1972 or 1973, even though he was born in La Grange, North Carolina, about 13 miles from Goldsboro. Born in 1931, Lucas, by all accounts, had as tough a time growing up in the segregated South as did Ike, who is six years older. Whereas Ike entered the military as a teenager after forging his mother's signature on a consent form, Lucas spent his teenage years pursuing a life of petty crime before migrating to Harlem, ragged and penniless. Ike entered the highly competitive world of drug trafficking but never carried a gun and took care of business using his charisma and business skills. On the other hand, Lucas's bully tactics and violent approach to criminal business made him feared, not liked. Lucas was one of thirteen people indicted as part of a drug conspiracy case in June 1974. However, within the next several months, at least six witnesses turned up dead. The prosecutor in the trial complained to the judge that the murder spree was making it hard for him to prosecute the case.

While the facts of Ike's early life can be documented, we must depend on Lucas's 'recollections' for his, a problematic consideration given that Lucas's road to 'Superfly' status is pock-marked with questions. Take his relationship with Bumpy Johnson, Harlem's legendary black godfather, one aspect of his life that has been challenged and compels one to question other aspects of it. As Lucas tells it, he was on the streets of Harlem, stealing to survive when a pool hustler named 'Ice Pick Red' challenged him to a game of pool for $1,000 at a pool hall on 134th Street in Harlem. Lucas did not have any money, but Bumpy Johnson arrived on the scene and backed him financially, becoming his guardian angel. 'Bumpy didn't like me; he loved me,' Lucas boasted.

Bumpy died in 1968, so he cannot verify 'his love' for Superfly. But Mayme, Bumpy's widow, who was 94 years old and doing well, can do it. In *Harlem Godfather*, her book about Bumpy, co-authored with Karen Quinones Miller, Mayme called Lucas a liar and devoted space shooting down Lucas's claims about his relationship with Bumpy. 'Frank wasn't anything more than a flunky and one that Bumpy never did really trust," she told one web site. 'Bumpy would let Frank drive him around, but you better believe he was never in important meetings or anything.'

Mayme's assessment of Lucas's relationship with her husband is confirmed in the conversations I had with old time law enforcement officials who worked in Harlem and knew Bumpy. They do not remember Lucas being around Bumpy, let alone serving as his right hand man.

IKE SCOFFS AT Lucas's boast that he became so big the La Cosa Nostra had to come to Lucas to get their heroin supply. Ike recalled visiting Lucas once in New Jersey to collect some money owed to him. 'Before I went to see Frank, some people told me: "Be careful when you get around Frank, he owes the Italians money and they might be looking for him."' When Ike arrived at Lucas's place, a couple of his men stood guard outside, ostensibly to protect their boss against any trouble from the Mob.

DEA sources reveal that for most of his criminal career Lucas was constantly in deep financial trouble with La Cosa Nostra. He even owed two well-connected Mafioso $300,000 and only managed to avoid ending up in a dumpster or buried in concrete because the two mobsters were arrested and carted off to jail. Ike also recalled the time two members of La Cosa Nostra visited him in jail in Atlanta. 'At the time, Frank was dead broke and he expected me to help him out. I was in the Atlanta penitentiary when these two Italian mobsters came to see me. He said: "Frank owes us $80,000, and one of them said you would take care of it.'" Both Ike and the mobsters broke out laughing at the absurdity of Superfly's claim.

Lucas and the La Cosa Nostra did not trust each other. In fact, Lucas had a tempestuous relationship with La Cosa Nostra, which helps explain his fervent campaign to forge a reputation as 'The Man' who was the first to break with the Mob and to establish the Asian drug pipeline to the U.S. In an interview with Lucas for my book *Gangsters of Harlem*, I asked him if he got his heroin from the Italians. 'Superfly' got testy and barked: 'I was not going to have no motherfucking fat guy leaning back in the chair, smoking a $20 cigar and bragging about how he had another nigger in Harlem working for him. I don't play that game. The Italians were charging $60,000 to $65,000 a kilo, and I was getting it at $4,000 a kilo. My junk (heroin) traveled from the Mekong Delta and the Ho Chi Minh Trail to the U.S.'

But DEA sources confirmed that Lucas had dealt with the Italian mobsters for most of his criminal career. Joe Sullivan, a retired DEA agent who worked drug cases in East Harlem in the 1970s, recalled: 'All the big drug traffickers, including Lucas, were getting their heroin from the Italians. The French Connection was in the process of being dismantled and the supply was tight and expensive. Lucas was getting it for about $200,000 a kilo.'

LUCAS THOUGH, STILL made his money by getting down and dirty on the streets of Harlem. 'The Italians were very risk-adverse,' Sullivan revealed. 'They trusted their foreign-contacts and were satisfied with bringing the heroin into the country. But the Italians thought it beneath them to whack the heroin, mix it, put it in glassine envelopes, and hawk it on the street. They preferred to sell the heroin (wholesale) to the black dealers. A few black dealers, such as Barnes and Lucas, became successful at controlling the drug business on the street while still being able to insulate themselves from the actual distribution.' Lew Rice, a retired DEA agent who interviewed Frank Lucas when he agreed to cooperate with the authorities after he was busted, said Superfly readily acknowledged to the DEA after he was busted that he was getting his heroin from the Mafia. 'Ralph Tutino (aka "The General") was his major source of supply,' Rice revealed. Press reports indicate that Tutino was one of few members of the La Cosa Nostra who was able to buy and deal in heroin brought from Southeast Asia.

SO WHAT ABOUT Lucas's claim that he pioneered the Asian drug connection? The way Lucas has told it, he traveled alone to Bangkok where he did not know anybody but still managed to establish the Asian connection. In his account, he checked into the Dusit Thani Hotel in Bangkok where he hailed a motorcycle to take him to Jack's American Star Bar.

In his *New York* magazine letter to the editor, Atkinson offered a different account of how 'Superfly' first came to Bangkok, revealing that it was through his efforts the arrangement was made. 'Frank wanted to go to Bangkok with his wife, Julie, and his brother Shorty but did not even know how to get a visa,' Atkinson explained. 'I helped by taking them to the Thai Embassy in Washington, D.C.'

A DEA intelligence report confirms that Lucas got a visa for Thailand from the Thai Embassy in Washington, DC, in October 1974. But in an interview for this author's *Gangsters of Harlem* book, Lucas claimed that he went to Bangkok as early as 1969 or 1970 to begin establishing the Asian connection. It is likely that Lucas did indeed travel to Bangkok earlier than 1974, perhaps entering on a 30-day tourist visa routinely issued at Don Muang Airport, because Atkinson recalls taking

Lucas to Jack's American Star Bar in his first visit to Bangkok. Jack's American Star Bar was closed in 1973.

However, as late as October 1974, Frank Lucas had not appeared on the DEA's 'radar screen' in Bangkok. Peter Davis is a retired DEA agent who worked on special assignment in the agency's Bangkok office in the early 1970s. 'We didn't know who Lucas was, nor did we have information that he was operating in Southeast Asia,' Davis recalled, adding: 'Of course, there is a possibility that he could have slipped under the radar screen, although that would be tough to do if he was a big drug trafficker in the region as he has claimed to be.'

Chuck Lutz transferred to the DEA's Bangkok office nine months before Lucas was issued his Thai visa in 1974, but he could not recall his office having any reports about Lucas or members of his drug trafficking organization operating in Thailand. 'We believe the Jackson-Atkinson drug ring was the only Black syndicate moving Asian heroin to the United States and that Lucas was probably getting his heroin supply from Ike Atkinson,' Lutz said.

As for that mysterious drug supplier, 007, he was, in reality, Luchai 'Chai' Ruviwat, Ike's Chinese-Thai partner. By 1974, Luchai was acting as the middleman between Ike's drug ring and the source of supply in the Golden Triangle of Laos, Burma and Thailand. According to Lucas, however, "When I began to do business with 007, I didn't see Atkinson. He wasn't important to me at all." Assuming Lucas was dealing with Luchai, how could Lucas have used his sources without having to deal with Ike?

'When we (Frank, Julie and Shorty) arrived in Bangkok, I checked them into the Dusit Thani Hotel,' Ike explained in his letter to the *New York* magazine. 'Frank won't admit it, but during the time he was there, we put him to bed, woke him up and took him where he wanted to go. The snake farm was his favorite attraction. After that, we would go back to my bar and restaurant (Jack's American Star Bar), and Frank would talk with the Green Berets (who) frequented my bar.' Ike believes that this is where Superfly heard about the fighting in Vietnam and got the material for some of his colorful accounts of how he started the Asian connection.

Ike was uncertain about the length of time Lucas spent in Bangkok, but it was not long—from three to five days. 'He slept most of the time,' Ike recalled. 'I told him I would take him anywhere he wanted to go in the city. The only thing he wanted to do was go to the zoo and look at the snakes.'

On the third day, according to Atkinson, Superfly came to his house and said he wanted to buy some heroin. Atkinson recalled the meeting: 'Frank said: "I heard there are two types of 'rice' (heroin) over here, and I want you to sell me the best one." In fact, the "rice" I was selling Frank was the best, but he said he wanted to try it himself. I told Luchai to bring two samples of "rice." Luchai went and got two samples and brought them back. Frank held his hands out. Luchai poured the contents of one bag in each of Frank's palms. Frank licked one hand and took a drink of water. He then licked the other hand and took another drink of water. He then raved about how much better the 'rice' in his left hand was and stated that he wanted that "rice."' Not surprisingly, both samples were taken from the same batch of "rice," and there was absolutely no difference between the two samples.

Lucas's second or third day in Bangkok, Ike took him to a Buddhist temple. When Lucas saw people bringing food and gifts for the Buddha and leaving it at the temple, he said he had to go and buy some apples and leave them for the Buddha. Then according to Atkinson, 'Lucas commenced crying and asked me: "Does Thailand border the Holy Land?"'

As for Superfly's wild claim that he once used a plane carrying Henry Kissinger to smuggle drugs from Bangkok to the U.S., Ike called the concept 'absolutely absurd,' explaining, 'We never put anybody or anything on Mr. Kissinger's jet, although Frank might have heard such tales while in Bangkok.' Bill Slaughter, a North Carolina State Bureau of Investigation (SBI) agent who investigated both Atkinson and Frank Lucas, said he heard the Kissinger story from Ellis Sutton. 'The story was floating around in North Carolina's criminal circles, so it's a good guess Lucas could have picked it up on one of his trips to the state,' Slaughter explained.

Given how little time Superfly spent in Bangkok and his lack of local contacts, Ike wonders how Lucas could get away with conning people with the idea that he could operate a cadaver-heroin connection. But he thinks he knows how the rumor of the conspiracy got started.

As pointed out in the *New York* magazine article, Lucas claimed that he flew a 'country boy North Carolina carpenter' over to Bangkok to make twenty-eight replicas of U.S. government-issued coffins with false bottoms, big enough to load six to eight kilos. First of all, as I have reported earlier, there were no 'government-issued coffins' made of wood. They were all constructed of aluminum and the military refers to them as 'transfer cases.' Secondly, yes, there was a carpenter named Leon, a lifelong friend of Ike's. 'He (Leon) never had any association with constructing coffins for transporting heroin or drugs,' Atkinson maintained. 'On the contrary, Leon was in Bangkok making false bottoms for teak furniture.'

And that is how Ike believes the story of transporting heroin via coffins got started: his use of the teak furniture to move heroin into the U.S. 'We used teak furniture to smuggle the heroin and we were getting a shipment ready,' Ike recalled. 'Frank barged in and went right to the back. "What are you doing?" Frank asked me: "I was caught off guard, and the only thing I could think of to say was: "We are making coffins.""

ALTHOUGH IKE FELT he needed to keep an eye on Lucas, he did develop a business relationship with him. 'After Jack went to jail, Frank asked me if he could be my partner. I said "Only if I handle the supply from Thailand and you handle the distribution from the New York end."'

By this time, figuring blood would be thicker than water, Lucas had built a network of relatives and dependable homeboys from his hometown area. The network, dubbed 'The Country Boys,' included brothers Ezell, Larry, Leevin, John Paul and Vernon Lee, who was known as 'Shorty.' Ike worked more with Shorty than he did with Frank, and Ike believed he was the man who held 'The Country Boys' together. 'I liked Shorty,' Ike revealed. 'He was a lot more easy going than Frank and good to work with.'

Unlike Ike's drug ring, which was nonviolent, the Country Boys were exceedingly violent. In 1973, Newark, New Jersey, detectives started getting complaints about the Country Boys. According to police intelligence, members of the drug ring were strong-arming local youths into using and selling dope. 'We got ten to fifteen complaints every day,' said Eddie Jones, one of the three Newark detectives assigned to investigating "The Country Boys." People were afraid to walk out of their houses.'

For Ike, though, working with Frank Lucas was often frustrating. 'When it came time to get my money from him, he would always take the $100 bills and leave me the $10 and $20 bills—the street money,' Ike recalled. 'I didn't think that was a classy thing to do.'

Ike and Lucas became partners in a farm near Stem, North Carolina. That was the property Lucas called 'Paradise Valley' in the *New York* magazine article, 'a several thousand-acre spread back on which ranged 300 head of Black Angus cows, including a big-balled breeding bull worth $125,000.' Ike fronted the money for the property, although the property was put in Lucas's name (that, in itself, another indication that Lucas was likely the subordinate of the two: the boss normally not wanting to put assets in his name to avoid notoriety and possible government seizure).

'The property was worth about $800,000 and it was a money-making proposition,' Ike revealed. 'At the time the farm had the biggest tobacco allotment in Granville County. Frank's big dream was to open two or three meat markets in New York City. The plan was to slaughter the meat in North Carolina and haul it to New York City. I thought it was a good idea because Frank was always squandering his money.'

One DEA intelligence report described an incident in which Ike tried to get his money from Lucas. In May 1975, four months after Lucas was busted at his home in Teaneck, New Jersey, an informant visited Lucas while he was in the hospital in Englewood, New Jersey. Lucas asked the informant to go to Goldsboro to pick up a package of heroin from Ike, and he would pay him $3,000 for the assignment. Several days later, the informant went to see Ike, who complained that Lucas owed him $246,000 for a large shipment of heroin that had recently arrived from Bangkok. The unpaid money, Ike said, was Lucas's part of the investment, and if he was not going to pay him soon, he would claim Lucas's share of the heroin. The debt was a big deal and could have become a big problem for the Atkinson-Lucas business relationship. But by this time, collecting the money would not be Ike's biggest concern. He was having bigger problems of a legal nature to worry about.

CHAPTER 10

New Kid on the Block

IKE ATKINSON HAD spent less than a year in jail for the 1969 offense of failing to pay a duty on heroin imported into the U.S. and, fortunately for him, he had not been involved in William Herman Jackson's plan to smuggle heroin to Denver, beginning in late 1971. Nevertheless, Ike began running into big-time legal problems in his home state of North Carolina. It began in 1971 when the North Carolina State Bureau of Investigation (SBI), in cooperation with Federal law enforcement, launched Operation Eagle, a major eight-month drug trafficking investigation.

A division of the North Carolina Department of Justice, the SBI got its start in 1937 when the North Carolina State Legislature ratified Public Law 349, which established the State Bureau of Identification and Investigation. The SBI's primary role has been to assist local law enforcement with criminal investigations. To accomplish this objective, the SBI works closely with both local and Federal authorities. The Bureau has legal jurisdiction over drug cases in North Carolina and through the years has launched several significant drug initiatives. Operation Eagle was the first major drug investigation in its history, and Ike Atkinson and his criminal organization was the major target.

Charles J. Overton III had joined the SBI in 1970, the ninety-ninth agent hired after graduating from the Bureau's second academy class. The need for agents and for an Academy to train qualified SBI agents was largely a response to the growing drug trade in North Carolina. Stationed in Fayetteville, North Carolina, Overton began working for an interagency narcotics task force comprised of one other SBI agent and law enforcement officials from the Cumberland County Sheriff's Department, the Fayetteville Police Department and the U.S. Army's Criminal Investigation Division (CID). 'We didn't have too many resources, but we started making (drug) buys, arresting the sellers, making them flip, then making more buys, trying to move up the chain,' Overton recalled. 'We began hearing that heroin from Asia was being smuggled into North Carolina through military couriers, but it took us a little while before we figured it out. Informants began telling us that there were four or five big drug dealers in North Carolina, and they were getting their heroin supply from the same source—Ike Atkinson.'

Operation Eagle led to the arrest of several suspected drug traffickers who were operating in North Carolina, including Ike Atkinson. On July 5, 1973, Ike and eleven others, including his old pal Eddie Wooten from Washington, DC, were indicted for heroin trafficking. U.S. District Judge Frank T. Dupree set Ike's bond at $250,000, an indication, SBI officials believed, of his importance in the national drug trade. 'This is the most extensive and effective investigation in North Carolina history,' SBI Director Charles Dunn told the press at the time. 'The quality and quantity of the heroin is down on the streets while the price is up.'

The Operation Eagle indictment came in October 1972, just eight months after Ike beat his 1969 conviction in the New York City heroin trafficking case. Ike had pleaded guilty to unlawfully distributing 2.2 grams of heroin in 1969, and Judge George Rosling sentenced him to ten years in prison and slapped him with a $2,500 fine. But on 30 October 1972, a Federal appeals court overturned the conviction after the government admitted that the search and seizure involved in the case may have been illegal. The following month, Judge Rosling 'vacated,' or overturned, his own decision.

Now, because of the success of Operation Eagle, Ike faced the sobering possibility that he would have to go to jail for a long time. Ike was not surprised that his long-time associate Ellis Sutton was the principal witness against him. By now, it was common knowledge in the North Carolina underworld that Sutton would sell out his mother or tell law enforcement any tall tale to stay out of jail. It was remarkable that the law did not find Sutton in some dark alley, dead, with a couple of bullets in his head. Sutton, though, was a master at snitching and staying alive—so good at it, in fact, that while in jail, he testified as a collaborating government witness in three trials, all of which resulted in convictions.

Elwood 'Spider' Newman was one alleged drug dealer who got too close to Sutton. North Carolina authorities arrested Newman and brought him to trial in September 1973 on the charge of allegedly running a $9,000 a week heroin ring in the Fayetteville, North Carolina, area from March through June of 1971. During the trial Newman became depressed at the way the trial was going, and he told his brother 'he wasn't going to serve time for something he didn't do.' At 4.15 pm on September 19 1973, Newman returned home from the trial. When Spider's wife asked him how he was doing, he replied, 'Not so good.'

Newman then tucked a revolver in his waste band and walked out to the nearby woods. A few minutes later, neighbors heard a single shot. Medical examiner William Berry ruled Newman's death a suicide.

Ike believed Sutton had a role in Newman's death. 'I warned anybody I knew to be careful about Sutton,' Ike recalled. 'But

Sutton had a way of gaining a person's trust. Spider got too close to him.'

In Ike's case, Sutton convinced a grand jury that he and Ike had met in Goldsboro on October 29 1971, to negotiate the purchase of six ounces of heroin for $5,000 and that Ike eventually sold him an ounce of heroin for $1,200. But Ike knew of what Sutton was capable, and with the permission of his lawyer, Howard Diller, he secretly tape-recorded a conversation he had with Sutton the day before the alleged drug transaction. 'We caught Sutton in a good one,' Ike recalled with a chuckle. 'The tape recording showed Sutton lied about what happened the day of the alleged heroin deal. We got Sutton on tape saying that I had not been there.'

Ike's trial lasted just two days, but it had the drama of a Perry Mason thriller, thanks to the secret tape recording. First, Diller stood up in court and revealed his October surprise. Second, Judge Arthur Stanley, Jr. allowed the tape to be played in court. Third, caught with their pants down, the prosecutors scrambled, trying to downplay the tape's importance. They rested their case, hoping to sneak out of court with a conviction.

Not so fast, ruled Judge Stanley, and he allowed Diller to re-call Sutton to the witness stand. Master snitch Sutton wilted under Diller's intense questioning and admitted that he had lied. The case was thrown out of court. Embarrassed prosecutor Thomas McNamara complained to the press that Ellis Sutton, the man who had fueled the bogus cadaver-heroin connection conspiracy, 'had led him astray.'

YET, NO SOONER had Ike beaten the Operation Eagle drug charge then another popped up. On January 22 1974, less than a month after embarrassing the Federal government in the Ellis Sutton affair, a Federal grand jury indicted Ike on a charge of attempted income tax evasion, claiming that he had understated his taxable income in 1965 by $31,832 and that he owed the IRS $12,281. Ironically, these charges had nothing to do with heroin trafficking and stemmed from Ike's days as a professional gambler. Ike was found guilty but, when it came time to be sentenced, he continued to look more like the African-American gangster version of "Teflon Don" John Gotti, the legendary Italian-American mobster whom the Feds had a hard time putting in jail. In other words, things legal had a hard time sticking to Ike. In this case, Uncle Sam was trying to take Ike of the streets; yet, the court gave him a veritable slap on the wrist—probation and a small fine.

IKE WAS SUCCESSFUL in fending off the law, but once again his drug dealing business was going down the toilet. After the court in Denver, Colorado, put William Herman 'Jack' Jackson away for a long time in Leavenworth Federal Penitentiary, Ike began working more frequently with Frank Lucas and his criminal gang, The Country Boys. But to paraphrase what the late Texas Senator Lloyd Bentsen said about Dan Quayle in a 1988 presidential election debate: Ike knew William Herman Jackson and Frank Lucas was no Jackson. In his 2000 letter to the editor of *New York* magazine, Ike explained: 'I told him (Frank Lucas) that we could only be partners with him running the New York operation and me continuing to run this end (Thailand). Superfly, however, was not Mr. Dependable. Despite making good money in the drug trade, he always seemed to be chronically broke, and Ike often would have to lend him money. As an ex-military man, Ike loved working with organized-type people, but Lucas invariably acted as if he had a hard time figuring how to get out of bed in the morning.

Jack's incarceration left a big hole in the drug ring that Ike needed to fill quickly. With Jack out of the picture, Ike had no choice but to put Smedley in charge of the Thailand end of his drug ring. Smedley, too, was no Jackson. Smedley, one of the co-owners of Jack's American Star Bar and its manager, would now have to wear two hats. But Smedley was in no way Mr. Reliable. He stayed drunk most of the time, and when he wasn't drinking, he was sleeping. 'Jimmy would get real drunk, pick up a girl and then try to drive home,' Ike recalled. 'I know he had at least three accidents while driving drunk in Bangkok, but he managed to bribe his way out of being charged.'

While Ike loved Smedley like a brother, he knew his friend was not the brightest bulb in his band of brothers. Later, Ike learned that Luchai 'Chai' Ruviwat, another one of his partners in Jack's American Star Bar, was stealing from their establishment. Still, when he learned how Chai did it, the drug kingpin had to laugh. As the bar manager, Smedley had to be at the bar every night minding the business. With Jack now out of the way, Chai saw an opportunity to make some extra money by pilfering the till.

One day at the bar, Chai said to Smedley: 'Jimmy, I got some serious news to tell you. I heard that some thieves are planning to rob your house.'

'Are you serious?' Smedley asked with concern. 'What should I do?' Smedley was known to keep a lot of money at his house, and he knew Chai had good sources on the street.

'I would go home and stay there,' Chai advised. 'That will scare the bandits off. I'll call you if I hear any news.'

Smedley hustled to his house to protect his territory; meanwhile, Chai helped himself to the till at the bar. A couple days later, Smedley called Chai and asked: 'Is it okay to come back to Jack's?'

'Not yet Jimmy,' Chai said. 'Stay put for a while. I'll let you know when it's okay to return.'

This went on for a couple of weeks—Smedley determined to protect his turf, while Chai stalled his partner, filled in as bar manager and padded his bank account. Eventually, Chai told Smedley it was okay to return to work. 'Chai played this con with Jimmy a few times,' Ike recalled. 'It's a funny story, but it cost me money.'

BY THE SUMMER of 1973, Jack's American Star Bar was not making much money for Chai to steal. On January 15 1973, the U.S. Government announced the suspension of offensive action against North Vietnam. Twelve days later, the Paris Peace Accords were signed, officially ending direct U.S. involvement in the Vietnam War and stipulating a sixty-day period for the total withdrawal of U.S. forces. After the declaration of a cease-fire across North and South Vietnam, U.S. prisoners of war were released.

Jack's American Star Bar had made Ike some money, but with the end of U.S. involvement in the Vietnam War, and its big pullout complete, American GIs were no longer coming to Bangkok for Rest and Recuperation (R & R). With Jack in jail and Smedley being unreliable, Ike, who was based in Goldsboro, could not be sure what was happening in Bangkok with his business interests, no matter how many trips he made there. Ike made a tough decision. It was time to close the bar down. 'It was a sad day,' Ike recalled philosophically. 'We had a lot of fun with the bar, but its time had come. It seems all good things must end.'

At this point, Ike had plenty of money and he could have quit the drug trade. After all, the heat was intensifying and the law enforcement pressure mounting. But he was not going to let go of his drug ring without first getting all the money he could squeeze out of it. The U.S. heroin market was still booming and his network of dealers still clamoring for the ultra pure white snow he sold, the China White. Besides, the adventure was in his blood; he still loved living on the edge.

IKE TOLD ONE informant he wanted to buy large quantities of heroin, but he did not have many suppliers because Jack and his brother Andrew Price, who bought the heroin for the Atkinson-Jackson ring from the suppliers, were now both imprisoned. Papa San, Nitaya Jackson's uncle, was one of Ike's main suppliers, but Ike did not know him well. In fact, he had only met him once. One day, while he was in Bangkok, Ike got a call from Nitaya. 'Ike, you must come quickly. Papa San wants to see you. He is very sick.'

Ike rushed to Chinatown. When he got to Papa San's place and entered his bedroom, Ike was surprised to see a frail, gentle old man, with a long wisp of beard, propped up in the bed, smoking a cigarette and looking like the paragon of perfect health. Ike and Papa San made small talk and then Papa San began sounding as if he was saying goodbye for good. 'I always respected you and I wish you well,' was Papa San's message; Ike left the meeting not sure if he would see the old man again. The next day, Ike heard the shocking news from Nitaya. Papa San was dead.

No longer having a reliable contact to the source of supply, Ike knew that his days as a big-time drug kingpin would soon come to an end. Rather than simply using couriers and the postal system, which were reliable but only moved small amounts of heroin, Ike decided he needed to find a way to smuggle bigger loads.

Ike loved teakwood, bamboo and the other exotic woods of Southeast Asia, but especially teakwood. Whenever he was in Bangkok, Ike would ship small quantities of the wood to Goldsboro, which he used to panel his home. One day, Ike ran into his old friend, Leon Ellis, a master of woodworking, and

Ike as a teenager growing up in Goldsboro. (*Ike Atkinson*)

Ike's military ID card that he used to travel the world. (*Ike Atkinson*)

Ike's military days. (*Ike Atkinson*)

Eddie Wooten examining a deck of cards in West German apartment. (*Ike Atkinson*)

William 'Herman' Jack Jackson, Ike's main partner in crime until Jack was busted in 1972. (*Ike Atkinson*)

Jimmy Smedley, Ike's buddy who managed Jack's American Star Bar in Bangkok and then joined Ike as partner in the Thai heroin trade. (*Ike Atkinson*)

Dan Burch, a member of Ike's band of brothers, sits with a girlfriend while he was in Germany. (*Dan Burch*)

Luchai 'Chai' Ruviwat: a Chinese-Thai who was a key associate of Ike, both as a partner in Jack's American Star Bar in Bangkok and later, after Jack was busted, as Ike's main source of heroin. (*Ike Atkinson*)

Ike Atkinson as he looked in the early 1970s during the height of his trafficking activities. (*Ike Atkinson*)

Thomas 'Sonny' Southerland: Ike's friend and band of brothers member who joined Ike on the infamous flight in 1972 from Thailand to the U.S. that led to Ike being branded as the instigator of the heroin-cadaver connection. (*Ron Chepesiuk*)

Chuck Lutz: DEA special agent who spearheaded the investigation of Ike's drug ring in Thailand. (*Chuck Lutz*)

Frank Lucas (left) and Jack Toal (right), retired DEA agent, on the set of a History Channel 'Mobsters' documentary segment about Lucas. (*Ike Atkinson*)

DEA agents Chuck Lutz (left) and Lionel Stewart (right) having received the 1976 Attorney General Award for Distinguished Service for the Leslie Atkinson/Luchai Ruviwat investigation.
DEA Administrator Peter Bensinger is in the middle. (*Chuck Lutz*)

Ike met New York City drug kingpin Leroy Nicky Barnes in the Marion Federal Peniteniary. (*U.S. DEA*)

Rudolph Jennings: Ike brought Jennings to Bangkok to stitch the AWOL bags that were used to transport heroin to the U.S.. (*Ike Atkinson*)

Herman Lee Gaillard AKA Peter Rabbit: a close associate of Ike Atkinson. (*Ike Atkinson*)

Larry Atkinson introduced Ike to Frank Lucas for the first time. Ike found the 'American Gangster' hiding from La Cosa Nostra in the closet. (*Ike Atkinson*)

Dennis Dillon: Assistant U.S. Attorney from Eastern District of New York who prosecuted Richard Patch and Dennis Hart. (*Dennis Dillon*)

Rufus Edmisten, the North Carolina State Attorney General and later North Carolina governor, oversaw the investigation of Ike Atkinson in North Carolina. (*Rufus Edmisten*)

Dennis 'Mike' Nerney, the San Francisco, California-based Assistant U.S. Attorney who assisted DEA agents Charles Lutz and Lionel Stewart in the Luchai drug trafficking investigation and sucessfully prosecuted Luchai in San Francisco. (*Mike Nerney*)

Paul Cooper: Assistant U.S. Attorney assigned to the Denver office who successfuly prosecuted William Herman Jackson in the 1972 Denver heroin case. (*Paul Cooper*)

Ike in prison. (*Ike Atkinson*)

Dan Burch and Ike Atkinson, still buddies after all these years. (*Thelma Scott*)

Ike in prison. (*Ike Atkinson*)

Ike sitting in a Hardee's Restaurant in Raleigh, North Carolina. (*Ron Chepesiuk*)

hired him to do the paneling. Leon had just got out of prison, and, as Ike recalled, he 'could carve a walking cane out of a tree limb.' Watching Leon re-panel his home, Ike realized he had the craftsman who could turn his teakwood smuggling scheme into reality.

He convinced Leon that he should come to Bangkok to help him build the false bottoms in teakwood furniture that he wanted to use for his heroin shipments to the U.S. Ike attracted the trim, handsome Leon with the allure that 'Thailand was a Blackman's paradise' and helped him get a passport and Thai visa. After Leon tied up loose ends at home, they were on their way to Bangkok. Ike helped Leon obtain some basic woodworking tools from Bangkok wood workers, and Leon made some special tools for his teakwood assignment. The 'Teakwood Connection' was born.

WITH THE TEAKWOOD furniture scheme in place and the postal orders still flowing to the U.S., Ike did not have to depend as much on the human element, which, with time, was becoming more and more a pain in the ass. Rudolph Jennings, Ike's life-long friend from Goldsboro had done a masterful job of fitting and re-stitching the AWOL bags so they could hold kilos of heroin in their false bottoms. Nobody in Ike's drug ring had ever been caught because Jennings had done shoddy craftsmanship, but he had a big personal problem. Jennings could not keep his pecker in his pants. He was another one of the band of brothers who had gone loco in paradise. He viewed Thailand as a sexual Dairy Queen, and like a glutton, greedily wanted to taste every flavor in the store. Jennings sexual addiction got so bad he did not need a Dr. Phil to recognize that he had a sexual problem.

One day Jennings told Ike that he planned to check himself into a Buddhist monastery where he hoped the solitude, the fasting and the monks' spiritual guidance would help him break his fixation on pussy. Ike knew his old friend had a sexual problem and he gave his blessing, but wondered if reaching out for nirvana could cure a healthy Westerner living in Thailand of his lusty demons. Ike did not hear from Jennings for several days. Then one morning, while Ike was in Bangkok and at Jack's American Star Bar, two Buddhist monks, clad in robes, heads shaven, wearing sandals, eyes downcast and looking humble, came to see him. They were from the monastery were Jennings was supposed to be undergoing therapy, Buddhist style.

'Mr. 'Udolph (sic) escape,' one of monks told Ike in broken English.

'What do you mean, Mr. Rudolph escaped?' Ike asked.

'He no longer with us, no longer be better, Mr. Ike,' the monk explained. 'Mr. 'Udolph go pong-pong.'

Ike was puzzled. 'Pong-pong? What do you mean "pong-pong"?'

One of the monks responded in their broken English while using hand gestures. Ike figured out that the monks had fitted 'Mr. Udolph' with a chastity belt to curb his sexual appetite, but he had broken the belt and fled the monastery in lusty pursuit of carnal pleasure.

'You can't find Rudolph?' Ike asked, laughing at the absurdity of the situation.

The monks shook their heads. Ike suggested a couple of places that Jennings might be. The monks hurried off in search of their 'patient.' They eventually found 'Mr. 'Udolph' on the infamous bar, nightclub and massage strip, Patpong Road (not 'Pong-Pong') and talked him into coming back to continue his 'therapy.' After a couple of weeks, Jennings returned to the bar and to his job of fixing AWOL bags for heroin shipments. He seemed normal, but given the opportunities for sexual pleasure in Bangkok, Ike was never sure that his friend had cured himself of his addiction.

IKE'S OPERATION WAS undergoing some tough times, but Ike thought he had found his dream operative when he re-established contact with Freddie Thornton in 1974. Thornton would become the man Ike designated to take Smedley's place as overseer of the Bangkok end of his drug smuggling operation in all its many forms. Ike liked Thornton the first time he saw him in Jack's American Star Bar in 1967 and they had a brief chat about Thornton's assignment in Thailand and life in Bangkok. Ike hoped that someday he could find a spot for Thornton in his organization. Trim and bespectacled, with short cropped hair and a military bearing, the airman carried himself well, was articulate and appeared to be the kind of military man who could undertake an assignment and complete it with efficiency.

Thornton was born in September 1935 in Alabama but called Detroit home. He was a career airman who was first assigned to Thailand at U-Tapao Air Force Base in July 1967. He eventually served three tours of duty in Thailand, rising to the rank of tech sergeant and position of crew chief responsible for the maintenance of KC-135 aircraft, a tanker-like plane that belongs to the Strategic Air Command and other aircraft while they are airborne.

Ike's first encounter with Thornton had been friendly and purely social, but that changed three years later when Ike told Jack to ask Thornton if he would be interested in smuggling some heroin into the U.S. at the end of his tour of duty. Thornton agreed to do so, but then law enforcement picked up the trail of the Jackson-Atkinson drug ring, and Jack cancelled the plans because, as he explained to Thornton, 'the heat is on me.' Then sometime in 1971, before his bust in Denver, Jack approached Thornton again at Jack's American Star Bar and asked him to smuggle some heroin to the U.S.

That same month, Jack gave Thornton, who was being re-assigned to the U.S., an AWOL bag containing heroin that he delivered to a black male he did not know and who was based at Travis Air Force Base in California. Jack had told Thornton that he would pay him when he returned to Thailand the following June. Thornton had no problem with that arrangement. He was eager to show he could be valuable to the Jackson-Atkinson operation. But when he returned, Jack claimed he could not pay him for his 'services.' The heroin that Thornton had delivered to the contact at Travis turned out to be 'bad' and was 'destroyed,' Jack explained. Thornton was pissed and did not know whether to believe the story, but he was one of those guys who seemed in constant need of money. So he agreed to make another heroin delivery. In July 1971, Thornton picked up a shoebox and a cheese box from Andrew Price, each of which contained heroin, and delivered the contraband to another black mule at Travis Air Force Base who he did not know. Jackson paid Thornton that time for the delivery.

In December 1971, Thornton returned to U-Tapao for a one-year tour of duty. He was still interested in making some easy money as a drug courier, but then heard that Jackson and Price got busted in Denver and decided against getting involved. After his tour ended in December, 1972, Thornton returned to the U.S., got married in Fairfield, California, and moved to Indiana where he was stationed at Grissom Joint Reserve Base, a military airport located about 60 miles from Indianapolis.

THORNTON WAS SCHEDULED to retire, but he re-enlisted in the Air Force and returned to U-Tapao for another tour of duty in February 1974. About a month later, Ike and

Smedley met with Thornton at the NCO club in U-Tapao after driving the 100 or so miles from Bangkok.

Freddie and Ike had a mutual friend named Eugene Evans who lived near U-Tapao, and they decided to go and say 'Hi' to him. While they were visiting Evans, Ike asked Thornton if he was broke. 'Hell, yes,' Thornton acknowledged. Ike gave $500 to Thornton who thanked Ike and told him he was planning to retire at the end of his current Thailand tour of duty. Ike and Thornton agreed to meet in Bangkok in two weekends.

They met at Smedley's house where Thornton asked Ike if he could have a job in Ike's organization once he got out of the service at the end of February (1974). By job, of course, Thornton meant work as a drug smuggler. Thornton was eager to please and to show his potential value, so he explained to Ike that he was looking for a good way to smuggle dope back to the U.S. 'If you find a way, contact Smedley,' Ike said. 'I'll make sure you get what you want.'

Thornton asked Ike, 'How long has Jimmy (Smedley) been working for you?' Instead of giving a direct answer, Ike lamented Jack's demise in Denver. Smedley was doing okay, Ike said, but with Jackson incarcerated he needed somebody to take care of his business in Thailand. Thornton left the meeting with the hope that Ike would find a lucrative place for him in his organization. In the following weeks, Thornton traveled to Bangkok several times and met with Smedley at the NCO club in the Luxury Hotel. Smedley and Thornton drank, played pool and shot the breeze, but to Thornton's disappointment, there was no talk of smuggling dope.

Then one day in the summer of 1974, Smedley asked Thornton how he was doing? 'Pretty good,' Thornton said, as he sipped on the drink Smedley had bought for him.

'You want to make some money?' Smedley asked

Thornton perked up. Maybe the time had come. 'Yes, what do I have to do?'

'All you have to do is take some leave in the States,' Smedley replied.

'Take some leave?' Thornton said. 'I sure can do that. There is a school back in the states that offers courses on quality control for inspectors. Let me check it out. Once I get a "yes" or a "no," I'll let you know.'

The following week, Thornton got approval from his superiors at U-Tapao to attend the school at Castle Air Force Base in California, but a date was not set. Thornton told Smedley that once that happened, he would give him a call. Thornton decided to level with Smedley.

You know, man. I am no longer a crew chief. I don't have any control over hiding stuff on the plane. I've been looking for a way to move some stuff.'

Smedley patted Thornton on the shoulder. 'Well, don't worry about that. It's all taken care of.'

'What do you mean?' Freddie asked with surprise.

'All you have to do is put all your clothes in an AWOL bag that we give you and take them back to the States.'

Thornton smiled. 'Well that's good if it's taken care of. I'll give you a call and tell you the time when you can get it to me. I'll give you plenty of time. Once I get the date I'll be ready to leave.' Thornton left the meeting excited but wondering what kind of luggage he would be using for the trip.

Thornton learned that the school at Castle Air Force Base would start August 30, 1974. He booked a flight to the U.S. for August 27 and went directly to Smedley's house. 'I need a $1,000 advance,' Thornton told Smedley. 'I need it to move across the country once I hit the States.'

'Are you broke now?' Smedley asked.

Thornton nodded 'Yes' and Jimmy gave Thornton $1,000, reminding him that he had advanced him $100 a couple of months ago. After the conversation, Smedley and Thornton went downstairs and looked under the stairwell where two AWOL bags were stashed. Smedley pulled them out and gave them to Thornton. They sat around and had another drink before Thornton went home and packed his clothes in the two AWOL bags. The next morning he was on a flight to the U.S.

THORNTON AND TWO kilos of heroin landed at March Joint Air Reserve Base in Riverside, California. Established in 1918, March, one of the oldest airfields operated by the U.S. military, is home to the Air Force Reserve Command, the largest air mobility wing of the 4th Air Force. Thornton cleared Customs and immediately flew cross-country to North Carolina where, as Smedley instructed, he left the two AWOL bags at a trailer court in Dudley, North Carolina, a small town located about nine miles south of Goldsboro. Hearing that Ike was in town, Thornton paid him a visit at his home on Neuse Circle. Excited by the ease with which he got the AWOL bags into the U.S. and by the prospect of making some real money, Thornton told Ike about his heroin smuggling plan that used the crew chiefs with whom he worked at U-Tapao.

'How can you do that?' Ike asked. Thornton explained that the aircraft with crew chiefs aboard were sent regularly from Seymour Johnson Air Force Base to U-Tapao for a period of about 60 to 90 days. 'When they (the crew chiefs) are ready to return,' Thornton explained, 'I'll go up to the guy and say, "Hey, I got a buddy at Seymour Johnson (Air Force Base). I was home on leave and borrowed two pieces of luggage from him. Would you drop them off for me when you get back? You can use them yourself, you know. You can put your clothes in them."'

'What happens when the crew chiefs get to Seymour Johnson?' Ike asked.

'My buddy Gil (Charles Murphy Gillis) will pick the bags up,' Thornton revealed.

Thornton first met the quiet, easy-going Gillis, who held the rank of master sergeant, in December 1966 during his first tour of duty in Thailand and they became good friends. By 1974 Gillis had served nearly 14 years in the military and was planning to make the military his career and retire with a pension. He had come to Seymour Johnson in 1969 to work as an aircraft mechanic. Thornton had actually worked under Gillis. 'I thought he (Thornton) was a good person, outgoing and in good physical shape,' Gillis recalled. 'We were close friends and drank and socialized together. He always liked to be in control, but in working with him I saw that he got things done.' Still, on this smuggling trip, when Gillis met Thornton at first upon his arrival in Goldsboro, Thornton did not tell his friend about his smuggling plan.

When Thornton did tell him, Gillis saw an opportunity to make some money. 'It was amazing what you could do with those AWOL bags,' Gillis said. 'You could buy two or three of them in the PX for just $5 or $6 each. There was little security and no X-Ray machines in those days. When they opened the bag all they could see was the personal items. They had no way of checking the bags to see if there was a false bottom where someone could hide stuff. Customs would have to tear up hundreds of bags a day to find that out, with no guarantee that they would find something.'

When Thornton talked to Ike about his smuggling plan, Ike revealed that his drug ring was now paying $8,000 for smuggling a kilo of heroin to the U.S. Thornton did some calculation and realized that Smedley had shorted him $3,000 for his first delivery. Thornton made a mental note to ask

Smedley about it when he returned to Bangkok. After Ike gave him $1,000 for this trip, Thornton left for Detroit and then headed cross-country again to Castle Air Force Base to begin school as planned.

AFTER THE COURSE ended, Thornton returned to Thailand on or about September the 22 or 23. The night of his arrival, he bumped into Smedley at the NCO club at the Luxury Hotel and told him he would come by his house the next day. Ike was there, and he told Smedley that Thornton had a good way of moving heroin to the U.S. and that he should give Thornton what he needs. Smedley agreed, but Thornton was still angry about being shorted $3,000 by Smedley and he jumped on him about it. But Smedley denied it and snapped, 'I ain't been paying nobody (sic) $8,000.'

'Well, I'm not going to take your dope until I'm ready to move it,' Thornton warned.

Smedley just shrugged and grumbled, 'Okay.'

Ike did not like the way the meeting had ended, but he was committed to making Thornton his main man in Thailand.

Thornton returned to U-Tapao and began checking the airplane schedule to find out when and to where they were heading. He chose the dates he thought would be best and gave them to Smedley. They agreed on a date in October. Smedley, however, had arranged to have some money sent to him so he could buy the heroin for the shipment. But the money arrived too late for the October date they chose. Thornton was broke and anxious to make the shipment. Ike gave Thornton $1,000 to tide him over until that happened.

In November 1974, Thornton made his first delivery of the two AWOL bags secretly containing one kilogram of heroin each, using an unsuspecting crew chief. Later, Thornton noted in court that since there was no black crew chiefs at U-Tapao at the time, he chose a "thin white guy about my height (5'11")" to be his courier. Thornton went by the crew chief's room at night and gave him the two AWOL bags and told him that a man named Charles Gillis would pick them up. The crew chief knew Gillis and said "no problem." Thornton wrote Gillis and told him the date the plane was leaving Thailand for Seymour Johnson and gave him the name of the crew chief who would give him the AWOL bags. Thornton instructed Gillis to give the bags to Ike.

The operation went smoothly, and Ike thought the use of unsuspecting crew chiefs was a great new way to smuggle dope. In December, Thornton was ready to use another crew chief who would travel from U-Tapao to Travis Air Force Base with two AWOL bags. Thornton's good friend Hosea Brooks was based at Mather Air Force Base in Sacramento, which is just 45 miles from Travis. Brooks was a tech sergeant whom Thornton had known since 1966. Brooks agreed to hold on to the AWOL bags until Thornton could come to the U.S. sometime in February 1975 and pick them up.

The crew chief's trip to Travis was successful but, when Thornton returned to the U.S. in February and went to see Brooks to pick up the bags, he bumped into a big problem. Brooks had only one of the two AWOL bags. He told Thornton that the roommate of the crew chief who had brought the heroin to the U.S. had the other one. The crew chief's roommate did not have an AWOL bag, so the crew chief allowed him to use Thornton's bag for a weekend trip home. When the roommate returned, the crew chief, who had brought the bag to the U.S., did not have an AWOL bag to take with him on an 18-day trip to Alaska, so he took the bag with him. Thornton later recalled: 'We got a bag of dope roaming all over the States and the kids didn't know what they got.'

'I'll just wait until the guy shows,' Thornton informed Brooks, silently cursing his bad luck. Finally, the crew chief returned from Alaska and left the bag in his room. Thornton got the passkey to his room, snuck in and retrieved the bag. Late with his delivery, he caught a plane for Goldsboro and called Ike's house the night he arrived. A man whose voice Thornton did not recognize told him that Ike was not home but to leave the bags in the bushes at the trailer court in Dudley. Thornton, however, got confused and could not remember the location, so he had to call Ike for directions. Ike sounded ticked off, but told Thornton he could pick up his payment in two or three days. It was Thornton's third successful trip and now it was payday. Ike gave him $12,000 for the four bags he delivered. Gil received an additional $4,000 for a bag Thornton had already delivered.

THORNTON SPENT FEBRUARY and March 1975 at Seymour Johnson Air Force Base waiting for the day he could retire. Meanwhile, he met frequently with Ike to discuss his future role in the drug ring as Ike's 'money man' in Bangkok.

Losing confidence in Smedley by the minute, Ike told Thornton he wanted him to be responsible for buying the heroin and that he should buy it directly from Chai, who had now become the main conduit to a supplier in the Golden Triangle. Thornton had no problem with this arrangement. He did not trust Smedley either, although he realized he might have to work with him if he wanted to make some big money.

Thornton retired from the U.S. Air Force on March 31 1975, and on May 2 returned to Thailand. Thornton had a U.S. passport but did not bother to get a visa before he arrived in Thailand. He had a 30-day tourist visa stamped in his passport upon arrival at Don Muang airport. Freddie Thornton was ready to enter the drug trade in a big way.

CHAPTER 11

Going Postal

WHILE IKE ATKINSON'S drug ring adopted Freddie Thornton's crew chief method of smuggling heroin into the U.S., Ike was still moving much more heroin via the postal system. The dapper Robert Ernest Patterson, who once used his motorcycle to bring Ike the money Ike mailed to Thailand to buy heroin, had been Ike's main contact for the postal connection since its inception. In March 1974, after serving a five-year tour of duty in Thailand, Patterson left the country for a new assignment at Langley Air Force Base in Hampton, Virginia. Patterson had been a dependable and valuable associate, but for Ike, Patterson's departure posed only a temporary glitch in his heroin trafficking operation. Ike replaced Patterson with Herbert Houseton, another Bangkok APO (Army Post Office) employee.

Herbert Houseton had been in the Air Force for thirteen years. He worked as an administrative supervisor in the APO, having arrived on June 1974, for his third tour of duty, Houseton was assigned to the postal and courier service at Don Muang Air Force Base, and by August 1974, Sergeant James McArthur began to bring packages to him for shipment to the United States. Houseton had gotten to know Mac, as McArthur's friends called him, at a poker game that had been going on for years that included Jimmy Smedley and a number of other players who were a part of Ike Atkinson's band of brothers. Houseton and McArthur became good friends. A native of Betsy Lane, Kentucky, McAthur worked in the APO's administrative office of the chief clerk and had a variety of duties, including overseeing all the financial and personnel work.

The Customs tag for the first package McArthur brought to Houseton read 'two bags of used clothing.' A couple of days later, McArthur returned again with packages for the U.S.; they contained more used clothing, according to the Customs tag. The third time McArthur came with packages to Patterson's counter at the APO he did not buy insurance for them, which McArthur thought was a little odd.

'What's in the box?' Houseton asked.

'Just some more old clothing,' McArthur explained.

McArthur left and Houseton, his curiosity piqued, put the package under a fluoroscope, a device that uses an x-ray source and a florescent screen to examine images inside an object. All he could see, however, was the outline of the clothing and the hangers.

One day, McArthur came by the APO and asked Houseton if he could talk to him in private. They went to the back of the Receiving and Delivery Department, where McArthur told Houseton he wanted to send a lot more packages to the U.S. in the future.

'How many?' queried Houseton.

'A lot.'

'Fine,' said Houseton. 'What are you sending?'

'Nothing but used clothing,' McArthur said. 'You don't have to know anything more.' Then he asked Houseton: 'Would you agree to being paid $400 for each shipment you make?'

Houseton stared at McArthur, wondering if he should press him for more information, but he decided to adopt a policy of 'don't ask, don't tell.' Later, Houseton claimed: 'At the time, I had no idea about what was being sent to the States. I had been thinking a little bit on my own and I figured, well, you know, maybe he's sending some valuables or stuff of that nature. I didn't have any reason to turn him down. I didn't think there was anything wrong with it. Four hundred dollars is a heck a sum, but I didn't ask any questions.'

Later the same day, McArthur returned to the APO and handed Houseton an envelope with $400. Houseton had never made such easy money.

ON OCTOBER 14, 1974, Houseton was transferred to a branch of the main APO in the Joint U.S. Military Advisory Group (JUSMAG) compound in downtown Bangkok. Two weeks after his reassignment, at about 11:30 in the morning, Houseton received a call from McArthur.

'Are you alone?' McArthur asked.

'No,' Houseton said, 'I'm here with another worker, but he will be going to lunch in about fifteen minutes.'

'Good. I've got some packages to bring over.'

'Okay, bring them after the guy goes to lunch,' Houseton replied. McArthur brought Houseton two packages with the Customs tags already filled out. Later in the day, McArthur met Houseton outside the post office and gave him another $400.

The packages from McArthur continued to arrive at Houseton's postal counter, but one day McArthur brought four black AWOL bags to Houseton's home. McArthur told Houseton that he, Houseton, would have to supply the clothing to put in the bags, and it would be up to him to wrap and prepare the shipment. Houseton had no problem with that, given the money he was making. McArthur also gave Houseton a list of addresses in North Carolina to where the boxes were to be sent. Houseton found two boxes and put two

AWOL bags in each one. He then sealed the box, addressed the package, indicated a return address, filled out a Customs tag and mailed the packages.

A few days later, McArthur came by the APO to tell Houseton that his Thai tour was ending. McArthur advised Houseton that the packages would still come to him for mailing; someone would contact Houseton to advise him of the arrival date. A few days later, Houseton got a call from Ike Atkinson who asked the postal clerk to come over to his residence on Soi 53, Sukhumvit Road in Bangkok.

After greeting Houseton in his charming manner, Ike told Houseton to have a seat, and they discussed Houseton's postal operation. Houseton gave Ike a "briefing" about how he had handled the packages. Ike was pleased, but he wanted to know more about the operation's logistics. How long did it take for a package to go from Thailand to the United States, and vice versa? When were the boxes picked up at the APO? By whom? After Houseton had filled Ike in on schedules and procedures, Ike showed Houseton a list of addresses to which he wanted the packages sent. Houseton noted the names of the North Carolina cities on the list (Fayetteville, Goldsboro and Raleigh).

'What kind of deal do you want?' Ike asked Houseton. 'I really don't know,' Houseton said.

'Did you know how much McArthur was making?' Houseton shook his head.

'You don't know how much money Mac was making?' Ike asked. 'Would you agree to the same thing he was making?'

Houseton said: 'Yes.' Ike told Houseton he would receive $4,000 for every package he sent out.

Ike took Houseton to a locked closet in the living room. 'Now, this is the closet where the bags are kept,' Ike said, unlocking the door. The closet had a little divider in the middle. 'The bags on the right-hand side are for Rudolph Jennings, while the bags on the left are your bags,' Ike explained. 'Only two people besides me will have keys to the closet: you and Jennings. When you come to the house and find the closet locked, take the bags on the left of the divider and send them off.'

If the closet door was unlocked and there were bags found only on the right, Houseton was to leave them alone because they were the 'unfinished products' for Jennings. Before Houseton left, Ike gave him the two packages and two of the addresses. 'When you finish addressing the packages, destroy the addresses,' Ike instructed. 'Come by every day to see if there are any boxes to send out.'

But the next day Houseton got too busy to show up. Ike called. 'What happened? Why didn't you show up?' Ike snapped. 'You got a schedule to keep. People back home are expecting those bags. When the bags don't show up at a certain time it screws up the flow.' The next day Houseton went by Ike's place and picked up four bags.

ONE DAY HOUSETON went over to Ike's house and found Rudolph Jennings and Ike in the bedroom sitting in chairs facing the bed. An AWOL bag and what looked like tools lay on the bed. They exchanged greetings and Jennings went to another room and closed the door. They were preparing bags for shipment, Ike explained. Houseton could see that they had unstitched the lining of the bag. Ike showed Houseton where they put the heroin in the false bottom. 'Rudolph is a real pro at this, but I'm giving him a hand because we're backlogged,' Ike explained. 'We sure have a lot of bags to go out.'

Houseton saw that Ike was wearing a thin pair of latex gloves, and he watched as Ike pressed hard on the plastic bags to make sure they fit nicely into an AWOL bag. When Ike was finished, he looked up, smiled and nodded as if to say, 'a job well done.'

Business was so good that Ike wanted Houseton to find someone else to help bring the bags to the post office. 'It would look better and be safer if someone actually could bring the bags to the APO for you to mail them,' Ike explained. 'Do you know anybody who can help out?'

'No I don't, but I'll ask around,' Houseton said.

JUST BEFORE LEAVING Thailand, McArthur had a car accident that prevented him from shipping his car back to the U.S. So he put the ownership papers to the car in Houseton's name and told his friend to keep it for him until he returned to Thailand after he retired or was discharged from the service. Houseton had some repairs done to McArthur's car because he was using the car and he knew Mac would be good for the money spent on the car. McArthur was now deep in debt to Houseton because Mac also owed Houseton $1,600 for some of the packages he shipped to the U.S. and for a gambling debt of $2,700.

Houseton had let Ike know about the money Mac owed him. One night, Houseton got a call from Jimmy Smedley who told him to come over to his house. Smedley had something for him. When he arrived, Houseton found Smedley, Thornton and Luchai Ruviwat in one of the bedrooms sitting in chairs counting a large stack of American money piled on the bed. Thornton asked Houseton how much money McArthur owed him. Houseton said he did not know the exact amount, but it was around $1,600. 'Give him his money,' Thornton told Smedley. Later, Thornton informed Houseton that the stack of money on the bed totaled about $180,000.

'Ike wants you to invest in a shipment that he's sending to the U.S. sometime in the near future,' Smedley told Houseton.

'What's that about?" Houseton asked.

'All I know is that Ike wants you to invest $4,100 in the shipment and you're goin' to get a $25,000 payoff,' Smedley said. Thornton verified the deal.

The next day around noon, Houseton did as he was told. He brought Smedley the money Smedley had given him the previous day and added $1,400 of his own money.

A FEW DAYS later at the Windsor Hotel's NCO club, Houseton spotted a friend of his named Sergeant Jasper Myrick. In his early twenties, the square-jawed Sergeant Myrick, a native of Alabama, wore a short Afro and worked at the Windsor Hotel, one of the several Bangkok hotels that the U.S. military leased from the Thai government. The two friends sat down and had a drink in the lounge. In chatting with Myrick, Houseton realized that his friend could fill the position that Ike wanted: someone to deliver the packages to Houseton at the post office. After all, Myrick always seemed to talk about how much he needed money. Houseton gave Myrick the same pitch McArthur had given him. Myrick was interested but asked, 'Is there anything I should know?'

'No, not a thing,' Houseton assured him. 'You will just be sending regular AWOL bags full of used clothing. Would $200 a package work for payment?' Myrick smiled. Houseton had struck a deal.

Houseton began going to Ike's place to pick up the bags and deliver them to Myrick's house. Myrick came by Houseton's counter at the APO with the bags ready for shipping. Houseton gave Myrick a receipt and shipped the packages out. Ike had supplied Houseton with some additional addresses, and Houseton gave them to Myrick. In all, Houseton sent fourteen packages. He kept a running tally of the shipments by logging them in a little black book, numbered one to fourteen.

One afternoon Smedley called Houseton and told him to come by his house. It was payday. Smedley gave Houseton a brown paper bag containing $10,000 in cash. But as Ike once said, 'All good things must come to an end.' Houseton did not know it at the time, but that transaction marked the end of the Houseton-Myrick postal connection. On January 28 1975, Ike returned home to North Carolina aboard Pam Am Flight 002 for the last time.

A FEW DAYS before Ike's return to North Carolina, some of the packages Houseton had helped prepare for shipment began arriving in Goldsboro, North Carolina. On January 22 1975, an elderly woman named Ethel Waters received a typewritten letter from an organization called 'People to People,' informing her that she would be receiving a package. The mail carrier who brought Mrs. Waters the letter told her he had delivered three such letters that same day. When the mailman left, the old woman read the letter. 'Congratulations, Mrs. Waters, you have been selected to receive a gift package of clothing.' The letter went on to explain that People to People was a tax exempt organization whose sole purpose was to help people. The letter was signed: 'Mr. James G. Smith, Director, People to People' and had the return address: 'North Carolina State Highway Patrol, PO Box, Cary, North Carolina 27511.'

Mrs. Waters was suspicious. She was the type of person who believed you couldn't get something for nothing in this world. She could not recall getting a letter similar to this one before and thought: what an odd address for a non-profit organization.

The next day a package arrived at Waters's house. Ike's drug ring, not an organization calling itself People to People, had sent it. Ike's plan was to have one of his associates stop by Waters' residence and retrieve the package, claiming that it had been sent to the wrong address. The drug ring had done this before with success, but Mrs. Waters panicked before one of Ike's operatives could come by and pick up the package. The strange letter she received the day before had already freaked her out. She thought the package might contain a bomb. So it did not take much for her to call the Wayne County Sheriff 's Department.

Sheriff's deputies came to see Mrs. Waters, and they examined the package. It had a Bangkok post mark, but Mrs. Waters explained: 'I know no one in Thailand.' The deputies decided to take the package back to their office for inspection. An x-ray examination revealed that the package did not contain a bomb. Now they needed a warrant to look inside.

'I got a call about two or three in the morning from the Goldsboro Sheriff's Department,' recalled Durward Matheny, who, at the time, was based in Raleigh as head of the SBI's Document Investigation Section. 'They told me to come to Goldsboro and examine a package that had arrived from Thailand. They had an example of Ike Atkinson's handwriting. They identified Atkinson as the person whom they thought had written out the address appearing on the package's label. They said that if I could identify the writing on the package as Ike's, they would have probable cause to get a warrant, open the package and look inside. I was able to verify that the handwriting on the package belonged to Ike.'

Inside the box, the authorities found two black AWOL bags containing some old clothing and a woman's purse. Upon further examination, the authorities noticed the stitching that held the lining had been re-stitched because several of the stitches had missed their original holes. In unstitching the black AWOL bags, the authorities found a hidden compartment and two plastic bags with what looked like a total of one kilo of heroin. The Sheriff 's Department notified U.S. Customs and the U.S. Drug Enforcement Administration (DEA). The authorities were now on the lookout for more packages from Thailand.

TWO DAYS AFTER Mrs. Waters received the package from Bangkok, another one with a Bangkok return address arrived at the Goldsboro post office. It was addressed to Delores Burney, a woman local and federal authorities had had under close surveillance for some time on suspicion of heroin trafficking.

The package was brought from the post office to the Sheriff's Department for examination. Authorities noticed that the color of the wrapping paper was the same as that used to wrap the package sent to Mrs. Waters. Moreover, the manner in which the box was wrapped was similar. A search warrant was served on the package, and Durward Metheny came to the Sheriff 's office once again to examine the handwriting on the package in order to gather evidence for a warrant. The authorities found another two AWOL bags with clothing just as they had with the package sent to Mrs. Waters. At this point, the authorities decided to make a 'controlled delivery,' meaning they would rewrap the package and put it back in the postal system for delivery to the intended addressee.

Every effort was made to pull the masking tape off the box without disturbing any possible fingerprints. The authorities were careful, too, with the four plastic bags in the AWOL bags that contained a white powdery substance. Although the authorities were certain the white powdery substance was heroin, they put the plastic bags back into the bag, the false bottom was re-attached on top of them and a heat sealer was used to seal the seam across the top. The clothing was put back in the false bottom of the AWOL bag, and the package was rewrapped.

The next day, the post office delivered the package to Burney's residence and the authorities served a search warrant. But when law enforcement entered Burney's house, they found Burney and an open package, but no heroin. The authorities turned the house upside down but could not find the dope.

They questioned Burney about the missing heroin; she claimed she did not know what they were talking about.

Surveillance of Burney's house continued. On July 26, shortly before midnight, the authorities stopped Burney's car on a Goldsboro street and found four pounds of heroin they estimated to have a street value of $3.35 million. One federal agent later described the heroin haul as the largest ever seized on the eastern seaboard. Burney and Jessie Thomas Horton, the other person in the car, were charged with possession of heroin with intent to distribute, and each was placed on $500,000 bond, which the court later reduced to $50,000 for Burney.

Meanwhile, the authorities questioned Mrs. Waters some more and learned that she had observed Horton driving slowly by her home while the mailman was delivering the package she had reported to the police. During the subsequent Burney-Horton investigation, law enforcement also discovered that Horton had visited Ike Atkinson on several occasions.

THE POSTAL DELIVERIES continued. A third package arrived at the Goldsboro post office on January 27 1975, addressed to a Mr. Dallas Lewis. The package looked exactly the same as the first two the authorities had seized.

The Sheriff's Department took custody of the package and obtained a search warrant so they could legally open it. Matheny was running ragged as he came once again from Raleigh to Goldsboro to help obtain this search warrant. The recently intercepted package contained the same contents as the previous two: a black AWOL bag with a false bottom that had the plastic bags filled with the powdery substance. Once again, law enforcement tried to make a controlled delivery, but they had learned their lesson. This time they replaced all but a small amount of the white powder in the plastic bags with confectionary sugar and delivered the package to the intended address. But nobody was home, so the postman took the parcel back to the post office, while the authorities maintained surveillance of the residence.

In a bizarre twist, later that day Nancy Brooks, who resided at Dallas Lewis's house, went to the post office and denied that she knew anything about the package delivered to Dallas Lewis. But in an interview with authorities, Mrs. Brooks admitted that Lewis was her son and resided with his grandmother at 625 Isler Street, Goldsboro. Mrs. Brooks also revealed that on January 24 or 25 she received a call from a male who told her that he was forwarding a package to her address through the mail and that he wanted her to hold on to it until someone came by and picked it up. Mrs. Brooks became suspicious and refused to accept the package when it arrived.

Brooks later implicated 'Peter Rabbit' (Herman Lee Gaillard), one of Ike's old friends and associates from his military days, as the person who had mailed the package to her residence. The authorities, however, were unable to prove it. The authorities also suspected that Peter Rabbit was responsible for having the packages sent to Dallas Lewis and to Mrs. Waters. Later it was determined that Peter Rabbit was the uncle of Dallas Lewis and that he had a girlfriend who was Waters' daughter. On March 21 1975, DEA agents interviewed Peter Rabbit, who acknowledged Waters' daughter was his girlfriend, but denied any knowledge of the heroin from the postal deliveries.

'Peter Rabbit screwed up the delivery of the package to the Waters residence,' Ike revealed. 'He was supposed to be watching the house and waiting for the postman to arrive so he could get the package. But no, he was off somewhere with his girlfriend (Mrs. Waters daughter).'

The original plastic bags containing the white powder were sent to the SBI lab for chemical and finger print analysis. The lab personnel found that although the powder contained trace amounts of caffeine, it was almost 100 percent pure heroin. They also found some interesting prints.

IKE VIVIDLY RECALLED the postal shipments to Goldsboro. He had actually helped pack the heroin in AWOL bags, although he was not supposed to do it. That was Rudolph Jennings's job. But Ike's drug ring was quite busy preparing the packages for shipment and, like a good boss, Ike came over to the stash-house to give Jennings a hand. He had to press hard on the plastic bags to get them to fit the false-bottoms of the AWOL bags. Of course, he was wearing latex gloves to ensure that he would not leave fingerprints on the package, but he forgot that a few days before he was to get out of the Army in 1963, the military had taken impressions of his palm prints. He did not use anything to protect his palms. It was his palm prints that the SBI found on the plastic bags containing heroin in the Delores Burney package and on a piece of cardboard used to support the false bottom in the package sent to Mrs. Waters. Having Ike's palm prints on file with the military made it easy for the SBI to find a match. With such solid evidence, authorities were confident the 'Teflon' drug kingpin would have a hard time beating this case.

The DEA believed that Houseton, who had watched Ike pack and press the plastic bag into the AWOL bags, was involved with Ike's postal scheme. In May 1975 law enforcement determined that Houseton was responsible for sending the three packages to the residences of Waters, Burney and Lewis. They did this by matching the postal meter tape numbers on the packages with the postal meter assigned to Houseton. An informant told the DEA that he had attended a poker game on two consecutive weekends during which Houseton lost $15,000.

Yet, despite losing the money, Houseton seemed happy and even celebrated after the poker games at the Windsor Hotel.

ON FEBRUARY 6, 1975, authorities executed a search warrant on Ike's Neuse Circle home and arrested him on a heroin conspiracy charge. The way Ike reacted to the arrest made it seem as if the authorities had come by to pick him up for a social event. Ike was polite and chatted with the agents, even revealing a few details about the drug trade in Thailand and how he was getting his heroin supply.

Nine days before, Frank 'Superfly' Lucas had been arrested at his home at 933 Sheffield Road in the well-to-do neighborhood of Teaneck, New Jersey. But the authorities involved in the Lucas arrest did not find the experience as pleasant as the one their colleagues had in Goldsboro. Acting on a tip from two East Harlem members of La Cosa Nostra, a strike force of 12 DEA agents and 12 NYPD (New York Police Department) officers, all heavily armed, surrounded Lucas's home. They kept a watch for any drugs or any other incriminating evidence that Lucas might throw from a window. Once inside the house, strike force members quickly broke up into teams of three. One team member looked for drugs, guns, and money. A second acted as a witness. A third took notes and documented the search.

As the teams began searching the house, suitcases filled with money came flying out of the bathroom window. The suitcases were brought into the house and put on the floor. The strike force then made a big circle so that everybody could see what was happening and they began counting the money. 'We went into the wee hours before we finished,' recalled Joe Sullivan, a retired DEA agent who was a strike force member. 'Lucas made most of his drug buys on the streets, so the money was in small denominations of $5, $10 and $20. But the important thing: Everybody in the room could see everybody else.'

As the money was counted, it was bundled into $10,000 lots and put into specially-designated bags in the center of the room. When the count was finished, each strike force member was searched before he could leave the house. 'At the time, I was insulted, but now I realize that searching us was the smart thing to do,' said Sullivan. 'The strike force told Lucas that the money they were confiscating totaled $585,000, and he did not appear to have a problem with the count.'

Later, however, once Lucas had a chance to talk to his lawyer, he changed his tune. Superfly claimed a lot of money from the house was missing—millions, in fact. Later, Lucas recalled his version of events for *New York* magazine. 'Five hundred and eighty-five thousand. What's that? Shit. In Vegas I'd lose 500 Gs (grand) playing baccarat with a green-haired whore in half an hour.'

'Lucas lied,' Sullivan said bluntly. 'No way could any money be missing. We had strict safeguards in place because management was sensitive to recent corruption scandals in New York law enforcement and the publicity surrounding the Knapp Commission, and we wanted to protect the strike force against any charges of corruption.'

On August 27 1975, Julie Lucas, Frank's wife, pled guilty to charges related to throwing the $585,000 from the bathroom window while agents were searching the home. Two days after the raid on Lucas's house, the authorities indicted the drug lord and 18 other people. According to the indictment, Antonio De Lutro delivered a package of about 11 pounds of heroin to Anthony Verzino in November 1973 and received, as payment, $250,000 in two installments. Then in December 1973, Mario Perna and Ernest Maliza delivered a package containing 22 pounds of heroin to Lucas at the Van Cortlandt Motel in the Bronx.

Records of the bust showed that Lucas was getting heroin from the La Cosa Nostra. Lucas faced a maximum penalty of 40 years in prison and a fine of $50,000.

MEANWHILE, IKE WAS arraigned before U.S. Magistrate Martin Lancaster for heroin trafficking and incarcerated in the Wayne County jail under a $500,000 bond. Federal authorities also charged Ike with heroin trafficking. In all, the authorities had seized six pounds of heroin worth about $5.1 million in potential street sales. While Ike awaited trial, he got more bad news. The IRS was after him again for allegedly failing to report income from Jack's American Star Bar. This time, Ike was convicted of under-reporting his income for 1969 by $34,937.63; the government claimed he owed the IRS $11,421 in additional taxes. The IRS's investigation determined that while Ike's bank deposits totaled $4,744.09, his cash expenditures exceeded $88,000. U.S. District Judge John D. Larkins, Jr. gave Ike a five-year suspended sentence and fined him $10,000 plus court costs as a condition of Ike's probation. He pleaded no contest to the charges and agreed to pay all of his 1969 taxes.

On March 27 1975, a federal grand jury indicted Ike on a charge of importing two of the six pounds of heroin that had been seized coming into the United States from Thailand. The press noted that Ike had been previously indicted four times for importing heroin into the U.S., and each time he was found innocent of the charges. Facing the legal battle of his life, Ike hired Stephen Nimocks, a top-flight lawyer out of Fayetteville, North Carolina. Nimocks was white, but Ike heard through the grapevine that he had successfully defended some young black soldiers who had fragged a white officer in

Vietnam. Ike also believed Nimocks was close to Judge Larkins. He had heard that Nimocks had served in the judge's unsuccessful 1960 campaign for the governorship of North Carolina as a Democratic candidate. 'I knew Nimocks would give me the same type of excellent representation that he would a white man,' Ike explained.

THE TRIAL BEGAN in early June 1975. Ike had pleaded not guilty at his arraignment, but he changed his plea to no contest after Stephen James, the SBI's chief fingerprint examiner, testified that he found Ike's palm prints on one of the plastic bags containing heroin and on the false bottom of one of the AWOL bags. On June 12 1975, in the Eastern District Court of North Carolina, Judge Larkins sentenced Ike to 19 years in prison. The judge divided the sentence into 15 years for the charge of importation of heroin and four years for using the U.S. postal system to smuggle the contraband. The prosecution was upset with Judge Larkins acceptance of Ike's plea of no contest and the length of sentence he imposed. They were well aware that Ike had a lot of money to hire the best defense lawyers who would use the law to get him free in a relatively short period of time. Indeed, Ike was convinced he could possibly get out of jail in 18 months.

That was why Ike was surprised to learn that the authorities claimed they had evidence indicating he was preparing to leave the country to avoid serving his prison sentence. On June 12 1975, U.S. Attorney Tom McNamara told the *Raleigh News and Observer*: 'Certain members of his (Ike's) family were seen transporting two suitcases full of cash by private charter flight to some place in the Grand Bahamas. With a man facing a 19-year prison sentence, especially when we've been after him as long as we have Atkinson, I'm just afraid now that he has been caught, he might not want to go to jail.'

When McNamara made this statement, Ike was free on $1 million bond, and he still had eighteen days before he was to report to jail, for up to 19 years. So he had plenty of time to flee. But the drug kingpin punctually appeared before the court to begin serving his sentence in Atlanta Federal Penitentiary, confident his lawyers would get him out of prison within a reasonable period of time.

IKE'S TRIAL AND conviction spurred the DEA to take much more aggressive action against him and his drug ring. On October 1 1975, three months after Ike went to prison, the DEA established Central Tactical Unit (CENTAC) 9 whose overall objective was to destroy Ike's drug ring once and for all. The DEA had created the first CENTAC unit in April 1975 to concentrate enforcement efforts against major drug trafficking organizations. The first eight CENTACs investigated heroin-manufacturing organizations in Asia, Lebanon and Mexico. CENTAC 9, which included eight DEA agents and one NYPD detective, operated, for the most part, from the DEA's Wilmington, North Carolina District office, but it worked closely with other offices in Bangkok, San Francisco, Los Angeles, New York City, Pittsburgh, Atlanta and Savannah, Georgia.

'When I came to North Carolina, everybody in law enforcement considered Ike to be untouchable, 'explained Don Ashton, who headed the DEA's Wilmington office, beginning in 1974, and coordinated the CENTAC 9 investigation. 'He had an amazing ability to get people to work for him. I asked someone we believed to be connected to Ike's organization who was the closest person to him in the organization? They all said the same thing. "I am." We really had to focus our effort if we were to smash Ike's organization. That's why the DEA created CENTAC 9.'

CENTAC 9 estimated that between 1968 and 1975, Ike's drug ring had smuggled heroin into the U.S. at a rate of one thousand pounds per year, an amount that could be worth as much as $400 million on the street. Two independent sources told CENTAC 9 investigators that Ike may have as much as $80 million in the Cayman Islands. 'This may well be an exaggeration,' one CENTAC 9 investigative report conceded, but one investigation has identified two particular shipments of money to the Grand Cayman Islands in a two-month period of time accounting for an estimated $500 thousand to $1 million dollars. Ike was behind bars, but the DEA knew that he was still pulling the strings of his drug ring.

CHAPTER 12

The Teakwood Connection

WHEN IKE ATKINSON was imprisoned in the Federal Penitentiary in Atlanta on July 1975, he hoped his crack team of defense lawyers would get him out soon. 'I was in a serious situation, but I felt confident I could get out of it and not have to serve more than a third of my sentence before going up for parole,' Ike recalled. 'I'd never been convicted of a serious crime. I could prove I was a good family man. All I had to do was keep my conduct in prison clean.'

Meanwhile, Ike was determined to make the best of his bad situation. Opened in 1902 as the country's second federal prison, Atlanta Penitentiary had the reputation of being one of the country's toughest. In the mid-1970s, the Federal Bureau of Prisons had six security levels, five and six being maximum security, two to four being medium and one being minimum security. At the time, the Federal Penitentiary at Marion, Illinois, was the only level-six prison in the system. The Atlanta Penitentiary was level five.

Arriving at the gate and entering the bleak-looking structure, Ike had no doubt that he had arrived at a prison. The transfer-holding unit was large and imposing and devoid of natural light; the hallways were dark, cold and dangerous. At the Receiving and Discharge (R & D) Department, Ike had to turn over all of his possessions and clothing to the prison guards, who reminded him of some of the drill sergeants he had met in the military. He was strip-searched, fingerprinted, photographed and given some drab gray garb that every prisoner had to wear. Ike had come prepared, though; he brought an extra pair of glasses and enough money to open a personal account that he could use to buy items not supplied by the prison authority or to bribe favors from underpaid but corrupt guards.

Ike quickly noticed one big change since he was last incarcerated in the Atlanta pen for the tax conviction in New York City. 'In the early 1970s, the Atlanta pen's population was mostly white,' Ike recalled. 'Now I saw many more black faces. You could see that the U.S. Government was waging its war on drugs, and blacks were bearing the brunt of it.'

Ike walked down the long narrow corridor to his prison cell without receiving much notice from the other inmates. As Ike learned, an air of excitement would ripple through the prison population when a 'star' inmate showed up. As the word spread of the arrival of a notorious new inmate, the other inmates pressed up against the bars of their cells to see the arriving celebrity, and they would shout his name. But such was not the case for Ike. 'Nobody but a few guys from North Carolina really knew who I was when I arrived at the Atlanta pen,' Ike recalled. 'Gradually, that changed. The word spread about who I was and what I had done.'

BY PUTTING IKE in prison, Uncle Sam had won a battle in the War on Drugs, but Ike still had not surrendered. He remained determined to retain control of his drug trafficking ring and smuggle as much dope as possible out of Southeast Asia while the U.S. still had a presence there. In 1975, Uncle Sam began a three-day operation to withdraw the last of its B-52 bombers from Thailand. The B-52s were leaving under an agreement between Thailand and the U.S. that mandated the total withdrawal of U.S. troops from Thailand by March 1976.

Ike planned to take advantage of the U.S. withdrawal from Thailand to ship the largest quantity of heroin he had ever smuggled out of the country since he entered the drug trade in 1968. Always an over-achiever criminal-wise, he even hoped that one day, before his drug trafficking days were over, he could smuggle a 1,000-kilo load of heroin in a single shipment. He could not do that, though, by smuggling heroin in the false bottom of AWOL bags, one or two kilos at a time. Instead, he planned to use teakwood furniture with specially built false bottoms that departing U.S. military personnel could send back to the U.S. with their household goods after they completed their tours of duty in Thailand. The teak furniture could carry as much as 50 kilos of heroin, or more.

While in jail, Ike chose Freddie Thornton to be his second in command and to implement the teakwood smuggling plan. Thornton's first experience with the emerging teakwood connection came in March 1975 after Ike had paid him $12,000 for three successful deliveries of heroin using the crew chiefs AWOL bag smuggling procedure.

'Could you do me a favor?' Ike had asked Thornton.

'What is it?' Freddie replied.

'Could you go to California for me and pick up some stuff?'

The 'stuff' was some heroin that Ike's drug ring had smuggled from Bangkok to California inside teakwood furniture for the first time. The smuggling operation marked the launch of a new phase for the Atkinson drug ring: the 'Teakwood Connection.'

Thornton picked up the furniture and delivered it to the home of Ronald Ward, who was stationed at Beale Air Force Base near Maysville, California. Established in 1943 and located about forty miles from Sacramento, Beale Air Force Base is the home of the 9th Renaissance Wing of the Air

Combat Wing. The base accommodates about 4,000 military personnel stationed there.

Ronald Ward, a staff sergeant and military police officer with thirteen years service, had known Thornton since 1968. Ronald's wife, Delores, was like a sister to Thornton; in fact, Thornton called her 'Sis.' Thornton phoned Delores about once a month to see how she and her family were doing. The Wards had two teenage sons, one of whom was mentally retarded and required expensive special education. As the bills piled up, Freddie tried to help. One time, Thornton gave Dolores $1,000; another time, he gave Delores $200 to buy her kids bicycles.

One morning in early March 1975, Delores returned home from a shopping trip to find her buddy Freddie Thornton sitting in a U-haul truck parked in the driveway.

Delores and Thornton hugged each other and Thornton said: 'Sis, I've got something for you.'

'What is it?' Delores said.

'I'm going to show you,' Thornton said. He lifted the back end of the truck and revealed two heavy dining room buffets, each about six feet long.

Delores was not surprised. Thornton was always bringing her exotic gifts from his overseas assignments. The previous time Thornton had called, he asked her what she wanted from Thailand. Delores had said 'china.' This time, in buying the buffet furniture, Freddie had bought something extra special for Delores, and she was delighted.

Ronald Ward helped Thornton lug the buffets into the house. They put one piece in the hallway and the other in the dining room. Thornton gave Delores $100 and told her to go shopping. For the next two and half hours, Ward helped Thornton with carefully removing the dope from the false bottoms of the buffets. One of the plastic bags broke and Thornton used a brown paper bag to clean up the white powder that had spilled on the floor. When through, Thornton paid Ward $1,000 for his help

It was now 2:30 in the afternoon, and Ward had to go to work. Thornton said he would wait for Delores to return home so he could get a ride to the airport. When Delores returned, Thornton put the brown paper bag in the back seat of Delores's red 1973 Buick and asked his friend to get rid of the bag after she dropped him off. When Ronald Ward returned home from work at 11:30p.m., his wife was not home yet. Still, Ward was not concerned. The Wards were planning to move off base to nearby Atwater soon, so they were getting a place they had rented in the city ready. Delores planned to go there later in the day and stay the night. So, while Thornton traveled cross country to North Carolina carrying Ike's dope, Delores drove to Atwater, stopping only to throw the brown paper bag in a dumpster.

GIVEN THE LIBERAL visitation policy at the Atlanta pen, Ike knew he would have no problem communicating with Thornton, even though Thornton was spending a lot of his time in Thailand. Relatives who visited Ike in the penal institution could smuggle his messages out of the prison and give them to Thornton. By the time Thornton retired at the end of March 1975, he was delivering what Ike called 'notes' to Luchai 'Chai' Ruviwat, Jimmy Smedley, Rudolph Jennings and other drug ring members based in Bangkok. In the first note Thornton delivered to Ike's gang in Bangkok, Ike stated unequivocally that, in his absence, Thornton was in charge of the Thailand end of the operation. The notes also provided instructions as to how many pieces of furniture Thornton needed to get for future shipments. Ike put Chai in charge of buying the heroin and the furniture. 'Money would be coming shortly to pay for future shipments,' Ike assured. The notes acknowledged that

Ike owed Chai and Smedley money and that Thornton would repay them soon. Luchai and Smedley had no doubts that the orders came from Ike, for in reading the notes, they recognized Ike's handwriting.

THE MONEY FOR the teakwood drug shipments arrived in Bangkok in three postal service boxes five to eight days after Thornton had brought the first set of instructions from Ike. The money was stored at Smedley's house at Soi 53 in one of the bedrooms. Thornton came over to wake up Smedley so he could help him count the money, but Smedley was sound asleep. Thornton busied himself for a couple of hours before he finally woke Smedley up.

'Jimmy, good news, the money has arrived,' Thornton said.

Dressed in a white undershirt and flowery designed boxer shorts, Smedley reached for a cigarette and propped himself up on the edge of bed. 'Bring it over to me,' Smedley ordered, acting as if he was still the boss in Thailand.

When he saw the boxes, Smedley blew up. 'Who opened the box,' he snapped.

'We did; I mean I did,' Thornton said, taken aback by Smedley's aggressive manner.

'You don't open the boxes when you are by yourself,' Smedley said.

'Well, you wouldn't get up.'

'You still shouldn't have opened them,' Smedley insisted.

'Why?' Thornton asked.

'Because I'm responsible for the money.'

'How are you responsible for the money?' Thornton asked. 'Nobody sent you anything.'

Smedley stopped arguing and lit his cigarette. Thornton phoned Chai and asked him to come over and help count the money. Thornton had to wait about two hours before Chai finally arrived.

WILLIAM KELLEY BROWN was the second soldier that Ike's drug ring recruited for his teakwood smuggling operation. On his second tour of duty in Thailand, Brown worked in Bangkok at SEATO (Southeast Asia Treaty Organization) in an Army medical research facility that collaborated closely with the Thai Government. There he met Wallace Walker (not his real name), a co-worker, ten-year military veteran and a friend of Ike's. Walker and Brown belonged to the Black Masonic Lodge in Bangkok and they had developed a friendship and socialized on occasion.

A native of the Washington, DC area, Walker was a Chief Warrant Officer in the U.S. Army on his second tour of duty in Thailand. Walker was fluent in Thai and had a Thai wife whom he married in 1969 during his first tour of duty. Walker was hard working, and while in Bangkok, he attended night school, studying business. Despite his tight schedule, Walker still found time to join the regular weekend poker game at Jimmy Smedley's place. Walker would also socialize with Ike at the poker game at Smedley's house at one of the NCO clubs, whenever Ike was in Bangkok.

In the spring of 1975, about two or three months before he was going to be re-assigned back to the States. Walker got into a financial bind, the result of a car deal in which he was supposed to sell a car to a Thai movie star for $9,000. But when the movie star backed out of the deal in July, Ike helped Walker out by buying his car for $8,000 cash and allowed Walker to keep it until he left for the U.S. in the early fall.

When Smedley saw Walker at the poker game or NCO club, he would invariably ask: 'When are you going home?'

'I don't know,' Walker would say: 'Maybe February or March (1975).'

'Well, I may have something for you to ship'

One day, Walker agreed to do it and told Smedley: 'Yeah, I got the weight; I'll ship something for you.' As a Chief Warrant Officer, Walker was authorized to ship up to 1,100 pounds of household goods to his next duty station. For the U.S. military in Thailand, it was not unusual for someone with some spare weight to ship things to the U.S. for other people.

Smedley said: 'Let me tell you about it.'

"What do you mean?' Walker asked. 'Tell me about it?'

Smedley took Walker to the back of the house in a secure area near the kitchen and the maid's quarters. Walker saw Thornton standing next to a piece of furniture that was turned upside down.

'What are you all doing?' Walker asked.

'Look, let me tell you,' Smedley said. 'It's a sure thing.' Then with a sly smile, Smedley added, 'We are going to put dope in this thing.'

Walker watched as Thornton drilled screws into the bottom of the furniture. Later, Walker explained to a Federal court in Raleigh, North Carolina: 'I told him (Smedley) he was crazy. At this point he never mentioned it again.' Walker also claimed that while he delivered $10,000 for Smedley to Herbert Houseton at the post office, he did not get paid anything for doing it.

However, Walker, in fact, had agreed to find someone else to smuggle the heroin-laden furniture to the States. After work one day, Walker dropped by the NCO club at the Windsor Hotel for a few drinks and some conversation with William Brown and Joyce, his wife of fifteen years, Joyce Watson, and some other friends. Walker explained to the group that he was going back to the U.S. soon and that before he left, he wanted to buy some furniture, although he didn't know exactly what he wanted. Joyce Brown said: 'Well, if you want to buy some furniture, we will be glad to show you around Bangkok.' By "we" Joyce meant herself and Joyce Watson, the wife of Major George Watson, a military doctor.

Walker thought it was a good idea and asked William Brown: 'If I get some furniture, would you ship it for me back home?'

'That would be no problem,' Brown said.

A few days later, Joyce Watson came by Walker's house in a red black-topped Pontiac and picked Walker and his wife up before stopping by Joyce Brown's house to pick her up. The shopping excursion lasted all day and ended on Sukhumvit Road where they checked out a number of furniture stores and Walker bought some teakwood furniture.

On 8 July 1975, the day William Brown was preparing his furniture and household goods for shipment to Fort Gordon, near August, Georgia, Chai came by his house and explained that he had some furniture for him from Wallace Walker: seven pieces of heavy teakwood furniture. Brown shipped the furniture that day and it arrived at Fort Gordon in Augusta on 3 September. Hidden inside the false bottoms of the furniture that Brown had shipped was an incredible fifty-two kilograms (114.2 pounds) of heroin. For being a drug courier, Brown had been promised $100,000.

SOMETIME IN JUNE 1975, while setting up the Brown shipment, Thornton stopped by the NCO club at the Windsor Hotel for a drink. Jasper Myrick, a young GI who worked at the club and had earlier helped Houseton with the postal drug smuggling connection, approached Thornton. Myrick told Thornton that before Rudolph Jennings left for the U.S. to attend Ike's trial in North Carolina, Jennings had asked him if he wanted to make some money.

'I'm always interested in making some money,' Myrick told Jennings.

'Talk to me or Thornton about it when you are ready,' Myrick said Jennings had told him: 'If I'm not available, don't talk to anybody but Freddie.'

Jennings had said nothing to Thornton about his conversation with Myrick, so Thornton was wary about saying too much to Myrick. 'I will get back with you,' Thornton told Myrick.

Thornton thought it would be a good idea to write Ike a letter to find out how he should deal with Myrick. Ike sent Thornton a note back, giving him the go ahead to recruit Myrick, but advising Thornton to let Smedley handle it when Smedley returned from the States. After reading the instructions, Thornton burned the letter.

Smedley went by the Windsor Hotel to see Myrick. Although there was a big difference in their ages, the two men hit it off. Later, Myrick described how Smedley became almost like a father figure to him. Smedley began dropping by Myrick's house for a drink. In one of their conversations, Smedley learned that Myrick was going to be transferred to Fort Benning in September 1975. Smedley asked his young friend if he would be willing to ship some furniture for him through the U.S. postal system. Myrick did not see any problem with that. They agreed on a fee—$500.

IN THE LATER part of June 1975, Ike's drug ring received more money from the States—the $180,000 for the Jasper Myrick heroin shipment. Chai came by Smedley's house to pick up the money he needed for his part in the operation. Thornton told Chai to buy forty-two kilos of heroin as well as the teakwood furniture that would be used for the shipment.

But Chai began grumbling. 'Ike owes me some money,' Chai complained to Thornton.

'How much?' Thornton asked.

'About $12,000.'

'Well, we'll have to get it straight with Ike,' Thornton said. 'Let me write him to find out what's going on.'

'Well, I need the money,' Chai insisted.

An exasperated Thornton gave Chai $3,000 and said he would contact him about the rest of the money when he heard from Ike.

Soon after, another $25,000 arrived in Bangkok, money Thornton planned to use to buy six more kilos through Chai. Thornton phoned Chai to tell him that the money had arrived. Chai's wife answered the phone and told Thornton that her husband had gone 'up country.' The next day, Thornton called Chai's house again, but he still had not returned from his trip. 'Have your husband call me when he returns,' Thornton told Chai's wife. But Chai did not call. The following day, Thornton called Chai's house again and left another message for him with his wife. Still no response.

Thornton could not believe it. Here he was trying to put together a major drug shipment and his main man had done a disappearing act. The next day Chai's wife paid Thornton a visit. 'The police have my husband and he needs $25,000 to get out of jail,' she explained.

Thornton looked at Mrs. Chai with amazement. 'Well, you are in Thailand and you don't need that kind of money to get Chai out of jail. Why don't you ask the gentleman Chai is working with to get him out of jail?'

'Well, we can't get in touch with him,' she explained.

Mrs. Chai seemed to have an answer for every question Thornton fired at her. So he put $5,000 in a brown paper bag and gave it to her.

'Here's some money. Can't you post bond?' Thornton asked. 'See if this will do it. If not, bring the money back.'

A couple of days later, Chai's wife returned the money to Thornton. After she left, Thornton checked the bag. About $1,000 of the $5,000 was missing.

Thornton was getting more and more pissed about how the operation was going. Three days later, when Smedley returned from a trip to the United States, Thornton complained to Smedley about how Chai was acting. Smedley got on the phone and called Chai, but he was not at home. Smedley left his name and phone number with the wife and told her to have Chai call him as soon as he arrived.

Meanwhile, a friend of Thornton's named Lamb came by Thornton's place to borrow some money. Thornton told the friend about his problem in locating Chai. 'I really think the police must have Chai,'

Thornton said. 'He's been gone so long.'

'But I've seen Chai,' Lamb revealed.

'Where did you see him?' Thornton asked, surprised.

'Over at his house,' Lamb said. 'He told me not to tell you that I had seen him.'

'So it's a rip off !' Thornton shouted.

'Chai needs the money but is mad at you,' Lamb explained. 'What did I do to him?' Thornton asked.

'Chai said you're too busy,' Lamb replied.

Too busy! Thornton was livid. Here they were trying to arrange major drug deals that have to move half-way around the world and one of his key people is angry because he thinks he's 'too busy.' Was he running a nursery or a drug ring?

Thornton pushed Smedley. 'You need to see Chai and get him to come over and talk. We can sit down and work out our problems. There is no need to have a mess.'

Smedley caught up with Chai and persuaded him to come over the next day to talk with Thornton. But Chai had another surprise in store for Thornton. Smedley told Thornton that

Chai wanted $4,900, not $4,100 as previously agreed, for each kilo of heroin Thornton bought from him. Moreover, Chai was demanding that Thornton pay that amount not only for future shipments but also retroactively for the Brown shipment that was about to go out.

'He can't do that,' Thornton exclaimed. 'It will screw up our finances.'

Thornton asked Smedley to intercede with Chai so he could get the operation back on track. But as Thornton later explained; 'Jimmy wouldn't talk. He wouldn't say anything. He just didn't feel like talking to nobody (sic). When I would say something to him, he would snap.'

Thornton was frustrated and concerned about the developments at perhaps the most critical time in the Atkinson drug ring's history. It sounded crazy to Thornton when he thought about it, but it looked like Chai and Smedley were working together to screw up the operation. He also suspected that Chai and Smedley were planning to steal Ike's money. Thornton needed to talk with Ike to let him know about the disturbing turn of events.

IN JULY 1975, Thornton returned to the U.S. to get further instructions from Ike. Thornton's plane landed at Hickam Air Force Base in Honolulu, Hawaii, and he went through Customs for what he thought would be a routine check. But when one of the Customs agents saw Thornton's ID, he asked Thornton to step out of line and to follow him to a room in the back of the airport terminal. Thornton had to strip while Customs officials took the papers out of his AWOL bag and photocopied them. That was it. No interrogation, no probing questions. He was escorted back to the plane and allowed to continue his journey. Thornton did not know what happened, but he decided to go to the bathroom, take the papers that the Customs officials photocopied out of the AWOL bag and burn them.

Thornton's plane landed at March Air Force Base in California and he immediately flew from there cross-country to North Carolina, arriving in Goldsboro around August 1st. Thornton wrote a letter and had it delivered to Ike. In the letter, Thornton described the problems he was having in Bangkok. Thornton wrote that it seemed to him that Chai and Smedley were conspiring together against the best interests of Ike's drug ring.

Ike sent six 'notes' to Thornton, five of which he was to deliver to Smedley and Chai. In the letter to Thornton, Ike told him that as soon as his job was complete in Thailand, Thornton was to return to the U.S. to control the stateside operation. A second note to Smedley told him to send his maid, Missy, to the United States to work at Ike's house in Goldsboro. The third note informed Chai and Smedley that Thornton was in charge of the operation. A fourth note warned Smedley to "take care of business the way you are supposed to and stay low because the Feds were looking for you.' The fifth accused Smedley of being the cause of all the heat on Thornton. In the sixth note to Chai and Smedley, Ike warned: 'If any of my stuff comes up missing, somebody's ass is going to hang.'

Thornton then went to the Thai embassy to get his visa stamped. He returned to Thailand about August 4.

Thornton gave Ike's notes to Smedley and Chai, and after they read them, Thornton made sure the notes were burned. He then moved to exert his leadership. 'Do you have the Myrick shipment together?' Thornton asked Chai.

'No, but it will be ready in three or four days,' Chai said.

'Have you bought any more dope for the Myrick shipment?'

Thornton asked Smedley.

'Yeah, I did,' Smedley said.

Thornton revealed that he had promised Myrick a $3,000 advance, but he hadn't seen him and so hadn't given him the money. 'Could you pay Myrick off?' Thornton asked Smedley.

'I'll take care of it,' Smedley said. Thornton was satisfied. It seemed as if Chai and Jimmy had gotten the message.

THORNTON WAS ALSO waiting for an additional $10,000 to arrive from the States. Lorenzo Martin, a member of Ike's drug ring who was working at the Army Post Office (APO) in Bangkok, would receive the money. But in an odd coincidence a junior clerk at the APO who worked for Martin had the same last name as Martin. Moreover, the clerk had a brother in Washington, DC, with the same initials as Lorenzo Martin ('LM'). The junior clerk had written his brother and asked him to send him some 45-RPM records. The money that Thornton was expecting arrived at the APO in a box that looked a lot like the size of the box that his 45 RPMs would come in from DC. The junior clerk almost fainted when he opened the box that he thought his brother had sent him and instead found $10,000 in crisp $100 bills. Fortunately, Lorenzo Martin discovered the screw-up before it could get out of control, and he paid the junior clerk $100 to hand over the money and keep quiet. Thornton used the $10,000 to buy two "joints" (kilos of heroin) from Chai.

IN JULY 1975, Smedley sent five pieces of furniture (two small end tables, a cabinet, a buffet and a dresser) to Myrick's house. In August, a Thai-Chinese gentleman who called himself 'Vichai' delivered a sixth-piece of furniture, a wooden cabinet, to Myrick's house in a blue van. Vichai was an alias for Luchai 'Chai' Ruviwat. Myrick helped Chai take the cabinet off the van and into the house.

Valerie Myrick, Jasper's wife, was impressed with the furniture's beauty, and she kidded Smedley, saying that if he was not going to pick up the furniture, she would keep it for herself. Smedley was not amused. 'You can't keep it,' he said. 'There is no place too far for me not to come and get it.'

CHAPTER 13

The Sting

IN LATE 1974 Ike Atkinson had made a serious mistake by leaving his palm print on a drug shipment sent through the U.S. Postal Service from Bangkok to Goldsboro, North Carolina. In June 1975, that 'mistake' got Ike a 19-year sentence in a Federal courtroom in Raleigh, North Carolina. While Ike hoped to be out of jail in no more than 18 months, it was a good bet he would remain behind bars much longer. Still, he remained in charge of his drug ring. Ike directed his subordinates from prison to smuggle even larger shipments of heroin using teakwood furniture with specially made false bottoms and using the 'services' of military personnel who, as the U.S. military decreased its Southeast Asia presence, were moving from Thailand back to the U.S. after completing their tour of duty. While it was true that Ike's drug ring was experiencing personality and organizational problems, evident in the clashes between Thornton on one side and Luchai 'Chai' Ruviwat and Jimmy Smedley on the other, law enforcement officials were still seemingly light years away from taking Ike's drug ring down.

Chuck Lutz, who headed the U.S. Drug Enforcement Administration (DEA) Atkinson drug ring investigation in Thailand, had redirected three Thai undercover surveillance agents to follow members of Atkinson's organization still operating in Thailand. 'We had bought them motorcycles so they could move unnoticed among the thousands of motorbikes and gather intelligence,' Lutz said. The surveillance team was able to document the movements of the Atkinson drug ring, but the authorities did not have the intelligence, let alone the evidence, to make any arrests. In February 1975, the investigation was still an open case. While the DEA was intent on taking down the drug ring, the investigation in Bangkok was essentially 'dead in the water.'

'I was writing up the surveillance reports, hoping to keep the case active, but I didn't have the informants who could provide information on the group's activities or help us to infiltrate them,' Lutz recalled. 'We were on the outside looking in. I was also busy working on several other cases that monopolized much of my time. Then I got a call that changed everything.'"

The call came from Lionel Stewart, a black DEA agent, who, by all accounts, was one of the best undercover agents in the Administration's history. Stewart was a retired Army Criminal Investigation Division (CID) Warrant Officer, who, like Ike, had lied about his age to get into the military service at age 17. Both served in the Korean conflict, but unlike Ike, Stewart saw combat, having received a Purple Heart and the Bronze Star Medal. Stewart took advantage of the opportunity offered him while in the Service to earn a degree in military science from the University of Omaha in Nebraska. In 1975 when Stewart retired from the Army and joined the DEA, he was about 37-years old, a lot older than many of the DEA agents with whom he worked and even some of those who supervised him.

Stewart had a charismatic presence, according to DEA agents who served with him. Muscular, of medium build, with an engaging smile, Stewart wore a short Afro, which was in vogue among many African American men at the time, and he looked as if he could step into the role of a leading character in one of the many so called 'blaxploitation' movies of the time, such as 'Shaft,' 'Superfly' or 'Black Caesar.'

'He was a remarkable person who rose from the hood in New York City to the highest levels of the DEA,' recalled Lutz, who worked with Stewart on the Atkinson investigation and became a close friend. 'He had a very engaging personality and could talk a hungry dog off a meat wagon.' Paul Wallace, a retired special DEA agent who was Stewart's partner in the San Francisco office in the 1970s, recalled Stewart as being 'a Type-A personality who was always on the go and loved undercover work.'

Stewart mixed with all kinds of company. 'He could speak like a street thug, but at the same time, he was cultured and articulate,' recalled Mike Nerney, a former Assistant U.S. Attorney in San Francisco who worked with Stewart on several drug trafficking cases. 'As an undercover agent, he could do anything and everything.'

Stewart was as good at the more humdrum task of completing office paper work as he was in the field. 'To get wiretaps approved, I had to write affidavits that went on for page after page,' Wallace recalled. 'They were very complicated and time consuming to do, especially for a young agent like me. But Lionel did those documents with ease. He guided me through the process until I could do them myself.'

Stewart was one of a handful of black agents in the DEA at the time, but he became a mentor for many DEA agents from different ethnic backgrounds. 'He was respected by state and local police in the San Francisco Bay region as well,' Lutz revealed. 'That was unusual for a federal agent.'

LUTZ DIDN'T KNOW Lionel Stewart when Stewart called him in February 1975, but he listened with keen interest to what his colleague had to say. Stewart explained that he was working on a drug investigation that had a connection to Thailand, and he provided Lutz with background on the case.

Four U.S. airmen turned drug traffickers (Cleophus J. Kearney, Andre W. King, Fred Neal Powell and Eugene Lemon, Jr.), who collectively became known as the 'Japanese Connection,' were arrested in a scheme to smuggle $1 million worth of heroin from Thailand through Japan to the U.S. via American military bases. U.S. Navy investigators uncovered the smuggling operation when drugs started turning up on the streets of Yokosuka, a city on Tokyo Bay, and in the snack bars in the Dubuita Alley district of Tokyo. Investigators believed that as many as 70 people were involved in the drug ring.

In an unusual move, a U.S. prosecutor went to Tokyo to take the video deposition of Thomas Adams and Thomas Gamble, two Americans involved with the Japanese Connection and already in prison convicted of violating Japanese narcotics laws. Adams and Gamble agreed to cooperate because they did not like the conditions in the prison at Yokosuka and were hoping that by testifying they could get out of the Japanese prison system early.

'This case was unusual in a number of ways,' explained Mike Nerney. 'It was the first time that the U.S. Government took depositions of U.S. prisoners imprisoned outside the U.S. that were admitted as evidence in a U.S. criminal trial. It was also the first time U.S. prosecutors were able to get a conviction under 21 USC 959 for having distributed illegal drugs in another country while knowing that the intended destination for the heroin was the United States.'

Adams and Gamble also revealed that the Japanese Connection had bought its heroin in Bangkok through a deal brokered by a man named Chai at Jack's American Star Bar in Bangkok before it closed in 1973. According to the informants, members of the Japanese Connection were introduced to Chai through a young Black intermediary named Carl Dunlap (not his true identity), who was in his 20s, an employee of an American corporation based in Bangkok and an amateur musician who sang and played the guitar at Jack's Bar on weekends. Sources described Dunlap as 'a good kid who hung out with the wrong crowd.'

'Dunlap later said he told the Japanese Connection guys that he had nothing to do with heroin, but they kept pushing him,' Lutz re-called. 'Finally, Dunlap agreed to introduce them to Luchai Ruviwat.'

The bottom line of the phone call—Stewart wanted to know if Lutz was interested in trying to get Dunlap to cooperate so he could put Stewart in touch with Chai. Am I interested? Lutz thought. 'I would have hugged him if we were in the same room.' This could be the big break that Lutz was waiting for—a chance to penetrate the Bangkok end of the Atkinson drug ring.

IN EARLY MARCH 1975, Lionel Stewart and Mike Nerney traveled to Bangkok to meet with Chuck Lutz. Nerney, who was known as a hard-nosed, capable prosecutor, became an Assistant U.S. Attorney in San Francisco in 1971 and was assigned to the General Crimes Unit. Among other notable successes, Nerney had been a member of the team responsible for prosecuting the government's case in the kidnapping of newspaper heiress Patricia Hearst.

The three American law enforcement officials met at Lutz's office in the U.S. Embassy in Bangkok to devise a game plan that would get Dunlap to cooperate. The plan began with a flimsy arrest warrant that Nerney had gotten issued against Carl Dunlap for 'aiding and abetting a conspiracy.' The DEA did not have enough evidence to prosecute Dunlap in the Japanese Connection heroin case, but the warrant's purpose was to get his attention. They needed a 'safe' place to meet. American services are performed on Sathorn Road, about a mile from the U.S. Embassy. The Consul General was a friend of Lutz's. He agreed to allow Lutz to use his office for a meeting with the man they hoped would be their ticket into the Atkinson organization.

Lutz phoned Dunlap and said in his best official tone: 'I'm the head of the DEA in Bangkok and I want to talk to you. Come down to see me at the U.S. Consulate on Sathorn Road tomorrow morning.'

'The Consulate was a good place to meet with Dunlap,' Lutz recalled. 'We didn't want to create any problems for him or for us by having someone think he worked for the DEA. A lot of Americans were coming and going from the U.S. Consulate on passport and visa matters, so nobody would get suspicious seeing Dunlap there.'

When Dunlap arrived at the Consulate, he was directed to a large office where Mike Nerney sat behind the Consul General's imposing desk. Lutz and Stewart were also seated in the room. 'Have a seat,' Nerney offered Dunlap. With a solemn expression, Nerney explained: 'I got a warrant for your arrest in my left hand and a get-out-of-jail-free card in my right. Cooperate with these two gentlemen (pointing to Stewart and Lutz), and I will tear up what I have in my left hand. If you don't cooperate, I will make sure that you are kicked out of Thailand and prosecuted in the States for drug trafficking.'

Dunlap tried to stand up. Nerney walked around the desk, shoved Dunlap back in his seat and barked: 'Sit down, asshole.'

Dunlap began shaking. To Nerney it looked like the young man was about to wet his pants. Lutz saw him trembling and felt sorry for him. Dunlap needed no more persuasion to get him to cooperate fully. By then, he might have done anything, even gone on a secret Cold War mission to the Soviet Union in order to make his three interrogators happy. Dunlap agreed to introduce Stewart to Chai. Their initial mission completed, Stewart and Nerney returned to San Francisco while Lutz completed the paper work that would make Dunlap an official DEA informant and used Dunlap's information to fine tune the surveillance of Smedley and his associates.

A few weeks later, Stewart returned to Bangkok to begin the undercover operation that, hopefully, would lead to Chai and through him, the penetration of the Atkinson drug ring. Stewart used the nickname 'Johnny,' and, for his cover story, he posed as a mid-level drug trafficker from San Francisco who claimed to have a good way of smuggling heroin into the U.S. 'The ultimate objective of the investigation was to have Chai arrested outside of Thailand,' Lutz recalled. 'The Thai government wasn't extraditing their citizens to the United States on drug trafficking offenses in those days, and we knew if Chai was arrested in Thailand he would bribe his way out of jail.'

ON MARCH 8 1975, Dunlap arranged the first meeting between Johnny (Stewart) and Chai in front of the Windsor Hotel off Sukhumvit Road in Bangkok. To gather evidence, Stewart was outfitted with a recorder taped to the inside of his thigh and with the mike taped to his chest. He recorded each undercover conversation. Dunlap told Chai that he had met Johnny while in the Army and that his friend was in town to make a heroin connection. After Dunlap made the introductions, they drove to Lumpini Park in the center of Bangkok and walked first to a bar and then to a restaurant, getting to know each other. Lumpini Park is about three-square blocks in size and surrounded by high-rise apartment and office buildings, shop houses and hotels. Many people spend their early morning hours exercising in Lumpini Park, jogging, roller skating, doing Tai Chi and even practicing ballroom dancing. During the day, children romp in the playgrounds and office workers take breaks from the searing heat under the shade trees. During morning and evening rush hours, the sidewalks around the park are crowded with hawkers selling everything from soups and curries for workers to take to work or to take home for dinner, to snake's blood drained from live snakes for use as a tonic.

'Lumpini Park was like New York City's Central Park, and it was near our Embassy,' Lutz recalled. 'I chose that place for the initial meeting because it was busy and had lots of foreigners hanging around. So our surveillance agents could blend in.'

During their conversation, Stewart told Chai that he had just arrived in Bangkok and wanted to buy a large quantity of heroin. 'I've got a system, man,' Stewart bragged, 'I can get any dope back to the U.S.' Stewart explained that his system involved the use of a Pan American airline cargo supervisor who acted as a courier and another Pan Am employee in San Francisco who could substitute the heroin with a dummy package to get it through U.S. Customs.

Chai was impressed, but he told Stewart: 'I've got my own system.' Stewart insisted that he wanted to use his own system, and he assured Chai that it worked well. Chai acknowledged that he had previously delivered a load of three or four kilos of heroin to the U.S. but conceded that he did not want to do it again because he feared he might become too well known to U.S. Customs officials. The prospective partners discussed a purchase by Stewart of 700 grams of heroin to test Stewart's smuggling system. They then negotiated the delivery date, the price and the availability of more heroin in the future.

'I'm interested in developing a lucrative long-term relationship,' Stewart said.

'I can get heroin anytime,' Chai boasted.

But Stewart complained that the $4,700 per kilo price Chai wanted was a little too steep.

After more haggling, Chai and Stewart finally agreed that Stewart would choose the delivery site (to ensure it would be in a public place) and that the transfer of heroin would take place in Chai's car. But Chai said there was one more thing. 'I've been cheated before,' he revealed. 'I need an advance to show your good faith. You can pay the balance on delivery.' Playing his role to a T, Stewart reluctantly agreed to front a $2,000 advance, but added: 'In the future, I'm not going to advance you any money.'

Trying to impress Stewart, Chai boasted that he was '70 percent sure' he could get Stewart out of prison should he ever be arrested because the Thai police had to 'go through my man in the police department.' Chai also said he would include some extra heroin in the package for testing purposes. 'This is a business for me,' Chai said.

Stewart reported back to Lutz. His meeting with Chai had gone better than could be expected. But fronting the money in those days was a big deal in the DEA, and special authorization had to be obtained. 'Considering who Lionel was dealing with, Atkinson's source of supply, headquarters gave us permission and Lionel fronted the $2,000 to Chai,' Lutz recalled.

Lutz's surveillance team had placed Jimmy Smedley and the band of brothers most nights at the Thermae Massage Parlor restaurant and bar. 'While working the Luchai side of the investigation, we also thought that Lionel would be able to befriend other members of the Atkinson ring if he began hanging out at the Thermae at night,' Lutz said.

The Thermae massage parlor on Sukhumvit Road between Soi 13 and Soi 15 was a Bangkok fixture in the 1970s. It was a popular place where young girls sat in a glassed-in room upstairs with numbers on their blouses. A customer drank a Singha beer while studying the girls as they sat and read, sewed, or listened to music. The customer would then pick the one he wanted, her number would be called and the two would retire to a private room for a massage. Downstairs was a twenty-four hour restaurant and bar with more young prostitutes as hostesses. One could eat, drink, socialize, and/or buy a girl out of the bar. The girls received part of the money paid to the bar, and the customers usually tipped the girls in accordance with the services rendered.

'I conducted surveillance of Lionel's activities at the Thermae every night for at least a week while he got to meet and know Smedley, Thornton and the others,' Lutz recalled. 'It is standard procedure in DEA that no one works undercover without surveillance. After an evening of socializing at the Thermae, Lionel would make his own way back to his hotel, and I would stay for a few more minutes to ensure no one followed him. Then I would go home to get a few hours sleep. I would pick Lionel up at a pre-arranged location in the morning, after he had determined that he wasn't being followed, and I would smuggle him into the Embassy on the floor in the back seat of my car.

'Bangkok was a small town when it came to foreigners, particularly when it came to black foreigners. So we were very careful not even letting the Marine Security Guard at the Embassy see Lionel. Lionel would write his undercover report from the night before, and I would write my surveillance report. We'd then spend most afternoons playing golf. That night, we would start all over again.'

One night after an undercover meeting, Lionel did not go back to his hotel room, and he did not contact his colleagues to tell them where he was. Nerney, who was in Bangkok for meetings and registered at the same hotel, telephoned Lutz through the Embassy switchboard, and they agreed to meet at the U.S. Embassy to figure out how they should go about trying to find Stewart. 'We were concerned, but about six in the morning Lionel comes waltzing up to the back gate of the compound,' Nerney recalled. 'He said he couldn't find us at the hotel. We told him we were worried; he called us a bunch of sissies. Lionel lived on the edge and did some real dangerous shit. But we couldn't have made the Japanese Connection case without him.'

AT 11.30 AM on March 11 1975, Chai delivered one kilo of 98 percent pure heroin to Stewart in the open-air parking lot of the Bangkok Siam Center, one of Bangkok's first interior shopping malls, while the DEA recorded the meeting on videotape. After the delivery, Chai and Stewart walked to a hotel coffee shop, where Stewart paid Chai $2,700, the balance he owed. Chai was getting comfortable hanging with Stewart and revealed that a Thai policeman was his source for the heroin.

Stewart and Chai agreed to have a third meeting at which time Stewart would let Chai know what happened to the heroin on his end of the deal. The third meeting took place on March 15 1975, again in Lumpini Park. Stewart had good news for Chai. His system had worked perfectly; Stewart said he had successfully smuggled Chai's heroin back to the States.

'I have to be careful,' Stewart said. 'I don't like to use my system more than three or four times a year. I'm afraid something will go wrong if we use it too many times. How about if we use your system next?'

Chai demurred. 'Yeah, sure Johnny, my system could work, but right now I'm making changes to it. It won't be ready to use for several months.'

Stewart did not push. 'Well, if that's the case, you can use my system if you want.'

'When will you be able to buy some more stuff?' Chai asked.

'I'm not certain, but when I do, I will want about ten kilos,' replied Johnny, aka Lionel Stewart.

'Could I include one or two of my own kilos in your shipment?'

Stewart moved to take the initiative. 'If you are going to use my system, I want you to reduce the price you're charging me. What do you say to $3,700 a kilo?'

Chai had no problem with that price, given that Stewart was willing to allow him to use his transportation system. Finally, Stewart was in complete control of the sting.

On March 19, the partners met again at the Lumpini Park restaurant. Stewart told Chai that before he could use Chai's system, he wanted to know who would be receiving the heroin in the U.S.

'I don't have anybody to pick it up in the States,' Chai revealed. 'Why can't you sell it for me?'

Stewart played coy and asked Chai: 'How do you expect to get paid for the heroin if I'm going to sell it for you in the U.S.?'

Chai thought about it and then suggested that Stewart could bring the money to him. Or better yet, Chai said he could come to the U.S. to pick it up and even bring along three or four more kilos for Stewart to sell.

It was a remarkable suggestion and showed how well Stewart was playing his undercover role. Chai completely trusted Stewart, and he was willing to leave Thailand and risk making himself vulnerable to arrest in the U.S.

Stewart further enticed Chai, saying, 'Yeah, since you are going through a lot of trouble to help me out, I'm going to show you a good time, my friend. When we finish the deal, I'll take you to Las Vegas, and we will check out some show girls. How about that?'

Chai realized he could have a great time in the States while making a lot of money and thought it was a great idea. Stewart left Thailand the next day and returned to San Francisco. Stewart had other, totally unrelated cases going on in San Francisco that needed his attention. 'Lionel was not assigned to our Bangkok Regional Office and could not remain there indefinitely,' Lutz explained. 'He and I flew between Bangkok and San Francisco numerous times during the Luchai investigation. On one occasion, I carried the heroin that Luchai had sold to Lionel in Bangkok to San Francisco and placed it in evidence.'

That trip produced a bonus. Lutz had a friend who was the Pan American airline station manager at Don Muang Airport. Whenever Lutz flew from Bangkok, his friend would upgrade him to first class, but he could only do so for the Bangkok-Hong Kong leg. 'When I boarded in Bangkok, there was a black male sitting in first class. I vaguely recalled seeing his picture before,' Lutz recalled. 'When we got to Hong Kong, I discreetly checked with Pan Am ground personnel and got his name. I called San Francisco and learned from a check of the NADDIS (the DEA's Narcotics and Dangerous Drugs Information System computerized database) that he was a fugitive from a DEA case in Los Angeles.'

'He was on the continuing flight to Los Angeles, so I used my credit card to upgrade to first class on his flight, instead of continuing on to San Francisco, and managed to get a seat next to him. We talked at length as we flew over the Pacific with the box of Chai's heroin sitting on the floor between us. I gave him a line that I was in the import-export furniture business and alluded to him that I was smuggling gems out of Burma to the States. I hoped he would bite and ask me if I could smuggle drugs for him back to the U.S. Unfortunately, I was no Lionel Stewart. When we got to LA, I pointed him out to the waiting

DEA and Customs agents, and he was arrested. I caught a flight to San Francisco with the package of heroin.'

ON JUNE 27, 1975, Lionel returned to Bangkok. Without telling Chai, he and Dunlap paid a 'social' call on Freddie Thornton, by then Ike's main man in Thailand who 'Johnny' had met several times at the Thermae. 'It was through Lionel that we first learned about Thornton,' Lutz explained. 'At some point Lionel had introduced himself to Thornton at the Thermae. We didn't think Thornton and Smedley knew that Carl Dunlap had already introduced Lionel to Luchai and that Lionel was buying dope from Luchai. Luchai was apparently selling heroin to Lionel on the side. And Luchai did not hang out with the band of brothers at the Thermae. So we decided to try and keep the two matters separate as long as we could. But Chai showed up unexpectedly at Thornton's residence and was surprised to see Johnny. But the two did not discuss their heroin dealings in front of Thornton.'

Hanging out at the Thermae, Lionel portrayed himself as a high roller from San Francisco, throwing money around, buying drinks for other patrons and the hookers, trying to get known and trusted by the band of brothers. It was not an easy task for an undercover agent who does not have an informant to vouch for him and infiltrate his way into a sophisticated drug trafficking organization. But it was easy for those with Lionel's talent. 'You can't just come out and say you're a drug dealer without people shying away,' Lutz explained. 'You have to talk the talk and walk the walk and make them feel comfortable with you. Lionel went into the Thermae cold and pulled it off.'

Later, Thornton recalled: 'He (Stewart) already knew Chai and had purchased some dope from him before I ever met him... we (Thornton and Stewart) just got tighter. I thought he was all right.'

On July 3 1975, Thornton had invited Stewart to meet with Chai at Thornton's house. By then it was clear that Thornton knew what was going on between Chai and Stewart. Chai told Stewart that he wanted to include a kilo or two of his own heroin in each of Stewart's shipments. Stewart had no problem with that, and they agreed on a price of $4,100 per kilo for the heroin that Chai would sell Stewart. They also planned for future deliveries. Thornton, however, did not incriminate himself during that conversation.

Five days later, Chai and Stewart met for dinner at a Bangkok tavern where they reconfirmed the sale of three kilos of heroin at $4,100 a piece. "That's all I can handle at the moment because I'm having trouble getting money from the U.S.," Stewart said. Chai was upset but Stewart assured him that his system would be in full force by September 1975, and that by that time he would be able to buy 15 to 20 kilos twice a month. But since he was only buying three kilograms, Stewart agreed to pay half the price up front and the balance on delivery. Chai was reassured and confirmed that he intended to include an extra kilo of heroin for Lionel to sell for him.

'There was no reason to buy more than three kilos of heroin from Chai,' Lutz explained. 'We already had one buy from him, and we expected he would smuggle another kilo or two to San Francisco when he met Lionel to collect his money from his consigned kilo. We didn't want to risk fronting more money when we didn't have to.' Stewart was playing his role brilliantly and Chai was going down hook, line and sinker.

Chai telephoned Stewart on July 18 and arranged a meeting for the following day at a coffee shop at the Nana Hotel on Sukhumvit Road. They agreed it was good to see each other again, and they reaffirmed their prior arrangement for the sale of three kilos of heroin and the consignment of Chai's one kilo. Stewart informed Chai that he would dilute

Chai's kilo four times once it reached the U.S. and could sell each 'stepped-on' kilogram of 25 percent pure heroin for $25,000. Stewart continued that the drug organization he worked for would return $80,000 of the $100,000, keeping $20,000 to pay for transportation and distribution expenses in selling his contraband. Chai agreed to pick up his money from Stewart in the U.S. Stewart told Chai that he would have a chance to meet his boss, Mr. Big.

During the next four days, Chai and Stewart had more meetings at the Nana Hotel and Siam Center where they further refined the details of their smuggling operation. Stewart gave Chai a copy of a code he was to use in subsequent telephone conversations to avoid using the term 'heroin.' They confirmed the delivery of heroin for July 23. Stewart continued to pry information from his 'partner' in crime. This time Chai revealed that he was working with the 'Fat Man,' Leslie 'Ike' Atkinson, and that he would have his new drug delivery system in place by August 15. 'I had to pay someone $7,000 to devise my system,' Chai revealed.

On July 23, Chai arrived at the Siam Center carrying a brown paper bag. While the DEA videotaped and recorded them, Chai rendezvoused with Lionel and they walked to Chai's vehicle where Chai opened the trunk of his vehicle to reveal a cardboard box containing four kilograms of pure heroin. The paper bag he carried to the meeting was a ruse. If the police were watching and they arrested him, they would only seize an empty paper bag.

THE PLAN HAD worked beautifully so far; now it was time to get Chai to travel to San Francisco and consummate the sting. The DEA devised an elaborate plan that, hopefully, would not only lead to Chai's arrest but also identify some of the contacts in the U.S. They made reservations for Chai at the

Holiday Inn, a busy, popular tourist destination in San Francisco's Chinatown. Chai's room was bugged to gather any incriminating conversations within the room. DEA Group Supervisor Peter Fong, Lionel Stewart's real boss, would play "Mr. Big," Stewart's boss in his fictitious heroin trafficking organization.

On August 29th Chai arrived at the San Francisco International Airport and telephoned Stewart. He had arrived safely. Later that evening, they met at the Holiday Inn for dinner. On the way, Stewart informed Chai that he had not only sold Chai's consignment of heroin and received the money for it, but he had also negotiated another $100,000 down payment for the heroin Chai was about to smuggle into the United States. Chai was ecstatic. Not only had he made a lot of money, but once the deal was completed, he could relax, enjoy himself and go to Las Vegas, as Johnny, his friend and associate, had planned. Later, during Chai's trial, the press made a big deal about how Chai was entrapped into coming to America because he was intrigued by the prospect of getting together with a blonde Caucasian woman in La Vegas.

'That story was blown up in the press,' Lutz said. 'Luchai's main reason for being in the U.S. was to make money selling heroin.'

After the dinner, Chai informed Stewart that he had a courier named Chalermphol Phitakstrakul, who, on August 31, would leave Bangkok for the U.S. with the heroin. The following day, Chai met Chalermphol after he arrived at the San Francisco airport and had successfully cleared Customs (as the DEA prearranged), and they returned to the Holiday Inn, where they delivered a half-kilo of 93 percent pure heroin to Stewart. To Chai, it must have looked as if the streets of America were indeed paved with gold—paved, that is, with the huge profits he would surely be making from working with Johnny and selling his potent China White brand of heroin.

Johnny picked up Chai and Chalermphol at the airport and drove them to the nearby San Mateo Hotel where they delivered the heroin to 'Mr. Big.' Chai, Stewart and Mr. Big, agent Peter Fong, were still talking in the room about future heroin shipments when the DEA agents in the adjoining room burst in and arrested Chai and Chalermphol. Chai stood frozen with a stunned look on his face as the DEA agents handcuffed him. 'You could tell that Luchai Ruviwat had absolutely no clue that Lionel was playing him,' said Lowery Leong, a retired DEA special agent who was involved in Chai's arrest at the hotel room. 'He was caught by complete surprise.'

STEWART'S WORK WITH the DEA's Bangkok's office was not finished. Lutz recognized a talented undercover agent when he saw one. 'While Lionel was working the "Chai" case and hanging out at the Thermae, another informant came to our attention who could introduce an undercover agent to Preecha Leeyaruk, a local travel agent with a long history of drug trafficking,' said Lutz. DEA intelligence indicated that Preecha had been active during the Vietnam War selling heroin to American GI's on Rest and Recuperation (R & R) in Bangkok. U.S. Customs considered him to be one of the most important Thai drug traffickers directly affecting the U.S.

'With his affable, easy-going manner, Lionel ingratiated himself with Preecha at their first meeting, enabling us to cut out the informant after the initial introduction,' Lutz recalled. 'Lionel even bought toys for Preecha's children with his own money. And since Thailand was not extraditing Thai citizens at that time, as was the case with Luchai, we cooked up another scheme that would entice Preecha to deliver the heroin outside of Thailand to a country that would extradite him to the U.S.'

'We had been successful in another undercover operation earlier in the year with me posing undercover as a Pan Am cargo supervisor, and my partner, Matty Maher, posing as a Pan Am mechanic. I had asked my friend, the Bangkok Pan Am station manager, to document us with Pan Am employee ID cards and give us the schematic drawings of a Boeing 747. We told the Chinese-Thai crook, Sukree Sukreepirom aka Chao Pei Sui, who was believed to be the first Asian trafficker to convert opium to heroin, that we had a way of concealing large quantities of heroin behind false panels in the bathrooms of 747's and a way to secretly remove the heroin from the planes when they went in for a routine maintenance in the States. Sukree and a top-level Malaysian trafficker, Hoi Se Wan, ended up delivering twenty-five kilos of pure heroin.

'I had asked Lionel to use a similar scenario in the Luchai Ruviwat investigation and again in the Preecha investigation. If it works, why not? So Lionel told Preecha he ran a clothing business in San Francisco that purchased suits from Hong Kong and over time had developed a relationship with some Hong Kong-based Pan Am employees who said they could conceal almost anything in a 747. Lionel told Preecha he wanted to test the system with a trial run of one kilogram of heroin, but that Lionel had no secure way of getting the heroin to Hong Kong. Preecha agreed to have the heroin delivered to Hong Kong by courier.

'Lionel said he would eventually cut Preecha in on his business in the States once it developed, giving Preecha 25 percent of the profits and helping Preecha expand his tourist business into Hong Kong. Preecha took the bait and agreed to deliver the one kilo of heroin to Hong Kong for $18,000, which included transportation costs, and that after the trial run he would deliver 20 kilograms of heroin to Lionel in Hong Kong for $400,000. The DEA office in Bangkok and Hong Kong, and the U.S. Attorney's Office in San Francisco reached agreement with Hong Kong authorities that, after their arrest,

Preecha and his courier would be extradited to San Francisco to stand charges there.'

Lutz continued: 'Lionel and Preecha flew to Hong Kong together. I flew on surveillance on the same flight to help identify them to the police when they arrived. We stayed at the Lee Gardens Hotel. The Royal Hong Kong Police had arranged adjoining rooms for Preecha and Lionel—with adjoining rooms for themselves.

'While Preecha had assured Lionel that he had a secure way of getting the heroin to Hong Kong through a "big cheese," we had no idea then that the couriers would be two former members of the Thai Parliament traveling on diplomatic passports. After the diplomats delivered a suitcase with the one-kilogram of heroin hidden in a false bottom to Preecha and Lionel. "The Royal Hong Kong Police arrested Preecha in his room, and then arrested the Thai politician smugglers while they were eating lunch in the hotel's coffee shop,' he explained. Due to the high profile of the couriers, and the publicity surrounding their arrests, the Hong Kong authorities reneged on their agreement and decided not to extradite them to the States but to prosecute the defendants in Hong Kong.

At the trial, Preecha told the panel of three judges that he never dreamed the smooth-talking Stewart was actually trying to 'frame' him. It was to no avail, however. Preecha and the corrupt former members of the Thai parliament were each sentenced to ten years in prison.

Mike Nerney had flown to Hong Kong for the trial and, in the interest of the economy, had been asked by the DEA to take with him the kilogram that had been purchased from Preecha in Bangkok and placed into evidence in San Francisco. 'The ever-playful Lionel Stewart arranged with his Royal Hong Kong Police counterparts not to have them meet me upon my arrival in Hong Kong but to let me sweat it out a bit at the

Airport's Customs and Immigration stations with a kilogram of pure heroin locked in my briefcase,' Mike Nerney recalled.

IN THE AFTERMATH of that sting and the highly publicized trial, Lionel Stewart's exploits became legendary in the Far East. In fact, the main character in a Hong Kong action movie made in the late 1970s was reportedly based on Lionel Stewart's exploits in the Preecha case. 'The movie was in Chinese, but they had a black guy playing Lionel, the "super narc,"' Nerney recalled. 'The Hong Kong film industry knew Lionel from his undercover work on the case of the corrupt Thai parliamentarians. Lionel stood out at their trial. When he was not in court, Lionel had four bodyguards with him wherever he went.'

Lionel Stewart eventually retired as a DEA senior executive in the DEA's Miami Field Division, and after two unsuccessful bids to be elected Broward Country, Florida, sheriff, died of a heart ailment. He never did go back to Bangkok to work undercover; someone in Thailand had put out a contract on his life.

CHAPTER 14

Takedown

THE ARREST OF Luchai 'Chai' Ruviwat was a major blow to the Ike Atkinson drug ring. Chai was 'The Main Man,' the supplier who knew where to buy the heroin, the confidant who could keep an eye on the local Bangkok scene and be counted on to fix any problems that arose. Ike trusted Chai as a partner and was perplexed about why and how he got busted in San Francisco. 'That thing about blonde girls in Las Vegas makes absolutely no sense,' Ike explained. 'It sounds as if Chai was obsessed with blonde girls. But that wasn't like him. He never showed any interest in any blonde girls while I knew him in Bangkok.'

It looked as if Chai was running a rogue operation that nobody in Ike's drug ring knew anything about and nobody could give Ike answers. Locked up in prison several thousand miles away from Thailand, Ike could not do his own investigation. He just hoped that nothing would go wrong with the William Brown and Jasper Myrick shipments, which would provide his biggest paydays in his seven years of drug trafficking.

By the time Chai left for San Francisco on August 29 1975, for his fateful meeting with Lionel Stewart aka 'Johnny.' Freddie Thornton had his suspicions about Johnny. Thornton realized he knew nothing about this smooth-talking stranger who had appeared out of nowhere. He wondered about the incident at

Hickham Air Force Base in Honolulu where U.S. Customs strip-searched him and rifled through his papers. That had never happened before. Was that search somehow connected to Johnny? Thornton sensed something was not right.

THE AUTHORITIES DIDN'T know that Freddie Thornton was Ike's right-hand man, but they knew he was deeply involved with Atkinson. With Ike in prison and Chai out of the picture, the Drug Enforcement Administration's (DEA) next objective was to go after Thornton, and, ideally, get him to the U.S. where they could pressure him to cooperate. On the morning of September 3 1975, Freddie Thornton was on his way to the NCO club at the Windsor Hotel in Bangkok. He was about to get into his car when the gate to the front entrance of his house flew open and a swarm of Thai police, followed by DEA agents, swept in. The Thai authorities shoved Thornton against his car and handcuffed him. Meanwhile, some of the raiding party fanned out through Thornton's house. Thornton waited for an hour and a half while the Thai authorities turned his house upside down.

One of the policemen approached Thornton and asked him if he had a gun. 'Yes, there is a .22 inside,' Thornton revealed. 'It's my wife's gun.' Thornton was confident nothing would happen because his wife was Thai and the .22 was registered in her name. Freddie had married her the previous May, and his wife had the weapon when he met her.

Then one of the officers showed Thornton a cigarette. It was not just any kind of cigarette. It was a marijuana cigarette. The Thai authorities told Thornton that they had found the joint in the latrine in the area where the Thornton's maid lived. Thornton protested his innocence. 'I don't know where that came from. I don't fool with that stuff.' The Thai authorities had heard that story many times before from foreigners they caught with illegal drugs. The police arrested Thornton and took him across town to the Crime Suppression Unit where he was booked for drug possession. The penalty for marijuana possession was a fine of 100 baht, or $5 American, but under the law, the authorities could keep Thornton in jail for 84 days while they conducted their investigation before bringing him before a judge.

Thornton did not have a resident visa for Thailand, but he did have a valid 30-day tourist visa, which had been stamped in his American passport when he arrived at the airport on August 14. Thornton had plans to fly to the U.S. on September 4, so he was well within the time frame in which he could stay legally in Thailand.

Incarceration in a Thai jail was not a pleasant prospect. Thornton would have to sleep on the cell floor with other prisoners with only a blanket and a bucket with which to relieve himself. Food would have consisted of rice twice a day with some soya-like sauce spread over it, and that is all he would have to eat unless his wife brought additional rations. Ghilo, Thornton's wife, paid the police U.S. $500 to get him out of his bind. The police brought Thornton before a judge, and he was given a 30-day suspended sentence. Later, Thornton attempted to explain the $500 he had given the police. 'The police didn't ask for the money. She (my wife) didn't ask them if they wanted it. So I guess you wouldn't call it a bribe. She just handed it to them.'

The police told Thornton they would hold on to his passport because they wanted to make sure the visa stamp for Thailand was valid and that he was in the country legally. Pick it up in two days, Thornton was told by the police commander. He did as instructed and sent Ghilo to the Crime Suppression Unit two days later, but she was told that her husband would have to pick up the passport in person. When Thornton showed up at the Unit, several DEA agents were waiting for him. They had some bad news for Thornton. Not only had his Thai visa been cancelled, but U.S. Immigration had cancelled his passport.

What's going on? Thornton protested. One of the agents read Thornton a warrant for his arrest for 'aiding and abetting heroin trafficking to the U.S.' 'It's only September 8 today,' Thornton, said 'My visa is good until the September 13.' But the DEA had asked the U.S. Consulate to cancel his passport. With Thornton's passport cancelled, there was no doubt now that he was illegally in Thailand, and he was locked up in the Thai immigration prison. Eight hours later, the Thai police came to his cell and handcuffed Thornton and took him to the airport where seven or eight DEA agents, by Thornton's count, were waiting to put him on the plane bound for San Francisco via Tokyo (in reality, there were only two agent escorts).

Although Mike Nerney had obtained an arrest warrant for Thornton in San Francisco, a formal extradition could have taken months. No warrant, however, was needed for Thornton's expulsion. The Thai police considered him an undesirable based on the gun and the marijuana cigarette found in his house. He was deported in what DEA agents referred to as 'an informal extradition.'

A first-class seat was the only one available on the flight. If this was his last plane trip as a free man, Thornton planned to enjoy himself, so he ate steak and got drunk on free booze. One of the two agents accompanying him on the flight wanted to talk to Thornton about co-operating, but Thornton fell fast asleep. On September 9 at about 8 p.m., the plane landed in San Francisco; Thornton was still half drunk.

Mike Nerney and Lionel Stewart were waiting in Nerney's office when the DEA agents brought Thornton from the airport. Thornton was not as surprised as Chai was to learn that Johnny was actually an undercover DEA agent. He wondered, though, if the authorities had enough evidence to put him in jail. 'I have a warrant for your arrest,' said Nerney. But instead of threatening Thornton, Nerney offered him a deal. 'You're guilty as sin,' Nerney said. 'But cooperate with us and I'll not press charges. We want you to go before a grand jury so you can tell them what you know. We want you to do it tomorrow.'

The street-wise Thornton saw an opportunity and agreed to cooperate and appear before a grand jury. Thornton gave his interrogators a carrot. 'I know of a big heroin shipment of at least 100 pounds and it's coming to the U.S. soon,' Thornton revealed. 'If you can give me some time, I can find out the details.' It was a good reason for the U.S. Government to make Thornton an unofficial Cooperating Individual (CI). But Nerney still had the 'stick.' If Thornton double-crossed them—an arrest warrant for violation of code 21USC 959.

Thornton was under oath while testifying the next day, but later admitted that he told the Federal Grand Jury 'just enough, lied a little bit, missed quite a bit and gave them just enough information so they wouldn't lock me up. They thought I was cooperating fully.' Later, Thornton claimed he lied to protect his friends, not to save his own skin.

With the hope of a big bust soon in the offing, and an arrest warrant that could be executed against him at anytime, the authorities let Thornton go. 'He told us enough that we didn't lock his ass up,' Nerney recalled. The prosecutor, though, ordered Thornton to phone his office twice a week to let him know how he was doing and what he was finding out. Thornton traveled to Detroit to visit family. He was free but broke. He called Charles Gillis in Goldsboro and told him he needed some money. Gillis came to Detroit with $ 5,000.

When Thornton called Nerney's office the first time, he was referred to Lionel Stewart who told him that Don Ashton, the DEA Special Agent-in-Charge of the Wilmington, North Carolina Office, wanted to talk to him. Thornton flew to

Wilmington where he met Ashton in a hotel. As the two men talked, Thornton decided that no way was he going to cooperate. There was no reason why he should, Thornton figured. He was going to go to jail sooner or later anyway. Just like that, Thornton decided to double cross Uncle Sam.

Later Thornton explained: 'I asked the authorities while they were talking to me: "If I cooperate like this and you don't press charges, could you or some other agency come up later and press charges on me about this stuff here that you are giving me a break about?" Don (Ashton) said: "We won't, but that doesn't mean another agency can't." I found out later that what he meant was that if they found out later that I didn't tell them everything I knew or something related to that, you know... (sic) if something that I hadn't told them that they didn't know before came up and if another outfit wanted to get me, they possibly could, you know. He (Don Ashton) didn't explain it that thorough, though. I said to myself: "well, it looks like I'm going to jail anyhow. I'll just go ahead and move this stuff, collect my money, party and then go to jail." That's what I was thinking.'

ON OCTOBER 14, Thornton decided to head for Augusta, Georgia, and see William K. Brown who was now assigned to Fort Gordon and working at the base hospital. He wanted to pick up the 114 pounds of heroin that Brown had shipped July 10th from Bangkok in his household goods. Brown and his family had left Bangkok on September 8th and arrived at Augusta on September 13 Brown's household goods, which contained the heroin packed in 30 to 34 plastic bags inside the teakwood furniture, were delivered to him on October 8.

Thornton did not have Brown's contact information so he went to the Dwight D. Eisenhower Medical Center at Fort Gordon where Brown worked. Located just a few miles southwest of the city of Augusta, Georgia, Fort Gordon is the home of the U.S. Army's Signal Corp. But, ironically, at the time Fort Gordon housed the Provost Marshal General's School and trained all of the Army's military police.

Thornton got the man on duty to look at the staff locator index and give him Brown's phone number. It was early in the morning and Thornton's call woke Brown up.

'Do you know who this is?' Thornton asked.

'Yes, I do,' Brown said.

'Could you come down to work a little early? I'm here to pick up the stuff.'

'I'll be right there,' Brown said.

When Brown arrived, Joyce, William's wife, was with him. Thornton thought it best that Joyce did not see him, and he stayed out of sight until Joyce drove off.

'When are you getting off work?' Thornton asked Brown.

'I can take some time when I get my break round 11 or 11:30 (a.m.).'

'I need some sleep,' Thornton said. 'I've been driving all night. Your wife has your car. You can drop me off at the hotel now and take mine. Here's $200 to buy some luggage for the stuff. I'll get some sleep. I'll see you at your break. We can move the dope then.'

Thornton stayed at a dumpy hotel, registering as Frank Scott. Brown picked up Thornton as scheduled and they went to work.

Seven of the pieces of furniture that Brown shipped from Bangkok had false bottoms containing heroin. That first day Thornton and Brown took the heroin from the false bottoms of the three nightstands. They turned the tables upside down, screwed off the false bottoms, took out the plastic bags containing the heroin and put it in the luggage that Brown had purchased. Brown and Thornton could not finish the job that first day, so they put the luggage with the heroin in them and the still empty suitcases in the loft and agreed to meet the next day during Brown's late morning break. Thornton returned to his dumpy hotel and spent the night.

The next morning, however, Brown was busy at work and did not get free until 12:45 PM Thornton picked Brown up and they rushed over to Brown's house to finish the job. They handled the furniture and contraband in the same way they did the first day. While they worked, Thornton discussed the money Brown had coming.

'I've no problem with that,' Brown said. 'Don't worry about it. I'm in no rush.' Brown was more interested in getting the furniture out of the way so his wife could organize the house the way she wanted it——and stop bitching.

'Let's put the screws back,' Thornton said. 'We'll leave the furniture here. Someone will come in two or three days to get it out of the way.'''

'Fine, the sooner the better,' said Brown.

Thornton put the heroin in the trunk of his car and drove the 260-odd miles to Goldsboro where he spent the night at a guesthouse. The next morning he drove over to Gillis's house and informed him that he had the Brown shipment in the trunk of his car. They took the heroin out and stored it in Gillis's carport. Later that day, the heroin was taken out to the country down a desolate road to a farmhouse. Here the dope was transferred to one of Ike's relatives.

Thornton was to be paid $100,000 for the job, but he was given half that amount less $10,000 he owed Ike. Thornton and Gillis returned to Gillis's house where they drank until Gillis had to go to work. Thornton left for Raleigh where he stayed at the Alamo Hotel on North Boulevard. On the evening of October 17, Thornton drove to Beckley, West Virginia, where he planned to spend the weekend visiting his sister. Thornton had been working hard, but it was not in the service of Uncle Sam.

ON OCTOBER 17, the day Freddie Thornton traveled to West Virginia, the Atkinson drug ring was about to make its second big heroin shipment using teakwood furniture and another U.S. serviceman who was relocating from Thailand to the States. U.S. military Customs officials were scheduled to come by Sergeant Jasper Myrick's residence at 270/23 Soi Ekkamai off Sukhumvit Road and conduct a routine check of the household goods and furniture he was sending to Fort Benning, Georgia, where he was being re-assigned. Fort Benning, a U.S. Army installation south of Columbus, Georgia, is home of the U.S. Army Infantry School.

Myrick had agreed to help out his friend Jimmy Smedley by taking some of his teakwood furniture back to the U.S. with him. The furniture contained false bottoms that hid 94 pounds of heroin. This would not have been a problem for Myrick except for Charles Winchester Thomas, one of the Customs officers inspecting the furniture, who took his job seriously and did it well.

The shipping list Thomas had with him showed that Myrick planned to ship six pieces of furniture: a teak desk, two china cabinets, a cedar chest and two end tables. Thomas and his assistant first inspected the household goods on the ground floor. Finding everything in order, the agents told Valerie Myrick, Jasper's wife, that she could start packing the goods. Then the agents went upstairs to check the furniture in the bedroom. Valerie did not accompany the agents upstairs because she was occupied with a Thai man who had come by to collect some money. Valerie did not fully understand the man, and she wanted her husband to come downstairs and translate for her.

Meanwhile, Thomas was inspecting an end table in the bedroom when he noted that the marks in the woodwork indicated the end table had been tampered with. 'What's this?' He asked. Myrick started to get nervous. 'Hey brother,' he coaxed the inspector, holding his arm. 'You don't need to look at that, do you?' Thomas, who was African American, tall, heavy and imposing, looked at the young GI and said, 'Step aside.' Thomas drilled through the bottom of the end table, and when he pulled it out, the drill bit had white powder on it. When he unscrewed the bottom of the end table and plastic bags filled with white powder fell out. He took a closer look and had no doubt. It was heroin. When Winchester began unscrewing the bottoms of some of the other pieces of furniture, he found more plastic bags filled with white powder.

When Valerie Myrick went to the bedroom to get her husband, she saw Thomas holding two plastic bags containing white powder. Thomas asked Valerie if she knew what it was.

'No, I don't,' she said.

'Well, it's heroin,' Winchester explained.

Valerie turned to Jasper and asked: 'Where is this from?' Her husband was as silent as the sphinx.

The Customs officers went downstairs and rechecked the other pieces of furniture and found more heroin. A routine inspection had become a major heroin bust, up to that point the biggest in Thai history. The Thai authorities estimated that the heroin found in Myrick residence, if cut and sold on the streets of the U.S., would be worth $22 million.

Thomas phoned the Thai police and the DEA and told them to come to the house. The police took Myrick into custody where he denied any knowledge of the heroin and insisted that he was shipping the furniture as a favor to Smedley. A few days later, investigators from the U.S. Army Criminal Investigation

Division (CID) interrogated him and administered a polygraph test. Myrick failed.

Gary Fouse, a retired DEA agent, was working in the DEA's Bangkok office when the Myrick bust went down. Fouse interviewed Myrick. 'He wasn't a bad kid but he struck me as naive,' Fouse re-called. 'He was in his early 20s, from Montgomery, Alabama, and a religious family. When we were taking Myrick in, he whispered in my ear: "come visit me in prison." I went to see him at the Klong Prem Prison, where I met with him in a small room that had a caged wire separating us. He told me Smedley had recruited him.'

Myrick came clean and gave a statement to the Thai police. The heroin in the furniture belonged to Smedley, who had hired him to ship it to the U.S. after Smedley learned Myrick was being re-assigned Stateside. Myrick said Smedley and Rudolph Jennings had bought the teak furniture at a furniture shop on Sukhumvit Road. The Thai police were able to find an employee of Sukhumvit Furniture who identified Smedley and Jennings from photographs as the two men who came to order some furniture that would have 'a lot space at the bottom.'

Fouse had the opportunity to interrogate Smedley, but unlike many people who warmed to the man many considered to be the 'Black Ambassador to Bangkok,' Fouse was unimpressed. 'Smedley was an asshole…just a big-time drunk. Yes, he was affable, but shifty. He denied to the end he was involved with the heroin shipment.'

IN THE WAKE of the Myrick bust, the Thai police widened their net. They claimed to have found seventeen witnesses, both American and Thai, who stood ready to testify against Smedley and Myrick. Police Lieutenant Kulachart Singhala told the press that he believed some 'American VIPs were behind the heroin trafficking.' 'The police knew some of them,' he said, but conceded that, 'although the police were willing to make more arrests if they could find witnesses willing to testify, it was difficult to do that in major cases since the witnesses feared reprisals.' Bail was set at 2.7 million baht ($135,000) each for Myrick and Smedley. The Thai authorities felt certain no one could raise that kind of bail money.

WHEN THE THAI authorities expelled Thornton in early September 1975, they searched his house and, among other things, found a permanent change of station order transferring Sergeant William K. Brown from SEATO (Southeast Asian Treaty Organization) to the Dwight D. Eisenhower Medical Center at Fort Gordon, Georgia. Not much was thought of the find at the time. But when Myrick's orders were found in Jimmy Smedley's briefcase, after he was arrested for arranging the Myrick shipment, it clicked. Was Brown also involved with the Atkinson drug ring? Could this be the heroin shipment Thornton had mentioned to Nerney and Stewart when they interrogated him on September 9 in San Francisco?

'I was in San Francisco when I got the call from Bangkok about the Brown orders,' said Addario the DEA Special Agent-in-Charge who oversaw the investigation of the Ike Atkinson drug ring in Thailand. 'I immediately called Don Ashton {of the Wilmington, North Carolina and a CENTAC 9 field coordinator} and flew the next day to Augusta. Don picked me up at the airport. It was a rainy day. CENTAC 9 agents had already set up surveillance at Brown's house in Fort Gordon.'

A large pile of furniture covered with canvas was sitting outside on Brown's patio. Could that be the teak furniture from Thailand? When Ashton and Lutz arrived at the scene, and Lutz saw the furniture sitting outside, he got a sinking feeling that they had arrived too late. Ashton got a search warrant from the United States Attorney's Office in Augusta while the other

DEA agents maintained surveillance. When Ashton returned, the agents served the warrant.

Fortunately for the DEA, Thornton had still not gotten the furniture removed and out of Joyce Brown's hair as he said he would. The DEA began examining the furniture out on the patio that was listed on the search warrant. They found that the false bottoms had been removed from the furniture, and that the furniture contained no heroin. Still, they spotted traces of white powder on the furniture and Thai newspapers that apparently had been used to pack the bags of heroin in the false bottoms had traces of white powder on some of the pages as well. Brown was read his rights and asked to produce the shipping documents for the furniture he had sent from Bangkok. Brown complied. The furniture and newspapers were delivered to the Criminal Investigation Division (CID) forensic lab at Fort Gordon and the traces of white powder were analyzed. Bingo! The analysis indicated that the white powder traces were 90 to 100 percent pure heroin. Sergeant William K. Brown and his wife, Joyce, were on their way to jail.

IN OCTOBER 1975, Chai and his drug courier Chalermphol Phitakstrakul were indicted in San Francisco for trafficking heroin intended for importation to the U.S. When Chai stood trial in late December 1975, the prosecution team portrayed him as one of the top five suppliers of heroin to the U.S. Chai's defense team, on the other hand, asserted that Carl Dunlap (true identity withheld) and Lionel Stewart had entrapped him.

Testifying on his own behalf, Chai admitted to being a partner in a Bangkok bar catering to black American servicemen. His American business associates, Chai revealed, were Ike Atkinson, Herman Jackson and James Smedley. Chai said he first met Carl Dunlap in 1968, and that in the following year, Dunlap approached him with an offer to buy 600 to 700 grams of heroin. At first, Chai claimed, he refused, but he was eventually persuaded to do so by Dunlap because Dunlap needed the money. Chai maintained he made nothing on the deal.

In 1971 Dunlap again allegedly persuaded Chai to procure two kilos of heroin for him because, as Chai put it, Dunlap 'wanted to get rich'. This heroin was for a Japanese friend of Dunlap's, and Chai admitted to making $300 to $400 profit on the sale.

Chai also described at his trial what he claimed were his heroin dealings with Ike Atkinson. According to Chai, Ike had offered him a $5,000 'gift' if he could supply Ike with some heroin. Chai admitted to making four to five sales to Atkinson, totaling fifteen to twenty kilograms. Chai, however, claimed that in November 1974 he told Atkinson and Smedley that he would arrange no more sales to them because 'heroin was bad business, and it hurt people.'

Chai told the court that he did not see Dunlap again until March 1975, at which time Dunlap asked the defendant to get him some heroin for an American friend. Chai testified that he refused several times, but was persuaded at last, telling Dunlap it would be his last time. Later that month, Dunlap introduced Chai to Lionel 'Johnny' Stewart, the undercover DEA agent. Chai admitted to selling Johnny slightly less than a kilo of heroin to 'help' Dunlap and claimed that Dunlap's influence was what persuaded him to charge 'Johnny' only $4,700 per kilo.

Chai testified that he saw Dunlap and Stewart three to four times in March 1975. At the end of March, he received a telephone call from Dunlap and Stewart in the U.S., pleading for more heroin.

The defendant also testified that he did not see Dunlap again until June 1975 at Smedley's house. According to Chai, Dunlap again requested that he secure heroin, but Chai refused because he was afraid. Finally, Johnny promised Chai some 'big money' if he allowed the agent to sell some of his heroin in the United States for him on consignment. Chai admitted he agreed to this deal.

Chai testified that it was Stewart's idea for him to come to the U.S. in August 1975, so the defendant could get his $80,000 because Stewart did not want to send that much money to Thailand. At that time, according to Chai, it was Stewart who suggested Chai bring a courier with two or three kilos of additional heroin. The courier was to get $5,000 for the trip. Chai further testified that Stewart promised that he would show him around San Francisco and Las Vegas and get him some blond women.

Chai also gave his version on the meeting with the 'Mr. Big' in Stewart's organization, played by Peter Fong, Stewart's supervisor. According to Chai, Stewart pressured him to deal with Fong. After the negotiations, Fong was supposed to take Chai to Las Vegas and get him the best hotel and a blonde girl. Chai also claimed that the DEA agents tried to get him drunk during this meeting.

The defendant further admitted on the stand that he had told the agent several lies in order to save face—a common Thai personality trait—that he had his own smuggling system and that he had a friend in the Thai police department. During the trial, Chai had continually asserted a defense of entrapment, but he could not recall any threats or promises made by Carl Dunlap. Moreover, he admitted paying for his own ticket to fly to San Francisco.

THE DEFENSE STRATEGY did not work, and Chai was found guilty as charged. Robert Marder, Chai's lawyer, literally and figuratively threw his client on the mercy of the court, reading to U.S. District Judge Oliver J. Carter a famous refrain from The Merchant of Venice, a play the bard, William Shakespeare, wrote.

The quality of mercy is not strained.

It droppeth as the gentle rain from heaven.

Upon the place beneath; it is twice blest.

It blesseth him that gives and him that takes.

The mightiest in the mightiest.

It becomes the throned monarch better than his crown.

Marder told Judge Carter that Chai's wife was dying of leukemia in Thailand and Chai wanted the chance to see her again. The lawyer poured it on, adding that Chai had a young son in Thailand who would not have a father if his client went to jail for a long time.

The judge then heard the government's side. Federal prosecutor Mike Nerney told the judge that the DEA believed Chai was one of the most notorious drug traffickers in the world and had sold 3,200 pounds of pure heroin that had been smuggled to the U.S. market from Thailand. 'You have been on the bench for twenty-five years, your honor,' Nerney said, 'and I'm sure you have never seen as big a drug dealer as this man before and it is not likely you will again.'

The judge obviously agreed with Nerney, for he sentenced Chai to sixty years in prison—15 years on each of the four counts of conspiracy to sell heroin and import it into the U.S.—two of the counts to run consecutively. Chai would have to serve at least thirty years in prison.

THE U.S. GOVERNMENT had a trophy in their War on Drugs, although its claim about Chai's drug-trafficking rank in the pantheon of international drug dealers has to be questioned. Chai was mainly a middle-man supplying heroin to Atkinson. He was not a dealer in his own right for much of his career and apparently had no distributors of his own. In fact, he really did not get involved with the drug trade in any significant way until after Herman 'Jack' Jackson was busted in 1972 and Papa San, the uncle of Jack's wife Nitaya, who was the original source of a large part of Ike's heroin supply, died. Although Chai supplied heroin to the Japanese Connection, Chai's dealings with Lionel Stewart appeared to be his first serious attempt to become a bigger player in the Thai-U.S. drug trade.

Still, it cannot be denied that at the time of his arrest Chai was the only reliable source of heroin for the band of brothers and that posed a serious criminal threat to American society. He had procured heroin twice for Carl Dunlap, numerous times for Ike Atkinson's AWOL bag and APO (Army Post Office) shipments, the furniture shipment that Thornton picked up in California and the huge Myrick and Brown furniture shipments that were by far the largest shipments Ike had ever attempted. Chai had become a serious criminal threat to American society and needed to be taken off the streets. It would be easy enough for Atkinson to replace the Smedleys and Thorntons in his operation, but without a reliable source of heroin it would be much more difficult for him and his band of brothers to continue to operate.

IN APRIL 1979, the DEA responded to a legal move for modification of Chai's sentence. Chai's lawyers requested a ten-year limitation. Chai had spent nearly four years in prison, so if his sentence was reduced, he would have been eligible for immediate parole. In a letter to Judge George B. Harris of the Northern District of California, Peter Bensinger, the head of the DEA, noted that Chai was 'one of the largest sources of heroin on record' and 'the source of supply for the largest Southeast Asian heroin smuggling and distribution ring in U.S. history.' Further, read the letter, 'DEA files show that this group is responsible for the importation of more than 1,000 pounds of heroin into the United States per year between 1967 and 1975.' The letter concluded: 'In view of the above and the fact that Ruviwat continues to pose a serious, potential threat, DEA strongly opposes any reduction in sentence.'

The letter contained one error. As we have seen, Ike and Jack began their drug smuggling operation in 1968, not 1967. Nevertheless, Chai would stay in jail and remain there until 1994 when he was finally released and deported to Thailand.

THE TRIAL OF Jasper Myrick and Jimmy Smedley was scheduled to begin on March 26 1976, in Bangkok Criminal Court, but the court granted the prosecution a stay until June 9 1976, because one of their witnesses, who it declined to name, was overseas. The wait had taken its toll on the 57-year old Smedley. When he appeared in court, he looked wasted and exhausted. Smedley complained about the trial delays. 'I've come here twice expecting the trial to begin and both times it's been put back,' Smedley grumbled. 'When is something going to happen?' When the much younger Myrick appeared in court, he looked as if he had experienced less wear and tear in the Thai jail.

IN MARCH, 1976, at about the time of the Smedley-Myrick trial delay, Peter Bensinger, the head of the DEA, announced in Washington, DC that, in a concerted operation, the DEA had arrested eleven people and that the arrests were related to the bust of Smedley and Myrick in Bangkok. Bensinger provided reporters with an indictment showing that over a 14-month period, from August 1974 to October 1975, these associates of Atkinson had smuggled more than 220 pounds of ultra-pure heroin into the U.S. from Thailand. Bensinger estimated the street value to be $100 million.

Bensinger said that 11 of the 14 people charged in the indictment were past or present U.S. servicemen who had served in Thailand. They smuggled the heroin in false bottoms of flight bags and later in furniture being shipped from Bangkok to the U.S. Although there was no indication that the U.S. Government prosecutors would bring the so-called 'cadaver-heroin connection' into evidence at the trial, the press could not help itself. Outlets like the *Associated Press* and *The Washington Post* reported that 'an early method' of smuggling by this group had included the stuffing of drugs into dead bodies of U.S. servicemen sent back to the United States after being killed in Vietnam.

The indictment said the ring mastermind was 51-year old former Army Master Sergeant Leslie 'Ike' Atkinson of Goldsboro, who, since June 1975 had been serving a 19-year prison sentence for heroin trafficking. The indicted included some familiar names—Rudolph Jennings, Charles Murphy Gillis, James McArthur and William K Brown.

IN JUNE 1976, the trial of Myrick and Smedley finally began in Bangkok. It was short, and the defendants were found guilty. The Thai court did not hesitate in throwing the book at them. The 57-year old Smedley was given a life sentence that might as well have been a death sentence. Myrick also got a life sentence, but it was reduced to thirty-three years because he fully confessed, and his testimony was helpful to the case. In its ruling, the court reasoned that Myrick would not accuse Smedley of being the furniture's owner if it was not true because the two men never had any personal conflicts. The willingness of Valerie Myrick to travel from the U.S. to testify on

Jasper's behalf no doubt helped her husband, but it was little consolation to him. He would be eligible for membership in the American Association of Retired People (AARP), the U.S.'s leading advocacy group for senior citizens, before he would be eligible to get out of prison.

For whatever reason, Myrick did not appeal his case, but Smedley did. And it got him acquitted. An appeals court overturned the lower court's ruling because it found that the evidence upon which the authorities issued a warrant in the case was insufficient and that Myrick's testimony was not sufficient to warrant Smedley's conviction.

The Appeals Court ordered Smedley's detention for another 30 days in case the prosecution filed an appeal to the Thai Supreme Court. But that didn't happen and Smedley walked.

How in the world did that happen? Living in Bangkok for some time, Smedley knew the ropes of the Bangkok legal system and how to grease the right palms. Peter Finucane, a reporter with the *Bangkok Post* at the time of Smedley's arrest, conviction, and subsequent exoneration, was a friend of Smedley and enjoyed a drink or two with him after he was released from jail. Smedley confided to Finucane about how he beat the wrap. 'At the time, Jimmy had a limited amount of money, so there was no point for him in trying to bribe the criminal court, which gave him the life sentence,' Finucane recalled. 'The lower court would have appealed, so he spent what money he had on trying to bribe one member of the Appeals Court. That member subsequently influenced his colleagues on the panel, and Smedley walked.'

Journalist John McBeth, who at the time was writing about the Atkinson drug ring for *Asiaweek* magazine, has a different take on what happened: 'I was told at the time that Smedley paid $50,000 to win his acquittal in Thailand and that to get the money his brother had to mortgage his house in Los

Angeles and a set of golf clubs. The money was apparently paid to the prosecutor. Smedley told me as much in front of two witnesses.'

After the trial Smedley returned to his high-profile lifestyle and was once again a familiar figure in Bangkok's bar and nightlife scene. How Smedley ended up being extradited to the U.S. is still unclear. According to Finucane, one day Smedley told a group of his friends, including Finucane, that he planned to go to Hong Kong. Why he wanted to do that nobody knew, but friends tried to talk Smedley out of it. 'He was advised to stay put,' Finucane recalled. 'Thailand did not have an extradition treaty with the U.S., Hong Kong did. He was safe in Thailand, but Smedley did not listen. He went to Hong Kong, and, as soon as he got off the plane, he was arrested and extradited to the U.S.'

According to McBeth, though, Smedley was arrested at his rented home in Bangkok and taken from there by Thai immigration officers to Don Muang Airport, where he was handed over to the two DEA agents. The flight they boarded went through Hong Kong to the U.S.

Whatever the true story, it is ironic that Jimmy Smedley, who had talked Myrick into the attempted smuggling venture, ended up spending his days and nights in a relatively plush U.S. prison while Myrick languished in Thailand.

CHAPTER 15
Behind Bars

BY MID-1976, IKE Atkinson's drug empire was in shambles. His reversal of fortunes took root in 1972 when William Herman Jackson, his partner, was busted in Denver. Jack had already spent four years in Leavenworth Federal Penitentiary and would remain locked up for several more years. Luchai Ruviwat, Ike's main heroin supplier, was in jail as well and scheduled to remain there for three decades. Jimmy Smedley was imprisoned in Bangkok but, in terms of Ike's drug ring, he no longer mattered. Ike had long since given up on his likeable friend and his inebriated ways. Besides, Ike would lose touch with Jimmy Smedley after he bribed his way out of Thai prison. Ike had made Freddie Thornton his main man in Bangkok, but that move was looking more and more like a big mistake. Ike believed that Thornton had done a good job, but he had heard through his lawyers that Thornton had struck a deal with Uncle Sam in the wake of the DEA's October 24 1975, raid on William K. Brown's residence in Augusta, Georgia.

Ike had been one of fourteen people indicted in March 1976 on a major Federal drug conspiracy charge. He and ten of the other co-indicted alleged conspirators had pleaded not guilty, while two, James Smedley and Jasper Myrick, were in prison in Bangkok awaiting trial on a drug trafficking charge and the possibility of being extradited to the U.S. for trial on Federal drug trafficking charges. Only one of the indicted, Freddie Thornton, had not been sent to jail.

On March 22 1976, two days before the indictment was unsealed, Federal prosecutors issued a warrant for Thornton's arrest. The warrant's purpose—to get Thornton into protective custody before the indictment became public. In becoming an informant, Thornton negotiated with Uncle Sam what many observers considered to be a sweetheart deal, given his role in Ike's organization and the fact that he trafficked in the more than 100 pounds of heroin stashed at the Brown residence while supposedly being in the U.S. Government's service. Thornton received a suspended five-year sentence, five years of probation, and a $10,000 fine. Thornton was released on a $100,000 personal recognizance bond.

Sometimes to ensure victory in court the prosecution must make a deal with the devil, law enforcement officials often rationalize. The physical evidence in the 1976 drug conspiracy case was impressive, but to tie all the pieces of the conspiracy together, the prosecution needed Freddie Thornton's testimony. He knew who did what and with whom and when. 'In a conspiracy case it is necessary to have someone, preferably someone on the inside, spell out the conspiracy, while we, as investigators, identify and document the overt acts and corroborate the witnesses,' explained Don Ashton, the DEA Special Agent who headed the DEA's Wilmington, North Carolina office and spearheaded CENTAC 9, the DEA agency that conducted much of the Ike Atkinson drug ring investigation. 'We do not always have a choice about who the witnesses are, but without a primary witness, the case is often lost and the organization continues. We spoke to a number of potential witnesses, and I told them that the first one on the bus gets a free ride; the rest go to jail. I guess, considering Thornton's involvement, some might say he got a good deal. But he was the first one on the bus, and without him, we would not have had the impact we had on this (Ike's) organization.'

The indictment led to the biggest drug trafficking trial in North Carolina history. The U.S. Government maintained that all defendants in the case where members in good standing of the Atkinson organization over a protracted period of time. 'I would say that this organization has to be classified as one of the largest heroin smuggling organizations in the world whose actions directly affected the United States,' Ashton told the press.

Mike Nerney had ceded the case to the U.S. Attorney's Office in Raleigh, and Joe Dean, an Assistant U.S. Attorney in North Carolina, prosecuted the case. Dean explained that the Atkinson organization had been under investigation for a number of years, and the case got a big investigative push in October 1975 when the DEA organized its tactical unit, CENTAC 9. The case was so big that it included investigators from Bangkok, New York City, Atlanta, Wilmington and Baltimore.

THE PROSPECT OF Ike manipulating a get-out-of-jail-early card from the American legal system was looking dimmer by the day. On October 24 1975, Ike made his first attempt to have his 19-year "palm print" conviction reduced. Ike had pleaded no contest, and Judge John D. Larkins, Jr. had structured the palm print sentence so that Ike could be eligible for parole within a relatively short period of time, given Ike's relatively clean record, family ties and what the court described as 'good personal characteristics.' Now, Ike's attorneys argued before Judge Larkins that their client should have his prison sentence reduced because of 'family problems.' Ike's wife, Atha, it seemed, had relapsed into alcoholism, and without a healthy mother, several of the children needed special care that only Ike could provide.

Given these personal problems, the lawyers contended, Ike's 19-year sentence (15 years on the first count and four years on the second to be served consecutively) should run concurrently. That would substantially reduce his prison time.

Assistant U.S. Attorney Thomas McNamara strongly opposed a sentence reduction, telling the court, 'Family problems should not interfere with justice.' Judge Larkins agreed. 'All criminal defendants have family problems, which they caused themselves and not the court or prosecution,' the judge ruled. 'In view of the fact that the defendant states that he has employed maids and nurses to help care for his family, it appears he is in a much better position than most criminal defendants.'

With the 19-year prison sentence remaining intact, Ike now had to go to trial again, this time for conspiracy to traffic and distribute heroin. Prosecutor Joe Dean told the jury: 'We have put evidence before you of 126 kilos of heroin, some of it has been brought and laid before you on the clerk's desk and in further testimony, you have seen pictures of 47 kilos of heroin in the Myrick shipment—103 bags of pure heroin shipped to this country... that's what the case is about; about the international big business of importing dope into this country.'

Later, the U.S. Government conceded that at trial it had only offered evidence of about some of the activities of the Atkinson drug ring—that for which they had evidence. The prosecution contended they could prove the defendants trafficked in about 354 pounds of pure heroin that could produce 54 million dosage units. According to Uncle Sam's calculation, the individual dosage units normally sold for $10 on the street, meaning that the approximate retail value of the heroin the Atkinson ring smuggled into the U.S. stood at approximately half a billion dollars. This staggering figure, the prosecution argued, showed the mammoth scope of Ike's drug ring activities, making the ring one of the largest heroin conspiracies in the United States over the past several years.

THE PROSECUTORS HAD a star witness and were confident they had a solid case, but they still expected a tough trial. 'The case was no slam dunk,' explained Christie Whitcover Dean, a now retired Federal prosecutor who assisted in the case's prosecution. 'You never know what a jury is going to do. It was tough to get Ike because like any good CEO he was insulated. But we did have a lot of evidence that could be corroborated.'

Freddie Thornton was the first witness the prosecution called after jury selection, and his testimony comprised more than 800 pages of transcribed court testimony. Thornton testified about how he headed the Thai operation of Ike's drug ring before it was broken up by the CENTAC 9 investigation. He revealed how he had used unsuspecting military personnel to help smuggle the heroin in military aircraft and how he helped buy and package the drugs. Under cross examination, Thornton admitted that he led the U.S. law enforcement to believe he could help them break a smuggling operation and that he lied to a grand jury in San Francisco after being arrested in Thailand and expelled from the country.

Ike watched Thornton's testimony in court impressively roll on and could not understand how he could be so wrong about a man. Ike considered Thornton to be the biggest mistake he had ever made in his life.

The prosecution called other witnesses besides Thornton. Lionel Stewart testified about his undercover work negotiating with Luchai 'Chai' Ruviwat and linked him to Atkinson. Herbert Houseton and Robert Ernest Patterson, who had participated in Ike's postal connection, where able to tie several of the defendants to the conspiracy. Many of the defendants testified in their own defense.

DEA Special Agent Chuck Lutz flew from Bangkok to testify at the trial. Lutz was a Thai speaker and prosecutor Joe Dean used him to introduce into evidence the Thai newspapers that had been found in the false bottom of Brown's furniture. When Lutz was handed the newspapers by Prosecutor Dean, Judge Dupree asked to see them. After examining the Thai Sanskrit writing, he quipped, "This looks like the voter registration forms we used to use here in North Carolina years ago."

Finally, on May 19 1976, the four-men and eight-women jury came back with its verdict. Nine of the 14 defendants were found guilty of participating in a drug conspiracy. Ike received a sentence of 25 years to be served consecutively with his 19-year palm print sentence, and a $50,000 fine. Without any successful appeals or court reductions in his sentence, Ike would not get out of prison until 2020. He would be about 95 years old.

Dressed in his military uniform and decked out with his ribbons, Sergeant William K. Brown stood at attention as Judge Franklin T. Dupree, Jr., sentenced the ten-and-one-half year veteran soldier to ten years in prison and fined him $5,000. Air Force Sergeant Charles Murphy Gillis was only months away from his 20-year retirement and was still assigned to Seymour Johnson Air Force Base. He asked the judge to give him time to determine whether the Air Force was going to discharge him and take away his retirement benefits. The judge told Gillis he would sentence him whenever that matter was settled. Eventually, Gillis lost his retirement and was given a ten-year sentence and a $5,000 fine. James McArthur, Ernest Patterson and Rudolph Jennings also received ten years and a $10,000 fine. Most of the convicted showed little emotion.

IN OCTOBER 1976, the DEA terminated CENTAC 9, one of the most successful of all CENTAC investigations. After a year of operation, it cost just $55,475.77 to fund the takedown of one of the biggest American drug trafficking rings ever to operate from Southeast Asia. Most of the money was spent on travel and per diem expenses. In Don Ashton's official report to DEA headquarters, he wrote about the impact of the operation on North Carolina: "CENTAC 9 had a very significant impact on the heroin availability in North Carolina. Prior to the operation, white heroin was both prevalent and immediately available throughout the State. After the completion of CENTAC 9, and to the present time, white heroin is rare and the overall availability of heroin in North Carolina has been significantly reduced." The impact was much broader, of course, considering Ike's heroin was supplying drug dealers primarily in New York, Pennsylvania, Washington, DC, and elsewhere

THE TRIAL WAS over and the authorities transferred Ike from the Wake County jail in Raleigh to the federal penitentiary in Atlanta. But he left behind a trail of rumors and innuendos of corruption. The press reported that while Ike was in the county jail in Raleigh, before and during his 1976 Federal trial, he had bribed his jailers to allow him to have parties in his cell with liquor, women and gambling. At the time, Stephen Nimocks, one of Ike's lawyers, said: 'If any of that happened, I was certainly not aware of it. The only time I saw him was when they brought him from the jail cell to the consulting room.'

That was hardly a ringing endorsement of innocence. But, fortunately for Ike's reputation, North Carolina Governor Jim Hunt appointed a special prosecutor to investigate the allegations. Joe Cheshire, a young 30-year-old lawyer who had graduated from Wake Forest University law school in 1973, conducted a thorough year-long investigation in which he interviewed the county sheriff's deputies, jail employees and prisoners in the Wake County jail. Cheshire also went to Atlanta to interview Ike. 'In my entire professional legal career—and I have been involved with defendants in hundreds of drug cases—I have never met a more pleasant person who was convicted of a serious crime,' Cheshire recalled.

Cheshire presented his findings to Governor Hunt. 'I reported that there was widespread corruption in the Wake County jail, but it was not because of Ike Atkinson or the other prisoners,' Cheshire explained. 'The jailers were responsible for it. My investigation led to a number of firings and convictions, and the state moved to clean up the jail system.'

FOR IKE, EXONERATION in the Wake County jail scandal was a small victory that did not change the sobering reality. He could spend the next 44 years in a 6" by 9" jail cell. He could continue to spend thousands of dollars in appeals to try to dig himself out of his hole, but, in all likelihood, he would likely never see the 'light at the end of the tunnel.'

'I always believed that as long as I did things right I would never get caught,' Ike recalled. 'So I never thought about the consequences. But I could not foresee how things would work out. Eventually, I depended upon too many people and a lot of things spun out of my control. Still, I wasn't afraid of prison because I knew I could do the time.'"

Ike had some good friends in the Atlanta pen who helped him learn the ropes of prison life. Thomas 'Sonny' Southerland, who had accompanied Ike and two cadavers on that fateful night in December 1972, was still in prison and at the Atlanta facility. Ike had always treated Sonny as a younger brother, and he took Sonny under his wing.

In a remarkable development, Herman 'Jack' Jackson was also transferred to Atlanta. Why would two partners in one of the 1970s biggest drug rings end up in the same prison? Could not such an arrangement help to create the conditions under which a criminal conspiracy could continue to function? Law enforcement officials say that the federal prison system is a huge complex, so it is difficult to keep track of who is in which prison, with whom.

When Jack showed up at Atlanta, Ike was already inclined to believe that his transfer was not a bureaucratic screw-up, but a move to bring Jack to the prison to snitch on him. After all, how often does a comet hit the earth? Unknown to Ike at the time, Jack had been singing to the authorities at the Leavenworth Federal Penitentiary and with U.S. Attorney's Office in Denver, where he had been tried and convicted of smuggling 21 pounds of heroin that had somehow disappeared from the hangar at Lowry Air Force Base.

Jack told Paul Cooper, Assistant U.S. Attorney in Denver, that he had information about drug trafficking in Philadelphia, and he was willing to share it if he could get a reduction in sentence. Cooper called Arlen Specter, the District Attorney in Philadelphia at that time, who would later become famous as a U.S. Senator, and Jackson's information led to the arrest and conviction of at least three-dozen people in Philadelphia. As he had promised Jack, Cooper went back to court to get his sentence reduced. Cooper and Jack, however, were in for a big surprise. Cooper recalled: 'I told the judge how Jackson's information had helped the authorities and why he should get his sentence reduced. The judge said to Jack: "You did all this while behind bars for several years? I can't let you out. You will still be a menace to society on the street. Request denied"'

But Ike was not going to let the threat of Jack being a snitch cramp his lifestyle. He was happy to see Jack—after all, he was still his best friend. Ike used his money and charisma to make life comfortable for Jack, Sonny and anyone else who became part of his circle. Ike bribed the guards for favors, such as getting them to buy him good pizza and cigars or a nice radio that he could use to keep up with world news. 'Ike could get anything he wanted in the Atlanta pen, and he was treated quite well,' said Talbot Smith, one of Ike's lawyers who visited Ike often. 'Ike didn't want drugs or women, just mainly food. He literally controlled the prison and the guards and prisoners, and they treated him with respect.'

Ike made friends easily, especially when other prisoners began learning about his place in the roll call of big-time drug dealers. One day the word came ricocheting down the prison corridor. 'Goldfinger is here!' Another celebrity gangster had arrived at the Atlanta pen. Jimmy 'Goldfinger' Terrell was one of the big-time Harlem drug dealers of the 1970s. Ike knew of Harry Terrell, Goldfinger's brother, but he had never met 'Goldfinger.' 'He turned out to be one of the nicest guys,' Ike recalled. 'We got along fine.'

Ike met Joe Stassi at the laundry. 'Well, if it isn't Mr. Atkinson,' Stassi said in his clipped, tough talking manner straight out of the 'Godfather'. Ike knew who Joe Stassi was—a well-connected mobster in La Cosa Nostra with powerful criminal friends in high places. Ike and Stassi hit it off and they became good friends. Ike thought Stassi was some kind of 'godfather' but came to learn that he was really a soldier in La Cosa Nostra. Still, Stassi had powerful connections in La Cosa Nostra. Stassi knew all the legendary gangsters—Lucky Luciano, Meyer Lansky and Bugsie Siegel, for example—and had killed many people for the Mob, and did it often.

During his testimony in 1962 before a Senate Subcommittee, Mafia turncoat Joseph Valachi named Joe Stassi a member of La Cosa Nostra. By this time, the FBI was already investigating him. A grand jury in Corpus Christi, Texas, indicted Stassi on a heroin importation charge, but he went on the run for three years before being captured in one of the

FBI's biggest manhunts at the time. Stassi spent the next 30 years in prison claiming he was framed.

'We would walk the yard together every day,' Ike recalled. 'They called the regular route that Joe took the "Stassi Trail." We would talk about life, our families, Joe's wife who was a former Miss California (beauty contest winner), his son, who was a professor at a university, and the mob scene in New York City.' Ike told Joe about the Italian mobsters who had come to the Atlanta pen to collect the $80,000 that Frank Lucas owed the Mob. Stassi had never heard of Lucas, but he had a good laugh anyway.

Walking the Stassi Trail became part of Ike's daily routine. He also worked as a clerk typist and barbershop orderly in Prison Industries where, according to prison reports, he received 'meritorious pay and meritorious time.' But while adjusting to prison life, Ike was also trying to keep an eye on the considerable assets he had left behind. He was receiving reports he did not like. Ike had a stash of heroin hidden in the countryside near Goldsboro. The location of the heroin stash was supposed to be a secret, but he heard that some members of his own family were stealing from it. 'I don't know how much dope I had out in the country, but it could have been worth as much as $50 million,' Ike explained. 'The frustrating part of it—I was locked up and I really couldn't do anything about it. I guess my situation made it too tempting for some of those close to me.'

Disloyal family members were not the only people who concerned Ike. He was also becoming suspicious of some of the people who were supposed to be handling his affairs while he remained behind bars. Ike hired Talbot Smith, a prominent criminal defense lawyer, to investigate. 'I came to see Ike several times,' Smith recalled. 'He said some things didn't seem right to him. He had concerns and wanted me to investigate the people who were working for him. I checked out one private investigator and found out he was ripping Ike off, so we fired him. I remember checking out Richard Mazur, a lawyer from San Francisco who was doing a lot of appeal work for Ike. Mazur checked out fine. He was doing an excellent job.'

One time, Ike wanted Smith to deliver a message to Frank Lucas about a twenty-kilogram deal. At the time Lucas was incarcerated at the Metropolitan Correction Center (MCC) in New York City. 'I said I wasn't going to do it,' Smith said. 'So he had a young lawyer named Wilbur Fuller go instead. Fuller got arrested because Lucas was an informant. Fuller was sentenced to four years in jail.'

LEON COHEN, AN Atlanta businessman, and Fred Sans, his accountant, were two of the individuals Talbot Smith investigated. Cohen owed more than $600,000 to the IRS due to several tax liens against him. Desperate for money, Cohen devised various schemes between late 1976 and mid-1977 to defraud Ike. It began in November 1976, when Cohen sent his attorney Stanley Galkin and an associate, John Tipton, to see Ike at the Atlanta pen. Cohen offered Ike a deal he did not refuse. Ike bought six kilos of quality heroin for $300,000. Ike and Cohen agreed to a time and place for the exchange, but Cohen arranged for fake cops to make a fake bust, and in a panic, Ike's people fled the scene without the money or drugs.

Sans and Tipton took the money to Cohen's house and counted it over a two-day period. Cohen then sent couriers to several Atlanta banks, ordering them to exchange no more than $5,000 at any one bank so as not to attract attention. In other words, Cohen was trying to launder his dirty money and avoid paying federal taxes. Over the next three months, Cohen also laundered money at the Palm State Bank in Palm Harbor, Florida, where he had corrupted bank officials.

In March and April 1977, Galkin returned to the Atlanta pen and conned more money out of Ike. Under Cohen's direction, Galkin convinced Ike that he had a high government official from the U.S. Attorney General's Office, who, for a $1 million fee, could arrange Ike's release from prison. After receiving a $100,000 'down payment' from one of Ike's associates, Cohen, himself, went to see Ike in prison impersonating Michael Eagan, then Associate U.S. Attorney General in the Jimmy Carter administration.

'I knew Griffin Bell (the U.S. Attorney General) was from Atlanta, so I thought I was making the contacts who would give me a hook into high places,' Ike said. 'Nothing was happening through the courts. I had the money, so I thought putting some money in the right high place gave me a good chance to reduce my sentence.'

Cohen conned Ike out of nearly another $300,000. Not satisfied, Cohen also forged Ike's signature on a note he sent to one of Ike's brothers authorizing payment of $260,000 to Cohen. Then Cohen sent Sans to the Cayman Islands where he arranged a wire transfer of $260,000 from one of Ike's accounts there, using a Canadian bank to send the money to a checking account in Sans's name at the Palm State Bank. Cohen now had close to $1 million dollars of Ike's money.

Uncle Sam, however, was hot on Cohen's trail and he and Sans were arrested and charged with four counts of fraud, money laundering and falsifying facts in a matter under the IRS's jurisdiction. Leon Cohen's case was separated from the other defendants because he was ill. A jury found Sans guilty of the conspiracy charge only.

ON APRIL 16, 1978, Ike was suddenly transferred to the federal penitentiary at Marion in southern Illinois. Built in 1963 on a wildlife refuge, Marion was a replacement for the less practical prison facility at Alcatraz. By the time of Atkinson's transfer, Marion was being touted as the country's most secure facility and the home of its most dangerous prisoners. Despite its reputation, the guard towers and the coiled razor wire cascading from the fences, the prison's look was unimposing. Still, Marion was a state-of-the-art prison for that time. It had new electronic detection systems, armed mobile patrols, remote-controlled gates and closed-circuit television. Each prisoner had his own cell, which included concrete fixtures and a stainless steel toilet.

Prison officials told Ike he was being transferred to Marion because the Atlanta penitentiary was overcrowded. But his transfer was actually part of the U.S. Bureau of Prisons's move to put all the prisoners it considered extraordinarily violent into one secure prison. Some U.S. cities were beginning to have a gang problem, and many of the transferees were gang members who had killed other inmates or assaulted prison officials while incarcerated. 'One day at Atlanta, I was simply told to get my stuff together; I was being moved,' Ike recalled. 'I was put on a bus, and we left Atlanta. Just like that.'

On the way to Marion, the bus stopped at the Lewisburg Federal Penitentiary, located in central Pennsylvania about 120 miles west of Philadelphia. Built in 1932, Lewisburg has housed many famous prisoners in its history, including Alger Hiss, John Gotti, Jimmy Hoffa and Whitey Bolger. The prison became known for its 'Mafia Row,' or G-block, a maximum-security wing that houses many Mafiosi.

'We were to stop at Lewisburg and stay overnight,' Ike recalled. 'While we were on the bus, some of the prisoners planned an escape. They didn't try to recruit me, but I could see what they were doing. The escapees were caught and the guards beat some of them up badly. The prisoners brought a lawsuit and I testified. I didn't know too much about Marion, but after what happened at Lewisburg, I was kind of happy to get there.'

Soon after his arrival at Marion, Ike was brought before the warden and his administrative team. 'The first question they asked me was: "What are you doing here?" I said: "Your guess is as good as mine." They reviewed my record and could see that I may have been a big-time drug dealer, but that I wasn't the violent type and I didn't belong in Marion. The team adjourned and then came back a little later. They said my file indicated I had been involved in a drug conspiracy, a serious crime, but that I had a good prison record at Atlanta. If I kept my nose clean, they would review my file at a later date, and I could get transferred. At the time, the guards at Marion weren't brutal, and there was no twenty-three hour lockdown. The prison wasn't actually that bad.'

Ike settled into his prison routine. He was assigned to the food service department where he worked in the dish tank as the lead man. On September 16 1978, Ike's food service supervisor wrote the following evaluation of Ike: 'Atkinson is an excellent worker who causes no problems whatsoever. He is courteous and polite to officers and inmates alike. This man works with a minimum of supervision, and he is cooperative in every respect. This man does not involve himself in any activities that are questionable. Atkinson is basically a loner, and he has done his own time. He is not a sniveler and accepts his present circumstances as a man who has made a mistake, but would never involve himself in any further criminal activities. Atkinson is friendly to all, but he has made no close ties within the institution.'

Actually, Ike did have some good friends at Marion. Joe Stassi was transferred from Atlanta as well, and once again, every day, the two pals took to a new Stassi Trail. Ike made one of his best friends at Marion in Veronza Bowers, Jr., a dread-locked, charismatic inmate who was in prison for life without parole. Bowers was a former member of the Black Panther Party who, in 1973, was convicted for the murders of a U.S. park ranger on the word of two government informants, both of whom received reduced sentences for other crimes. Since his incarceration, he has become the subject of a concerted campaign to get him released from jail. For Ike, Bowers was a Renaissance Man with many interests, including meditation and the healing arts, especially acupuncture and massage therapy. 'We became good friends and still are,' Ike recalled. 'Veronza is a health nut and into exercise. Veronza stayed after me to lead a healthier lifestyle. He was an inspiration. I tried to follow his advice.'

HARLEM GANGSTER LEROY 'Nicky' Barnes was at Marion when Ike arrived. Dubbed 'Mr. Untouchable' for his uncanny ability to avoid arrest, Barnes was considered so dangerous that, when he went on trial for his crimes in 1978, the court made the jury anonymous, the first time that had happened in American history. The popular song *Bad, Bad Leroy Brown* was supposedly written with Barnes in mind.

'Mr. Untouchable' Barnes was arrested in March 1977, but while on bond, he gave an interview to *The New York Times Magazine*. The article portrayed Barnes as a clever operator who enjoyed his popularity in Harlem, engaged in a lavish lifestyle and seemed to have made a career out of avoiding arrest and embarrassing law enforcement groups. On the front page of the magazine was the article's bold title: 'Mr. Untouchable,' with the subtext: 'The police say that Nicky Barnes may be Harlem's biggest drug dealer. Now the government will try to prove it.'

Uncle Sam reacted like a bull with a red flag waved in its face. The day after the article appeared, Robert Fiske, the lead prosecutor on the Barnes case, received a call from Griffin Bell, the U.S. Attorney General in the Jimmy Carter administration.

'Bell explained that President Carter said he considered the Barnes case the most important one in the country, and he wanted the government to put all of its resources towards it so we could get the arrogant drug dealer off the streets,' Fiske explained in this author's 2007 book, *Gangsters of Harlem*. Barnes was convicted and sentenced to life without parole.

Ike could see Barnes watching him whenever their paths crossed at Marion. Barnes, no doubt, knew who Ike was, but he made no effort to get acquainted. That was fine with Ike. The kingpin had no intention of paying homage to Mr. Untouchable. Then one day in the yard, while Ike and Joe were on the Stassi Trail, chatting, Barnes came up suddenly and tried to butt in on their conversation. The usually mild-mannered Ike got angry and scolded Mr. Untouchable. 'Man, I never saw anything like that,' Ike said. 'Someone had to teach Nicky some manners. I jumped on him and said he couldn't do that. He needed to introduce himself first.'

Ike later became friendly with Barnes and they would talk about their former criminal careers. Invariably, their conversation turned to Frank Lucas. 'Nicky was obsessed with Lucas,' Ike recalled. 'Frank was all he would talk about. Nicky really disliked Frank.'

Eventually, Barnes turned out to be a big snitch just like Frank Lucas. Indeed, Barnes turned out to be one of the most important and productive government witnesses in U.S. history. For fifteen months, he talked to his former associates, wife and girlfriend as the Feds listened in on wiretaps. And then he went undercover behind prison walls, exposing himself to great harm while gathering information as an informant.

When Barnes's 'tour of duty' for the Feds finally ended, his information was enough to put most of the associates from his old gang behind bars and put more than 50 other people behind bars. Barnes supplied information about a terrorist involved in robberies and prison escapes and testified before congressional hearings and presidential commissions about the inner workings of the narcotics industry and what the government could do about it.

When Ike and Barnes were transferred from Marion to the Federal pen at Terry Haute, Indiana, Ike began to have his suspicions about Barnes. When they were together, Ike would get the weird feeling that Barnes was trying to set him up. 'At Terre Haute, Nicky began to pry, trying to get my confidence,' Ike recalled. 'He was always going down to R and D (Receiving and Dispatch). I found out later he was going there to meet somebody from the U.S. Attorney General's Office. But you know what? If I had to make a choice between Nicky Barnes and Frank Lucas, I would take Barnes any day.' Given the events relating to Lucas that followed in Ike's life, his assessment is understandable.

CHAPTER 16

What Goes Around

IN SEPTEMBER 1978, five months after arriving at Marion Federal Penitentiary, Ike Atkinson was on the move again, this time to Raleigh, North Carolina, to stand trial as a high-profile defendant in the biggest drug trafficking trial in North Carolina history. The previous March, Ike was one of 14 people, nine of whom were his relatives, indicted on a familiar charge, one that had already put him in prison in 1976 for 25 years: conspiracy to traffic in illicit drugs. This time the indictment came from the state of North Carolina, not Uncle Sam, and stemmed from the seizure in the spring of 1977 of 13.3 pounds of 98 percent pure heroin worth $70 million. Others indicted were Ike's three brothers, Dallas, Ezzell, and Edward, Sr.; his three nephews, Larry, Philip Wade, and Dallas Edward; John McConnell and Wilbur Cleo Fuller, two attorneys for the alleged Atkinson organization; James Harper and Lawrence Fuller, who were identified as couriers for the Atkinson organization; and a woman named Laura Jones Holmes, whom prosecutors described as a business associate.

THE MARCH 1978 indictment was the result of a year-long investigation in North Carolina, New York, New Jersey, Ohio, and Georgia that involved 100 law enforcement agents from the North Carolina State Bureau of Investigation (SBI), the U.S. Drug Enforcement Administration (DEA), the District

Attorney's Office in Essex County (Newark) New Jersey and local law enforcement officers from North Carolina's Wayne, Lenoir and Johnston counties.

Once the State of North Carolina announced the indictment, the press went digging to find out more about the defendants. James Harper's arrest shocked his fellow workers at the Cherry Hospital in Goldsboro where he had worked 14 years and nine months as a health care technician at $10,596 per year. Harper supervised the employees who cared for alcoholic patients at the hospital. 'He was a good employee who got along well with his fellow employees,' stated Ida Mae Lucas, the director of nursing at the hospital and Harper's immediate supervisor.

THE FRAIL, PETIT Laura Holmes looked an unlikely drug dealer. Born in 1943 in Goldsboro, she had grown up with the Atkinson children and socialized with some of them. She spent time in New York City and Washington, DC, before returning in the early 1970s to Goldsboro where she began working at the telephone company. In the late 1960s, Holmes began hearing rumors about how Ike Atkinson was involved with illegal drugs, but she 'reserved judgment.' One day, she met William Herman 'Jack' Jackson at Ike's house on Neuse Circle. Jack was two decades older than her, but Holmes found him to be a charismatic and good-looking man with pretty eyes. Jack eventually asked her out, and she became one of his girlfriends. Looking back now, Holmes thinks Jack was 'setting her up.' She began doing 'favors' for Jack and Ike. After the authorities transferred Jack to the Atlanta pen, she visited him to pick up messages and receive instructions. As she continued to work in the Atkinson organization, Holmes worried about getting busted. 'The authorities didn't arrest me for a long time, but I knew they were coming,' Holmes recalled. By the time she was indicted in March 1978, the tension from her fear of arrest had taken its toll on Holmes's health. She began losing her hair, her skin changed color, and she tried to commit suicide.

SEEING THE NAME of John D. McConnell included in the indictment must have surprised many newspaper readers living in the Raleigh area. At the time, McConnell, a member of a prominent North Carolina family, was a partner in the major law firm of Broughton, Broughton, McConnell and Boxley. Law enforcement officials in New York City and North Carolina, though, knew McConnell as a money launderer for Ike Atkinson and Frank Lucas, and they had evidence that he helped the drug lords deposit their illicit profits in the offshore banks in the Cayman Islands.

McConnell had testified as a defense witness in Frank 'Superfly' Lucas's 1975 trial in New York City in which Lucas was one of thirteen people charged with drug conspiracy and trafficking. McConnell's testimony helped get Lucas acquitted, but, in January 1977 prosecutors charged McConnell with 35 counts of perjury for lying at that trial.

'I remember John McConnell coming to see me at the Atlanta pen,' Ike recalled 'He was really worried about the perjury charge. I felt sorry for him. My lawyer Steve Nimocks introduced me to McConnell and I introduced him to Lucas. I needed somebody to handle one of my IRS tax cases, and Nimocks said McConnell was good at that type of law. McConnell went from handling a tax case for me to moving my money to the Cayman Islands. McConnell was respectable and from a fine family. I blame myself for the bind he got him into.'

Prosecutors knew—and they could prove—that on at least one occasion, McConnell took two briefcases containing about $200,000 in cash to the Cayman Islands for Lucas. Lucas had instructed McConnell to bring the money to his brother

Shorty, who would be at the Miami International Airport with an associate named Otis Reid. Reid moved the money into the departure area and returned it to McConnell who then flew to Grand Cayman and deposited it in a bank.

Otis Reid worked in the Atkinson's and Lucas's drug rings but decided to cooperate with the Feds after DEA agents told him they had enough evidence to put him away for a long time. The DEA took Reid to their headquarters on West 57th Street for booking and then sequestered him in a nearby motel for interrogation. During the interrogation, Reid was allowed to leave the motel room and make a phone call. He called a girlfriend and explained that he had been arrested and was now in a motel room with two DEA agents. Unknown to Reid, a woman named Ann Fleming was with his girlfriend at the time. After Reid hung up, his girlfriend told Fleming about the call and what her boyfriend was doing. Unfortunately for Reid, Fleming was Frank Lucas's friend, and she told him about the call.

Lucas, who at the time was being held in the Manhattan Correctional Institution, told Reid he wanted to see him. Reid was afraid to go, but felt he had no choice. At the meeting, Lucas was low-key, almost sympathetic, when he asked Reid about the phone call. So Reid relaxed and managed to stay calm. He left the facility believing he had convinced Lucas that he was not a snitch.

On November 1 1975, Frank Lucas's brother, Shorty, called Reid and told him to meet him at 117th Street and Eight Avenue in Harlem. Reid arrived at 8.00pm. A half hour later, a blue Cadillac Eldorado with two men inside pulled up and Reid got inside. The three men drove to a battered tenement building at 348 West 118th Street where they got out of the car and took the elevator to the fourth floor. Reid's body was found later slumped in the elevator; he had been shot twice in the back of the head. The blue Cadillac Eldorado was last seen speeding toward Eighth Avenue. No one was ever arrested, let alone convicted, for Reid's murder.

'The murder conveniently eliminated a key witness who could have tied together everyone connected to the dirty money in the Cayman Islands,' said Bill Slaughter, a retired SBI agent who worked the investigation that led to the 1978 North Carolina state indictment.

IN OCTOBER 1977, McConnell pleaded guilty to four counts of perjury, which he admitted committing in Lucas's 1975 trial. After spending four months in federal prison at Eglin Air Force Base in Florida, he was paroled on March 15 1978, but the North Carolina State Bar disbarred him, and he lost his license to practice law.

In the 1978 North Carolina state case, prosecutors charged that in June 1975 McConnell, while a lawyer for Ike, deposited or helped deposit $600,000 in heroin profits in safe deposit boxes at the North-western Bank in Advance, North Carolina. McConnell was listed as trustee of the bank boxes. Prosecutors identified the Southern Bank and Trust Company, one of two offshore banks in the Cayman Islands that Lucas used to launder money, as a bank having a close working relationship with Northwestern Bank. Prosecutors believed that Lucas used some of the laundered money to buy a 540-acre farm in Granville County, which served as a stopping-off point for some of the heroin being shipped from Thailand to North Carolina. As the corruption scandal unfolded, embarrassed Northwestern Bank officials suspended two of its executives, Jack N. Crawford and Odell N. Wilson, who once managed the bank's Grand Cayman Islands branch.

In May 1978, a Wayne County grand jury re-indicted McConnell on expanded charges, accusing him of involvement in a conspiracy to sell and distribute heroin with Ike, members of Ike's family and others. McConnell realized that the handwriting was on the wall, and in September 1978, as the state was getting ready to go to trial, he plead guilty.

WHEN NORTH CAROLINA indicted Ike and thirteen others in May 1976 on federal drug conspiracy charges, 'Uncle Sam' confidently announced that it had finally dismantled the Atkinson drug ring. In January 1977, *The Bangkok Post* wrote what at the time seemed like a fitting obituary for the Atkinson drug organization. The newspaper predicted that the 1976 Raleigh trial that put Ike away for another 25 years marked 'the end of the biggest heroin gang in the world. During their long years of operation, they made themselves rich by several hundred million baht (millions of dollars), while, in the meantime, creating drastic problems in the homeland.'

In reality, though, Ike had never stopped dealing even though he was locked up behind bars. He knew how to use his charisma, money and 'people skills' to corrupt the system. He got an amazing variety of people, black or white, to do his bidding. It was easy for Ike to get messages out of prison, and despite the logistics problem posed by his incarceration, he was still able to run his organization. 'When people said Ike was in jail, that didn't mean a lot,' explained Cuyler Windam, a retired SBI agent who investigated Ike's drug ring in the 1970s. 'Any time someone came to visit Ike in jail, it wasn't to say hello. It was either for a meeting about drug money or to take care of this or that in his organization.'

IN MARCH 1978, at the time the indictment was unsealed, 32-year old Philip Wade Atkinson, the son of Ike's brother Edward, was living in a Howard Johnson's motel room in Atlanta, driving a late model Cadillac and serving as a kind of personal assistant for his uncle Ike whom he would visit often in the Atlanta pen. Ike took care of Wade financially so he did not have to work like a regular Joe. Wade's main responsibility was to keep an eye on Wilbur Fuller, a young black lawyer who had come to play an important role within Ike's drug ring. Slender and fastidious in his dress, Fuller, before his indictment, was enjoying the good life in the late 1970s. He lived in a million-dollar house, owned a fleet of luxury cars that included a Jaguar and a BMW, and had a stunning Puerto Rican wife on his arm. 'I thought Fuller would be useful because I believed he was well-connected to Atlanta's power elite, including Griffin Bell (U.S. Attorney General in the Jimmy Carter administration),' Ike recalled.

One day before his 1978 indictment, Wade went to see Laura Holmes in Goldsboro and picked up $800,000 that Ike planned to use for a drug deal. But the months rolled by and Wade still had the two suitcases full of cold cash and no instructions from Ike about what to do with it. As a precaution, Wade would put the money in the trunk of his Cadillac whenever he left the motel, once even taking the money with him when he went to see his parents in New York City. About ten months later, during a visit with Ike, Wade asked: 'What do you want me to do with the money?'

'What money?' Ike asked.

'Come on, Unc',' Wade said. 'I've got $800,000 of your money. I haven't spent a dime of it, but I know how much there is because I counted it. I got it from Laura.'

'Give it back to her,' Ike instructed.

'That was a bad mistake,' Wade recalled. 'I should have hung on to the money. Later, Holmes turned and became a witness for the State of North Carolina.'

Wade was at his parents's home in New York City, unaware that he had been indicted in North Carolina until the authorities came and arrested him and his father.

Bill Slaughter, a retired SBI agent, who worked with Cuyler Windam, said Ike and his family viewed their drug ring as a kind of family business. 'For North Carolina law enforcement, investigating Ike's drug ring was like working the moonshine liquor stills of North Carolina,' Slaughter explained. 'Many of the Atkinsons had been involved with the underworld all their lives, and they didn't see anything wrong with it. They looked at law enforcement as the ones who were messing with them. We were the bad guys.'

JIMMY ATKINSON, THE son of Ike's oldest brother, Dallas, recalled his involvement with the 'family business.' As a young man in his early twenties, Jimmy helped out William Herman 'Jack' Jackson during the time of the Dennis Hart and Richard Patch episode when Jack walked out of that New York police precinct in 1969 and went on the run. Returning to Goldsboro, Jack stashed some money in a chicken coop and hid out in an old folk's home. 'Jack told me and Peter Rabbit that he had about $25,000 there, and wanted us to get the money for him,' Jimmy recalled. 'We did and he paid us about $100.'

In 1971, Ike asked Jimmy to get himself a passport so he could go to Bangkok to bring about $100,000 back to him. Ike was tied up in litigation and needed somebody he could trust to do the job. Returning to Goldsboro, Jimmy began trafficking a kilo or two of heroin. He returned to Bangkok a second time, this time with Thomas Southerland on a military plane and with bogus military papers. He liked spending time in Bangkok. 'It was an exciting place; something was always happening,' Jimmy recalled. 'You could have as many girls as you wanted. Ike did not like me hanging around Jack's (American Star

Bar) out of concern that the bar could be under surveillance. So the girls would come up to our hotel room.'

By late 1974, Jimmy had become a street dealer, who was supplementing the money he earned from his job selling costume jewelry. 'I would move the stuff to Fayetteville or Rocky Mountain (North Carolina) and make about $300 a trip. I'd do it maybe once a week and not do it again for another couple of weeks.'

In July 1973, Jimmy went to his brother's house and met a man whom his brother introduced as 'a friend from Myrtle Beach.' Jimmy looked at the man. He was wearing a wool sport's coat and a wool shirt. Jimmy thought—'this guy ain't from Myrtle Beach. Nobody from Myrtle Beach dresses like that in July.' Jimmy warned his brother about his 'friend.' About three weeks later, the North Carolina SBI busted Jimmy at his home, where they found a couple of ounces heroin and about $33,000.

Jimmy was taken to a federal magistrate, booked and released on $25,000 bail. 'The agents put pressure on me to cooperate, but I didn't want to get killed,' Jimmy Atkinson recalled. 'So I kept my mouth shut.' In July, Jimmy went on trial. The man in the wool clothes who claimed to be from Myrtle Beach took the stand and testified that Jimmy sold him some heroin. Jimmy got 15 years in prison; his brother, 30.

Jimmy hired Ike's lawyer, Stephen Nimocks, to represent him and he went before Judge John D. Larkins, Jr. 'I knew Nimocks was Judge Larkins's good friend and that he had once been his manager in some political campaign,' Jimmy said. 'I knew that relationship would help me.' It certainly did not hurt him. On January 2 1974, Jimmy was released on appeal bond. The following month he took his family to Disney World to celebrate.

In 1974 and 1975, the heroin trade in North Carolina boomed; Jimmy was an active street dealer; and the money rolled in. He would arrange the sale of a kilo of heroin for $50,000 and sell it for $80,000. According to Jimmy's calculation, he did it 'fifteen or twenty times.'

By the summer of 1976, however, the heroin trade was in flux. Ike was in jail; the Asian heroin connection fragmented; and Mexican brown tar heroin was the smack of choice on the street, even though it was of poor quality compared to the Golden Triangle's ultra-pure China White.

Jimmy thought it was a good time to get out of drug dealing. He had made a lot of money, but he had to spend a lot as well and not necessarily on a good time. By his own estimate, over a three-year period, Jimmy spent $150,000 on lawyers to keep him out of jail. But eventually his lawyers finally told Jimmy he had to turn himself in; he had exhausted all of his appeals. He was sent to the prison near Asheville, North Carolina, to complete his sentence, but got out in August 1977. Jimmy went to Denver where one of his brothers was living. He was now out of the drug trade.

One day in March 1978, Jimmy's lawyer called him and said the SBI was coming to get him. He was being hauled in as part of the North Carolina's investigation of Ike's drug ring. 'I thought it was bullshit,' Jimmy stated. 'I didn't know any of the others who were indicted.'

BY THE MID-1970s the drug ring Ike and Jack started in 1968 was having a much more negative impact on North Carolina than the moonshine whiskey. When Ike launched his drug ring in the late 1960s, Goldsboro became the hub of his narcotics empire. The heroin may have gone through other parts of the U.S. after being transported from Thailand via couriers, the postal system, crew chiefs and finally teak furniture, but it always ended up in Goldsboro for distribution. 'In those days, any time I went to an intelligence meeting, all I heard was how a lot of dope was coming into Goldsboro,' revealed Steve Surratt, a retired SBI agent who worked the Atkinson investigation in the 1970s. 'I spent hours on surveillance. Informants would tell us that so-and-so from New York City or DC was in Goldsboro. Every work day, I would tour Goldsboro to see what cars were in town, and we'd run the plates to see to whom those cars belonged.'

By then, both heroin trafficking and addiction were big North Carolina problems, and Rufus Edmisten, the North Carolina State Attorney General, decided to establish a drug squad. 'I met with about six of my top SBI agents and they told me something illegal drug-wise was going on in North Carolina,' Edmisten explained. 'I decided we needed to go after the big-time drug dealers and gave the SBI and the state prosecutor all the resources they needed. In North Carolina no one was bigger than Ike Atkinson. I told the state prosecutor that he could have anything he wanted. I literally gave him a blank check.'

Ike's drug ring had the purest heroin in North Carolina, Surratt recalled. 'I never saw any of Ike's heroin that was less than 80 to 90 percent pure. We learned that Ike's goal was to have a $2,000,000 stash of heroin in North Carolina, but I don't think he made it.'

The North Carolina prosecutors publicized the 1978 indictment at a press conference in the Justice Building in Raleigh. North Carolina State Attorney General Rufus Edmisten said that the state's indictment was 'only the beginning' and explained how the investigation showed that 'Ike was running a continuing criminal enterprise.' Edmisten boasted: 'no other state had brought a case that we know of in the history of the country involving the charges we have presented and will prove in court.'

The case had national significance, Edmisten told the press, because 'it is fair to say that there have been literally millions of dollars made over the years and that it (the investigation) is an attempt on the part of all the people assembled here (officials at the press conference) to get the people in high levels who are in the business of distributing heroin. We can arrest hundreds of street people a day, and we do. That is not what we are really after. I think the case speaks for itself in that we are going to bring to justice a number of people who have been engaged in the business of distributing large amounts of heroin involving hundreds of millions of dollars.'

A week later, the defense lawyers jumped on the prosecutor for holding a press conference. Ethics rules for lawyers strictly limit the comments they can make about a case outside of court. Defense attorneys Robert Levin and Thomas Loflin charged that the press conference was a carefully orchestrated public circus. Levin called Edmisten the 'orchestra leader.' Judge Forest A. Ferrell took the defense motion to dismiss under advisement and said he would rule at a later date. Judge Ferrell eventually ruled against the defense motion.

Meanwhile, Don Jacobs, the North Carolina District Attorney who was prosecuting the case, added some melodrama by asking Judge Ferrell to provide protection for witnesses, since the judge had ordered that the prosecution share details of the prosecution's case with defense lawyers. SBI agent Bill Slaughter escorted Ike from the Marion prison to Raleigh for the state trial. He recalled telling Ike about the rumors that were floating around in North Carolina, claiming he might try to kill some witnesses in the case. Ike was sitting in the back seat. He leaned toward Slaughter, who sat in the front and said: 'Mr. Slaughter.

I'm not going to try to kill somebody when it's much easier to bribe them.'

WHILE IKE'S DEFENSE lawyers prepared for arraignment, they were also fighting an attempt by the State of Ohio to extradite their client to Akron where his old pal, Dan Burch, who taught Ike how to prepare AWOL bags for smuggling heroin and who had the bitter relationship with William Herman 'Jack' Jackson, was on trial, fighting a drug-conspiracy charge. Ohio prosecutors were trying to prove that Burch ran a widespread heroin network with North Carolina connections and that he, his brother, David, and three co-conspirators had brought 1,000 pounds of heroin annually into the U.S. from Thailand between 1968 and 1978, most it through Seymour Johnson Air Force Base in Goldsboro. The authorities also claimed that Burch used his business, Rare Elements Boutique, as a front to launder drug money. All of the defendants were found guilty and Dan Burch was sentenced to ten years in prison.

Burch was largely convicted on the basis of Ellis Sutton's testimony: 'Sutton testified that he hid in the closet of the Atkinson home in Goldsboro and saw me enter and get drugs from Ike,' Burch explained. 'Sutton lied. A lot of things were wrong with his story, including the timeline. I had lousy lawyers. Any decent defense lawyer could have picked Sutton's testimony apart. I didn't know that until I went to prison and began studying the law.'

Ike had no idea Sutton was testifying in Ohio. 'I didn't know he was a star witness in Dan's trial,' Ike recalled. 'Otherwise, I would not have fought extradition. I would have testified and showed that Sutton was a liar, just as he was in '72 when he lied about me selling him drugs.'

ON SEPTEMBER 12 1978, Ike Atkinson was brought from a two-man cell in Block D in the central prison to the Wayne County Courthouse for arraignment. Ike was handcuffed and his ankles shackled as he climbed from a vehicle escorted by two policemen to the conference room in the Justice Building where one of his defense lawyers, Talbot Smith, joined him. Ike waved and smiled to some of his family members who were at the courthouse. Smith asked for a ten-day delay to prepare his case. Judge Ferrell granted the request.

WHEN THEY INDICTED Ike and the other thirteen defendants, prosecutors revealed that some of the information leading to the indictments came from the conviction in New York City of Frank 'Superfly' Lucas, whom they described as a major heroin trafficker in the Bronx, Queens and Manhattan boroughs of New York City and in New Jersey. On September 19 1978, five days after the defendants were arraigned in Raleigh, Frank Lucas and his brother Vernon 'Shorty' Lucas signed a 'memorandum of agreement' with the State of North Carolina. In return for Lucas's truthful testimony in the trial of the 14, the State of North Carolina promised not to prosecute the Lucas brothers of any crime that they may reveal in testimony before any grand jury or at any trial.

By that time it was no secret that Lucas was singing to the authorities. In January 1975, a team of 12 U.S. DEA agents and 12 NYPD officers, acting on a tip from two East Harlem members of La Cosa Nostra, surrounded Lucas's house at 1933 Sheffield Road in the well-to-do neighborhood of Teaneck, New Jersey, and arrested him. The strike force confiscated $585,000 from the Lucas residence. Two days after the raid, the authorities indicted Lucas and 18 other people on drug conspiracy charges. A year later, a New York federal district court convicted Lucas, and he received a 40-year prison sentence and a fine of $200,000. In November 1976, a New Jersey state court sentenced Lucas to an additional 30 years in a New Jersey state prison for drug trafficking. The state sentence, however, would not begin until Lucas had finished his 40-year term in federal prison.

The prospect of spending the next 70 years behind bars did not deter Lucas from his life of crime. In September 1977, Lucas confessed to authorities that while incarcerated he had been running a multi-million-dollar drug ring with brother Larry and Ezell. The drug lord directed the operation through coded messages he passed to visitors who visited him in the Essex County jail in Newark, New Jersey.

It looked as if Superfly would be imprisoned forever, but he still had a card to play. He began contacting federal officials about working out a deal to reduce his sentence. In March 1979, one law enforcement source told the Newark Star Ledger newspaper: 'Lucas had been telling us everything from "day one" to now. A lot of the stuff was known to law enforcement, but a lot of it was new. We couldn't prove some of it, but he (Lucas) had agreed to testify everywhere he has to.' The source said most of the information Lucas was giving the authorities was about drug operations in New York and North Carolina.

Later, when the *American Gangster* movie appeared, which starred Denzel Washington in the role of Lucas, Lucas vehemently denied being a snitch. As part of the movie producers's efforts to soften Lucas's image, the movie portrayed him as only snitching on corrupt cops. That was not true; in fact, Lucas did not turn in a single law enforcement official. Lucas also claimed that he never took the stand as a witness. But that is also not true. Lew Rice, a retired DEA agent debriefed Lucas during his investigation of Leroy Butler, a big-time Harlem drug dealer who was convicted and sentenced to 15 years in prison largely because of Lucas's testimony. Rice confirmed that Lucas took the witness stand as a government informant.

In a memorandum dated March 13 1977, Lucas made a statement to two DEA officials, claiming he had dealt with Ike Atkinson on only two occasions. According to Lucas, in 1969 he purchased two kilos of heroin from Ike at his Goldsboro home. Lucas claimed the heroin was of such poor quality that a second delivery of two kilos was made in order to make up for the first package. He had no further dealings with Ike, Lucas said, although he did not deny reports that his brothers were involved with the Atkinson drug ring. Later, however, Lucas repudiated this statement, saying he had bought heroin from Ike on several other occasions.

While Lucas was incarcerated at Riker's Island, the authorities there allowed him to make more telephone calls than normal from prison and to have as many visitors as he wanted. Lucas used the arrangement to help keep his drug organization afloat. In early March 1977, Gino Gallina, a well-known criminal defense lawyer who represented several of the most powerful La Costa Nostra mobsters in New York City, as well as Lucas, Frank Matthews, and some other prominent black gangsters, visited Lucas in the counsel room at Riker's. Gallina was suspicious and attempted to search Lucas for a recording device. Lucas hit Gallina and demanded money that the lawyer allegedly owed him. On March 5 1977, Gallina was planning to dine with a lady friend at a restaurant in the vicinity of Carmine and Varick streets in Greenwich Village. As the lawyer stepped from his car, a lone gunman walked up and shot him eight times. An ambulance rushed to the scene, but it was too late. Gallina lay sprawled on the street, dead.

Not all of the people who visited Lucas in prison and pissed him off ended up dead like Gallina. Stanley Galkin came one day after the Gallina visit. Galkin was the Atlanta lawyer who represented Leon Cohen in Cohen's successful effort to scam Ike out of nearly $1 million while Ike was incarcerated at the Atlanta pen. As part of the scam, Cohen had visited Ike while posing as real-life Michael J. Egan, an associate U.S. attorney general in the Jimmy Carter Administration. Galkin had fallen out with Cohen, but Galkin decided to try the scam on Frank Lucas. He brought with him a real estate agent named Robert Charnock to pose as Micheal Egan, but the scam did not work and Galkin and Charnock were arrested. They pleaded guilty and were sent to prison.

Meanwhile, Galkin also pleaded guilty to a felony charge of criminal solicitation for conspiring to murder Leon Cohen and his accountant Fred Sans. 'Galkin was the worst lawyer I ever met,' Ike revealed. 'He was a real nightmare.' Sources say that Galkin was later murdered in a home invasion.

Joe Cheshire, a Raleigh lawyer who represented Ike's brother Edward Atkinson at the massive state trial following the March 1978 indictment and who conducted the special investigation of prison conditions in the Wake County jail, got a sense of the Lucas-Galkin relationship listening to an audio cassette tape. Cheshire, along with the other defense lawyers in the North Carolina State case, received about 300 tape-recorded conversations from the prosecutor.

'There were no transcripts and no indexes to go with the tapes,' Cheshire recalled. 'I wasn't going to listen to every tape, but I put one of them in a tape recorder to see what they contained. The tape happened to be a recorded conversation between Lucas and Stanley Galkin. Lucas was telling Galkin: "Stanley, you owe me money and I want it now." Stanley sounded nervous. He said: "I can't get it, I traveled all over the country. I've maxed out my American Express card." You could hear Galkin's children in the background. Stanley said: "I got to go and take my kids to the park." All of a sudden, Lucas's voice changed; it had a real chilling tone. Lucas said: "Stanley, you remember the story in the paper about how they found a lawyer floating in the river. Motherfucker, if you don't get my money, you and your family will be floating in the river, too!" I remember thinking. "I'm glad I'm representing the Atkinsons and not the Lucas family." The two families were so different. The Atkinsons were family people, pleasant and respectful. I never felt fear or danger.'

IKE SENT FULLER to Riker's Island to negotiate the deal with Frank Lucas that led to the sale of 13.3 pounds of heroin to an undercover SBI agent at a Holiday Inn in Selma, North Carolina. Frank Lucas would have been a star witness at the state trial, but the defendants, including Ike, pleaded guilty and received a sentence of 12 to 20 years to be served concurrently with his sentence in his 1976 federal conviction.

Lucas had provided enough information to make the North Carolina case against Ike and many of his relatives, but Ike was not going to let Superfly get away with it. And neither was Jack. The two decided they would get even with Lucas. During his period of incarceration, Lucas had adamantly denied any involvement in murder, even though during his efforts to fight a drug conspiracy case in 1974 he left behind a suspicious trail of dead bodies.

Lucas was one of 13 people named in an indictment that New York prosecutors unsealed on June 23 1974. Lucas and his co-defendants were accused of involvement in a conspiracy that had sold up to 20 pounds of heroin during the previous five years. Lucas faced the possibility of spending the rest of his life in prison for supervising the alleged conspiracy.

The prosecution looked as if it had a solid case against Frank Lucas. It presented a parade of witnesses, most of whom were informants and undercover detectives, and they provided impressive testimony about heroin deliveries and cash payments. Charles Morris, the prosecution's key witness, stayed on the stand for nine straight days, as the defense hammered away, trying to trip him up and blow holes in his testimony.

Still, the prosecution had a big problem. Important witnesses kept dying violently during the trial. The situation became so dire that Thomas M. Fortuin, the chief prosecutor in the case, complained to Judge Irvin Cooper that there is 'an extensive amount of blood in the case. We constantly have had more protection problems that any case I am aware of, really, in the history of the court.'

The series of murders were indeed disturbing and made witnesses look like casualties of war. The first victim cited by the prosecution was Marjorie Morris, who was murdered in 1973, two weeks after she had been interviewed by defense investigators. Next to die was Albert Pratt, who was shot to death in front of a Harlem bar shortly after he began cooperating in the case. On February 22 1973, Stanley Peek became the next witness to fall. He was an informant who tape-recorded conversations with Zack Robinson, one of the defendants in the trial. Robinson subsequently disappeared, and police did not know if he had fled or was killed.

Another victim was George Ford who had also been indicted in the case but had agreed to testify against Lucas before a grand jury. Police suspected Ford of trafficking as much as $12,000 worth of heroin a day from his candy shop in Harlem. On July 24 1974, the 'Candy Man' was shot dead at a block party in Harlem. Police had no suspects.

In September 1978, Ike and Jack told New York City detectives that Martin Trowery, who, at that time was cooperating against Ike and Jack in Pittsburgh, was the shooter in the George Ford murder and that Lucas was the buyer of Trowery's services. This new Lucas-Trowery-Ford lead convinced the New York special prosecutor to reopen the dormant Ford murder investigation.

Meanwhile, two days later and thousands of miles away, former Lucas employee Warren Sims was talking to the authorities. Sims told them that he had bumped into Martin

Trowery in the witness protection unit in a Chicago prison while they were both incarcerated. Sims telephoned the New York Special Prosecutor's Office and claimed that Trowery admitted to him that he had killed Ford on orders from Lucas. For the first time, Sims revealed that he and Lucas had a similar conversation three years earlier in which Lucas had admitted his involvement in the Ford killing. The new evidence from Atkinson and Jackson, on one hand, and from Sims, on the other, added to the information the authorities had in 1975. Lucas and Trowery were both indicted for Ford's murder.

But they both dodged a big bullet. As often happens at trial, the jury did not believe the testimony of convicted felons. Martin Trowery was found not guilty in July 1980. On November 26, Lucas was also found not guilty in New York state court in Manhattan, New York City.

In June 1981, Lucas walked out of jail a free man, after spending a mere five years in jail. The authorities revealed that Lucas would enter the Federal Government's Witness Protection Program because of threats against his life. 'He was unofficially in the program for years, living in the Protected Witness Section of the MCC (Metropolitan Correction Center) in New York City while in jail,' recalled Jack Toal, a retired DEA agent who interrogated Lucas during that period.

This meant a new identity and a new place to live for the man once described by a Federal prosecutor as 'unbelievably vicious.' Still, the authorities believed the deal with Lucas was worth it. They credited Lucas with supplying information leading to the successful prosecution of 70 drug traffickers, 34 of them in North Carolina.

Meanwhile, Ike was in prison at the Federal Corrections Institution in Otisville, New York, serving his 44-year sentence that would not end until 2020, unless he got early parole.

CHAPTER 17
Revival

LIKE A SHARK in a search of its prey, the North Carolina State Bureau of Investigation (SBI) pursued what it believed were the remaining members of the Ike Atkinson drug ring. By the time the SBI concluded its investigation in the late 1970s, more than 40 people (Atkinson relatives and friends, as well as lawyers and drug trafficking associates) were indicted. The SBI cast its investigative net as wide as possible, so many of those arrested did not get much prison time. 'My grandmother Rosetta was indicted,' recalled Wade Atkinson, the son of Ike's brother Edward who, himself, was indicted by the state in 1978. 'Why? I don't know. She could not tell a joint (of marijuana) from an ounce of heroin.'

The state of North Carolina even indicted Luchai 'Chai' Ruviwat, who, after being sentenced by a San Francisco court in December 1975 to three decades in prison, was serving time in a Federal prison in Washington State. 'We flew Luchai cross-country and took him down a North Carolina back road to jail,' recalled William Slaughter, a retired SBI agent who worked on the state investigation. 'We stopped the car by the side of the road so one of the agents could get out. It was really dark out, and I guess Luchai had watched too many movies. His eyes got really big and it looked as if he was going to wet his pants. For a moment, Chai actually thought we were going to take him out of the car and kill him.'

The North Carolina investigation did not come cheaply. In fact, it cost a small fortune and strained the North Carolina state budget. As a result, state travel funds were scarce for a while. The cost, in fact, became one of the major reasons why the state of North Carolina closed down the investigation.

A SIGNIFICANT FACTOR in making the state case was the cooperation of Frank Lucas and his brother Shorty. Frank Lucas had set up the sting that led to the seizure of 13.3 pounds of heroin at a Holiday Inn in Selma, North Carolina, and the guilty pleas of most of the 14 people indicted in the 1978 case. For Ike, the snitching by Frank and Shorty was a bitter pill to swallow, but he also learned that William Herman Jackson, his partner and best friend, also had been flown to North Carolina from the Atlanta Federal Penitentiary, not to be indicted but to be a potential witness for the state. 'Jackson cooperated with us, although he did not take the stand,' confirmed Steve Surratt, a retired SBI agent who worked on the North Carolina drug conspiracy investigation.

In return for Jack's cooperation, Sterling Johnson, Special Narcotics Prosecutor for New York City, recommended to the U.S. district court in Colorado in 1980 that Jackson receive special consideration for a reduction in sentence because of his testimony against Frank Lucas and Martin Trowery in the 1980 murder trial.

In the letter, Johnson wrote: 'Although the trial resulted in an acquittal, it was the view of this office that Mr. Jackson was truthful, cooperative and most helpful during the course of his cooperation. Additionally, the fact of that cooperation's discovery by others in the prison system poses a clear potential danger to Mr. Jackson, since he testified in part about revelations made to him by another inmate in the Atlanta Federal Penitentiary.' Johnson noted: 'It is my understanding that Mr. Jackson is completing part of his cooperation with officials in the state of North Carolina.'

'After I was indicted (in 1978), I learned that Jack had turned against me,' Ike recalled. 'He sent me a note saying he was sorry but that he was going to do it.' Remarkably, three decades later, Ike feels no animosity toward his old friend, 'Jack did what he had to do,' Ike explained. 'Man, he was crazy about his woman, Nitaya.'

AFTER THE TRIAL, the authorities returned Ike to Marion Federal Penitentiary, but on 28 April 1981, after spending a little more than three years there, he was transferred to the Federal correctional complex at Terre Haute, Indiana. Terre Haute is currently the home of the only death chamber for federal death penalty recipients in the United States, where they receive death by lethal injection. When Timothy McVeigh, the 'Oklahoma City Bomber,' was executed at Terre Haute in 2003, he became the first prisoner executed by the U.S. Government since the moratorium on the death penalty was lifted in 1976.

Ike wanted to get out of Marion, but his transfer to Terre Haute illustrated the old adage: Beware of what you wish for—it might come true. Ike's incarceration at Terre Haute morphed into the worse prison experience of his life. Members of Illinois street gangs infested the prison, and they were always fighting and trying to kill each other. The prison seemed to be in perpetual lockdown. 'Man, you were always concerned about being in the wrong place and getting in the middle of those fools,' Ike recalled. Fortunately for Ike, he did not have to endure the U.S. Federal Penitentiary System's version of Dante's Inferno for long. He was moved to the new Federal prison at Otisville, a medium security facility for male offenders located in the southeast part of New York State, close to Pennsylvania and New Jersey, and northwest of New York City. Opened in May

1980, the Otisville penitentiary looks like a campus and its low-rise buildings are built around a grassy area. 'The Federal prison system was looking for volunteers willing to transfer to Otisville,' Ike recalled. 'Given where I was, I jumped at the chance to move.'

As always when behind bars, Ike's charismatic personality made him many friends, and he was popular among inmates, young and old. He bonded with Steve Baker and Steve Monsanto, two young protégés of Robert 'Big Robbie' Stepeney, the legendary Harlem drug lord and so-called 'Godfather of Harlem.' Stepeney was known as the 'money man' in Harlem to whom even big-time drug dealers came for financial assistance. Ike also became friends with Clarence Jackson, who was nicknamed 'Scoop' because he always seemed to be on top of the news. Scoop played handball, but Ike got him to walk and they became walking buddies.

Indeed, Ike fit in well, no matter where the Bureau of Prisons sent him. Although Ike was not a black Muslim, the black Muslims invited him to one of their meetings and gave him an award for essentially being a nice guy. Native American prisoners invited Ike to 'sweat' with them in their sweat lodge, a ceremony that is an integral part of the religious life of many Native Americans. At the sweat lodge ceremony, Ike watched as coals were put in a pit and a fire started by using scraps of wood from the prison factory. When the coals turned white hot, Ike would take off his prison uniform and, dressed only in his briefs, he would get on his hands and knees and crawl into the sweat lodge. The purpose of the religious exercise is to cleanse the mind, body and spirit. 'It was such an honor to participate,' Ike recalled. 'You feel like a new man when you come out of the sweat lodge.'

BUT WHILE IKE endured prison life, he also pondered his future—that is, his life after serving time behind bars. By 1985, his drug ring was dead and his finances tapped out. The feds closed down his personal bank account, which amounted to a little more than $100,000, before he went to the pen in 1976. John McConnell had been Ike's bagman to the Cayman Islands, and he told authorities about the offshore accounts. The authorities closed them down, too.

Then in July 1985 the U.S. Parole Commission denied parole to Ike, in fact, keeping intact a sentence that would keep Ike in prison until the 21st Century. Joe Kovitsky, a U.S. Department of Justice spokesman, told the press that the Commission's decision was influenced by 'new adverse information' in the Atkinson case. Kovitsky would not say what the 'new adverse information' was.

Ike would be well into senior citizenry before he got out of prison, but what kind of life could he have without money and any employable skills? And Ike was the first to admit that he missed the excitement of the drug trade, the camaraderie, and the stature of being a big-time drug lord. And as wild as it may sound, Ike wondered if he could still beat The Man.

AT OTISVILLE, IKE got along well with Max 'Babe' Ruth, a loquacious, heavy-set white man who was incarcerated for bank robbery and who fancied himself an expert jailhouse lawyer. From prison, Babe wrote a lot of legal briefs that challenged the legal system. Ike noted that Babe often talked with another inmate named Norbert, a blond, stocky German whom Ike heard was in the pen on a smuggling conviction. Ike observed Norbert and liked the way Norbert carried himself.

One day, Ike asked Babe what he knew about Norbert.

'He seems to be well connected,' Babe said.

'In what way?" Ike asked.

'Norbert says he has a great contact, a German diplomat who's got diplomatic immunity. I think he may be his cousin. Norbert says his contact can get anything into the country. Nobody can stop him.'

'Really?' said Ike. 'Can Norbert's contact get dope into the country? '

Babe laughed. 'If money's involved, I'm sure he can.' The next day, Ike made a point of 'bumping' into Norbert at the mess hall where he worked in the kitchen. The two cons became friendly and soon were chatting up a storm. One day, after making some small talk, Ike laid it out for Norbert. 'I'm looking for a way to import heroin from Thailand to the U.S.'

Norbert smiled; Ike's bold confidence did not seem to surprise him. Through the prison grapevine Norbert had heard about Ike, the legend, who had used the military to smuggle hundreds of kilos from Thailand into the U.S.

'You mean smuggle don't you?' Norbert said. Ike laughed.

'How much are we talking about?' Norbert asked

'I'd say about 200 to 300 kilos,' Ike replied.

'I can do it through Germany,' Norbert replied. 'But gee, Ike, how are you going to finance it? You're in prison.'

'I got a distributor in DC who has made a lot money in the drug trade,' Ike explained. 'He has two record companies that are set up to launder money, but he can't launder all of it. So he's looking for other ways to invest it.'

'Well, I can help you,' Norbert said. 'I've got a well-connected friend in the West German consulate who has diplomatic immunity.'

'Really?' Ike said, not letting on he had already been briefed about Norbert's contact. 'Can you set up a meeting with him?'

'Let me get back to you,' Norbert said. 'I think we can work something out.'

IN REALITY, NORBERT did not have a well-connected diplomat friend and he was not whom he appeared to be. Yes, Norbert was charismatic, slick and smooth-talking, but he did not have enough sense to stay out of trouble with La Cosa Nostra. He owed a big gambling debt to the Mob and was afraid that a wise guy would kill him. While Norbert did not have a German diplomat friend, he thought he might have a big fish on the line that could help him out of his fix with the Mob. Scared and desperate, he approached the FBI (the Federal Bureau of Investigation) to see if the Bureau was interested in working out a deal that could catch a big-time drug trafficker trying to make a comeback. The FBI was interested, but since the case involved international drug trafficking, the Bureau contacted the U.S. DEA (Drug Enforcement Administration). Of course, the case interested the DEA. The DEA knew Ike Atkinson, the biggest American drug dealer to ever operate out of Asia, and knew it would be bad news if Ike could revive his network, even if he was in prison and still had a lot of time to serve. They knew that Ike Atkinson did it before and could do again.

The two Federal law enforcement agencies worked out a plan. First, they would need to get Norbert out of danger. So as not to attract attention, they transferred him to a halfway house. Next, they needed to find someone to play the role of Norbert's German diplomat. Special Agent Wolfgang Preisler would be the DEA's man. Of German ancestry and fluent in German, Preisler, a deliberate, no-nonsense type of guy, had been with DEA and its predecessor agency, the BNDD (Bureau of Narcotics and Dangerous Drugs), since the late 1960s. He was at that time a group supervisor in the DEA's intelligence division and had worked undercover numerous times both overseas and in the U.S., including Miami, one of the U.S. most dangerous cities. With the West German Embassy's cooperation, the U.S. authorities established a bogus office at the West German consulate for Preisler.

Norbert contacted Ike and gave him the name and address of the German diplomat and said his friend would be contacting him. Excited, Ike got on the prison phone and called his nephew, Wade, who by then was out of prison after serving two-and-a-half-years on the 1978 North Carolina drug conspiracy case. After his release, Wade lived in Queens, New York, and was working with computers at the Chase Manhattan Bank. Ike told Wade about Norbert and the plan he had to revive his heroin network.

'How much do you know about this Norbert?' Wade asked.

'He's a real nice guy,' Ike said. 'I've got a good feeling about him. But it's okay. Let's be safe. Why don't you go and check him out. See if his contact is working at the (West) German consulate.'

'Okay, but I think you should be careful,' Wade advised. 'You don't know too much about this Norbert guy.'

When Wade went to the West German consulate, he was stopped at the security gate. He gave his name to the guard and said he wanted to see Mr. Wolfgang Preisler. The guard said to wait while he went to see if Mr. Preisler is available. The guard made a call at the checkpoint and returned. 'I'm sorry. Mr. Preisler isn't in his office today.' So there is a German diplomat, Wade concluded. At least that part of Norbert's story checked out. Wade decided to do no further investigation; he was just too busy. He reported back to Ike; 'Yeah, Unc,' there is a German diplomat.'

WHILE THE DEA and FBI put their plan into motion, Norbert was working out his own deal with Ike through Wade whom he had contacted. By now, Norbert was out of the Otisville prison and in a halfway house. Using money from his DC distributor, Ike gave Norbert $100,000 in return for the assurance that his German 'diplomat' friend would arrange the transport of several kilograms of heroin from Germany to the U.S. Between April 15 and 18 1986, Wade called the halfway house three times, trying in vain to reach Norbert, but he had disappeared with the $100,000.

THE DEA WAS out a CI (Cooperating Informant), and Ike was out a lot of money. Wade's hunch had been right; Norbert was not the real thing. It looked as if Ike's misplaced faith in Norbert had dashed his big plans to revive his heroin smuggling network. But the DEA and FBI still believed they could keep their sting going. Preisler was instructed to contact Ike's nephew directly and offer his 'services.'

On April 25 1986, Preisler called Wade. 'How did you get my number?' Wade demanded.

Preisler kept his cool. 'Norbert gave it to me. Do you know what happened to Norbert? I've been looking for him.'

'We can't find him either,' Wade said.

'I would like to talk to you, but I don't want to do it over the phone,' Preisler said. 'Can we set up a meeting?'

'Let me get back to you,' Wade said. Preisler gave Wade his phone number.

On April 27, Wade went to the Otisville prison and met with Ike in the visiting room for two hours and forty-five minutes. He told his uncle about the diplomat's call. 'I tell you Unc', I don't get good vibes from this thing,' Wade said.

'Yeah, okay, but let's listen to what he has to say,' Ike said.

Wade called Preisler to set up a meeting. The call was routed to Preisler at the DEA's New York headquarters. They agreed to meet at the swank Waldorf Astoria Hotel on Park Avenue, a fitting place for a DEA undercover agent posing as a diplomat to have a meeting. It was a pleasant meeting and Wade was impressed with the German diplomat, but he still did not completely trust Preisler and the situation. To Preisler, Wade seemed like a nice kid who obviously respected his uncle and would do what he said. Wade told Preisler that he had given Norbert $100,000 for a 'package' (of heroin). The money belonged to several associates, Wade explained, and they were interested in finding Norbert. Preisler said he would check and get back to him.

Priesler did just that. 'I'm afraid Norbert is a con man and he's probably taken off with the money,' Preisler later told Wade. The undercover agent then suggested that they might still be able to work out a deal.

The same day that Preisler was to meet with Wade, a New York State judge was signing a court order authorizing the wiretapping of Wade's home phone in Queens for 30 days. The order was then extended for 30 days on 7 June and again on July 7. On May 9, Wade visited Ike again to report on his meeting with Preisler. Again Wade voiced his suspicions, but Ike decided to move forward and employ the 'services' of the 'German diplomat.'

DURING THE MONTHS of May and June, Ike continued to put his smuggling network in place, using Wade as his 'go-between.' Wade contacted and recruited Eddie Wooten, Ike's old friend from his gambling days in Germany who later became one of the main buyers of his heroin. Wade told Wooten that Ike wanted him to find Norman Young, whom Ike heard was living in Germany with a woman named Sylvia Bailey. Young was a friend of Ike's and they had served together in the U.S. Army in Germany. The DEA intercepted the call and checked their files for information on Bailey and Young. Both had been convicted of heroin smuggling but remained active in the business.

As we read earlier, Dan Burch, Ike's pal from Akron Ohio, who had worked the MPC (Military Payment Certificates) scam with him in Vietnam, had bought authentic military IDs from Sylvia Bailey in the late 1960s. Burch paid Bailey about $20 for a stolen ID and purchased as many as twenty at a time. On February 2 1974, Bailey and William Ward, her American common in-law husband, were arrested in Bangkok, Thailand, as part of a $10 million 'mail order' heroin smuggling operation. According to the DEA and Thai authorities, the operation involved more than 100 drug traffickers in the U.S. When the Thai police searched the duo's plush hotel room at the Hyatt Rama Hotel, they found 100 envelopes with the names of known U.S. heroin dealers and $1.6 million worth of ultra-pure China White heroin. The DEA concluded these many years later that Bailey and Young still had the connections that could make Ike's plan work.

Jimmy Smedley, the former 'Black ambassador to Thailand' who managed Jack's American Star Bar, had completed an eight-year sentence at the Lampoc Federal Prison Camp in Lampoc, California, after his extradition from Thailand or Hong Kong and conviction in the U.S. for conspiracy to traffic heroin. Ike had kept track of Smedley after Smedley was extradited to the U.S. Ike contacted him through Wade at Smedley's Los Angeles home. Smedley agreed that at the appropriate time he would go to Bangkok, with Savaneeya 'Ponsi' Batton, a former long-time employee at Jack's American Star Bar. A FBI check of the official authorized visitors list at Lampoc Prison Camp revealed that Ponsi and her husband, Cleophus Batton, had visited Smedley during his incarceration.

In 1975, Ponsi had married Cleophus Batton, an ex-GI who served with Ike in the U.S. Army in Germany. In 1979 Ponsi and Cleophus moved to the U.S.; six years later, Ponsi became a naturalized citizen. 'My initial plan was to locate Nitaya, (Jack's wife),' said Ike. 'Nitaya had helped set up the drug ring in 1968, but we couldn't find her. Ponsi was a good woman who had a good head on her shoulders and had done a good job (working) at Jack's American Star Bar.'

Ike's moneyman in Washington, DC, who owned the two record stores and who financially back Ike's criminal adventure, was out $100,000 already, thanks to Norbert, and wanted to recoup his investment. On May 27, Ike telephoned Wade and asked him to tell the moneyman that he needed a round trip ticket to Bangkok and about $450 in cash for Ponsi's hotel and travel expenses. By June 4, Ike made plans for Smedley and Ponsi to go to Thailand, and possibly Germany, to make arrangements to smuggle heroin to the U.S.

To coordinate his heroin network, Ike wanted to use the U.S. mail service as well as the telephone, so he recruited Samuel Arrante, a stocky Italian-American civilian prison worker at the Otisville federal pen. After working in the mailroom of the Records and Discharge Department at Otisville, Arrante became the laundry plant manager for the prison. Ike had worked for Arrante and the two were friendly.

Arrante had lamented to Ike that his wife wanted to start a restaurant, but that the interest charges on loans were outrageous.

'That's crazy, man,' Ike said. 'I'll loan you the money. How much do you need?'

At first, Arrante declined Ike's offer, but Ike persisted. 'Look, Sammy, no problem, no strings attached.'

Arrante slept on Ike's offer and the next day he agreed to accept a $2,000 loan from Ike.

'Don't worry about repaying me,' Ike told Arrante. 'We will take care of it when I get out of prison.'

In early May 1986, Ike gave Wade's telephone number to Arrante and told him to call his nephew and arrange a meeting so Arrante could pick up the loan. On May 22, Wade gave Arrante the $2,000. Returning to the prison, Arrante thanked Ike, not realizing he had unwittingly become part of Ike's heroin smuggling plan. Ike began putting his powers of persuasion to work, and Arrante began mailing letters for Ike, even though he knew he was breaking prison rules. Eventually, Ike gave Arrante $3,000 for his help in mailing the letters.

On July 8, Ike called Drayton Curry, his old friend from North Carolina who was living in Washington, DC. During their conversation, they talked about Norman Young. Ike had learned that Young was in trouble with the law in Germany, so he was going to have to find somebody else. Ike said his new contact turned out well and that they were 'in the move right now.' He should know something in a week or two, Ike revealed. He told Curry he would contact him again. During the conversation, Wooten arrived at Curry's house, and Ike spoke with him. 'Young's too hot,' Ike told Wooten. 'I'm going to get somebody else on that.'

In early August, however, another problem popped up. Ike's people could not find Wade. On August 3, Wooten told Ike that Curry had been unable to locate Wade and that his phone had been disconnected. Wooten had left messages for Wade to call either Curry or him, but Wade had not responded. Wade had not paid his phone bills, so on July 7 the telephone company disconnected his service. The federal authorities were also wondering what happened to Wade. They had not intercepted one of his calls since July 7.

Behind the scenes, Wade was having serious doubts about the prospects of Ike's plan succeeding and was avoiding his associates. He was now convinced that Wolfgang Preisler was some kind of law enforcement agent. He felt Ike had blinders on. It was almost as if his uncle was trying to will his plan to succeed. Disconnecting his phone was Wade's way of disassociating himself from Ike's plan.

Meanwhile, the authorities began intercepting the letters Ike was giving to Arrante to mail. Many of the letters were postmarked 'Bloomingburg, New York,' the town where Arrante lived and had Wade's name and address typed as the return address. The agents would tail Arrante, and, when he dropped off one of Ike's letters, they would seize it, copy it, reseal it, and put it back into the postal system, according to the requirements of the search warrant. On at least one of the letters, FBI agents found Arrante's fingerprints. Across the top of the envelopes, Ike wrote: 'GRAPEVINE LETTER—ATTENTION.' That was Ike's way of saying the letter was safe.

On August 22, the authorities seized a letter sent by Ike to Curry they believed provided information and directions about Ike's proposed heroin network. In the letter Ike wrote: 'Now let me get to business. I'm talking about the whole thing for $25. Now within six weeks, you can get someone cheaper than $25. I don't know how much cheaper just now until Wade and the people get together.'

The FBI analyzed the letter and later in a sworn affidavit, Raymond Kerr, a Special Agent of the FBI assigned the Atkinson-Otisville investigation, concluded; 'Based on my experience and in the context of this investigation, I believe that $25 means $25,000 and refers to the price per kilogram of heroin to be delivered to New York.'

On August 30, Preisler wrote a letter to Ike. He introduced himself as the person with whom Norbert had discussed providing the 'service you require.' Preisler explained that he had lost contact with Norbert and did not know how to reach him. He told Ike about his meeting with Wade. Although Wade seemed to be 'a nice gentleman,' he was 'not very responsible,' Preisler told Ike. 'I've had problems reaching him, and sometimes, when we have a meeting, he doesn't come.' Wolfgang told Ike to contact him, 'if I can still of service to you.'

ON SEPTEMBER 11, Ike wrote a letter to Preisler, which, remarkably, he sent through the regular mail service. In it, Ike told the 'German diplomat' that he had sent Jimmy Smedley, 'my oldest and most trusted friend,' to Thailand to renew an old connection. Smedley would visit Ike next week and report on his trip. At that time, Ike would have all the details for Preisler.

Ike mentioned Norbert and how Ike had paid off the debts that Norbert accrued while at Otisville. 'I tried several times to stop him from gambling, but he would not listen to anyone,' Ike wrote. 'I still like him, but he sure cost me a lot of money.' Ike ended his letter with: 'Don't be alarmed by the scotch tape on my envelope. This is a safe letter.'

Nearly six weeks later, Preisler sent Ike another letter, informing him that he had just returned from Germany. He had bad news to report. Norbert had died of cancer on October 4 1986. 'He was very sick and spent several weeks in the hospital at Quakenbruch (Germany) before he died,' Wolfgang revealed.

On November 12, Ike responded to Wolfgang's letter. 'Thank you for your letter. Norbert's death really messed up my mind. This guy played tennis every day he was here. Also, he walked the yard one hour each day. He was only thirty-seven years old. My god! I really liked Norbert more than anyone I met since I have been confined. I feel as if I knew him all my life. He was a real nice guy. I miss him. I hope he is at peace.'

By this point, Ike had gotten Wade back in the fold. He had sent Wade a check for $780 to pay off his telephone bill. 'You may call him (Wade) at any time next week if need be,' Ike advised Preisler. But in a letter dated December 12 from Preisler to Ike, Wolfgang complained that Wade's phone was still not working.

On January 19 1987, Ike sent Preisler another letter providing instructions on how to get to the Otisville prison and how to fill the visitor's request form included with the letter. Preisler visited Ike at Otisville with a tape recorder strapped to the inside pocket of his coat. Prison officials also videotaped the meeting.

Ike told Preisler to be prepared to travel to Thailand at the end of February. He had made arrangements through a Thai friend named Ponsi Batton who was going to pick up narcotics from an associate that Ike had used in the past when he was in Thailand. The money for the heroin was sent to Thailand (about $15,000) and placed in 'escrow' with his former Thai lawyer. Ike expected to make a return of $7,500 to $10,000 per kilo. Ike wanted the heroin to be 90 percent pure or he would not buy it. Ike considered this trip a trial run but, if it was successful, everybody stood to make millions because he planned to import no less than 50 kilos per shipment.

Ike told Preisler he would give him Ponsi's Bangkok phone number, and he gave him a code he had to use when calling her. The code: 'I know Ike.' Ponsi would respond with the other part of the code: 'I know Jimmy.' 'Use the name 'Norbert Mock' when you call the Thai woman,' Ike instructed Wolfgang. On February 12, Wade called Preisler and gave him four phone numbers: one for Ponsi's sister in Bangkok, another for Ponsi's father, and two phone numbers for Ponsi's place of employment in Delaware.

The following day, Preisler called Ponsi using the code Ike had provided. They agreed that Ponsi would leave for Bangkok on March 2 and Preisler the following day. Preisler would contact Ponsi on March 6, the day he would arrive in Bangkok.

FINALLY, IKE THOUGHT he had his plan in operation. Preisler and some FBI agents arrived in Bangkok and were met by DEA agents and Thai law enforcement officials. Preisler made contact immediately with Ponsi and let her know that he was staying at the Impala Hotel in room 602.

'Have you received a package yet?' Preisler asked.

'No I haven't,' Ponsi said. 'But I want to meet you first.'

At 9 pm the following day, Ponsi and Preisler met at the Impala for half-an-hour.

'The package arrived this afternoon,' Ponsi said, and she told Preisler to call her the next day to arrange a time to pick it up.

On March 8, Preisler and Ponsi met in the lobby at the Impala Hotel. Ponsi had a shopping bag with her. The two exchanged greetings and took the elevator to Preisler's room. Once inside, Ponsi wasted no time in opening the shopping bag and pulling out a plastic bag wrapped in a newspaper. It contained 5.28 pounds of heroin worth $450,000 on the street. Ponsi told Preisler that Wade had called her. She had assured him that everything was going to plan.

'If I want to purchase some heroin on my own,' Preisler asked Ponsi, 'could you get it for me?'

'Yes, I can, but I need two days notice,' Ponsi replied. 'First, though, I will need the money in advance.'

'I'll let you know if I'm interested,' Preisler said.

ON MARCH 7, 1987, Preisler and the two FBI agents arrived at John F. Kennedy Airport with the 5.28 pounds of heroin, the evidence they needed to bust the re-constituted Atkinson drug ring. After moving the contraband through Customs, it was brought to the DEA lab for analysis where tests showed the heroin to be 94 percent pure. Later, *The Washington Post* reported that it was the purest heroin ever tested at the DEA lab.

Two days later, Preisler called Wade. He said he had the package but was still in Germany. He would return to New York City on March 11. They agreed that Preisler would deliver the heroin to Wade the following day at the Waldorf Astoria Hotel. For Ike it would be the culmination of more than a year's planning and preparation and the revival of his international network. Meantime, the FBI and DEA prepared for the conclusion of their investigation.

Over breakfast at the Waldorf, Wade and Preisler discussed how things went in Thailand. Wade assured the DEA undercover agent that he would be paid for delivering the heroin to him. They went outside to Wolfgang's car where Wolfgang handed Wade a small silver-colored suitcase. Seconds later, DEA and FBI agents descended on the scene and arrested Wade. In Thailand, the local authorities, together with the DEA, arrested Ponsi and extradited her to the U.S. The FBI moved to arrest Smedley, Wooten, Curry and the other suspects in the U.S.

AS THE BUST went down, Ike waited in his prison cell. He knew Preisler had returned from Germany and that Wade was going to meet him and pick up the heroin. Before too long, the test run would be completed and he would be back in business.

'It was a shock to see the FBI show up at my cell,' Ike recalled. 'They told me what happened and said that I was under arrest. Prison guards were with them and they put handcuffs on me. Here I am in prison and they put handcuffs on me (laughs). They read me my rights and marched me out of my cell. It seemed everybody in the prison was watching me leave. I felt as if I was falling off a cliff. I wondered what went wrong. I thought I was on top of things and had the right people in place. We went to trial. We all got time. I got nine years that was to run consecutively with my other sentences. I thought I could beat the system, but I lost.'

EPILOGUE

THE FEDERAL BUREAU of Prisons (BOP) moved Ike Atkinson to the Metropolitan Correction Center in New York City for the 1987 trial stemming from the failed heroin smuggling scheme he had organized while incarcerated at Otisville Federal Penitentiary. Sitting in the courtroom and listening to the testimony, Ike could see that his scheme had been doomed from the beginning. 'I knew we should have checked out the phony German diplomat more carefully,' Ike recalled. 'I was angry with Wade (Atkinson), and I didn't speak to him at the trial. None of the others on trial did either. But I got over my anger. I never held it against Wade. I had to move on.' Since his incarceration in 1975 and prior to his bust at Otisville, Ike had kept his prison record clean. So he had a good chance of having a large part of his sentence reduced. But for now it seemed that Lazarus had a better chance of returning from the dead than Ike did of becoming a free man. 'I talked with Atha (Ike's wife) and she was really disappointed,' Ike recalled. 'She thought I would never come home.'

ON FEBRUARY 16, 1988, Ike was transferred to the Federal Correctional Institution at Petersburg, Virginia, a medium and low security prison for male offenders, located about 25 miles south of Richmond. Ike was lucky. Given his run-in with the law at Otisville, he could have been transferred to a much tougher facility. Opened in 1930 as Fort Lee, the Petersburg Federal pen is a well-manicured facility that looks like a college campus from the outside. With its large indoor and outdoor recreation areas, the penitentiary offers inmates plenty of opportunities to exercise.

So Ike did not mind the transfer, especially when he learned that he would be spending time once again with his old friend, Joe Stassi. By chance, the BOP had transferred the old mafia soldier from Marion before Ike arrived, and he had about three years to serve before being eligible for parole. Ike also met William 'Dog' Turner, the prominent Washington, DC, drug dealer who, in the early 1970s, had bought heroin from Ike's drug ring. Ike played handball with Dog and walked the trail with Stassi. Since Goldsboro was just a couple of hours away from Petersburg by car, family members were able to visit him regularly on the weekends.

Resourceful as ever despite his setback at Otisville, Ike adapted well to his new prison conditions. But every three months he had to appear before a prison board that reviewed his record. Inevitably, whenever they discussed his criminal record, the rumors about the coffins, heroin and dead bodies would pop up. At Petersburg, Ike finally got tired of hearing the lies that, in Ike's words, had 'blackballed me from the get-go,' and he decided to try and clear his name. In 1988 Ike got a fellow inmate to file a civil lawsuit in the U.S. District Court in Richmond challenging the validity of the cadaver-heroin connection theory. It was a quixotic attempt at redress, and the court threw out his suit.

For Ike, being away from his wife and close-knit family was always tough, but it got tougher on May 19 1991, when Ike's wife Atha died of heart failure at their home on Neuse Circle in Goldsboro. Ike desperately wanted to attend Atha's funeral, but the BOP callously denied his request, although it was in its power to allow it. Ike wanted to know why, but the BOP refused to give him a reason.

ABOUT A MONTH later, Ike was transferred back to the Terre Haute Federal Penitentiary. A decade had passed since Ike was last incarcerated at Terre Haute, but the prison had changed little. The gangs from Chicago and Detroit still dominated the prison, and it was still in a perpetual state of conflict. On the positive side, many of Ike's old friends were still there, including Veronza Bowers and some of the Native Americans who once again invited Ike to 'sweat' with them. A model prisoner, Ike was allowed to live in the honor unit in a cell of his own with a TV.

After a few years at Terre Haute, the BOP told Ike he would be transferred to a Federal penitentiary in South Carolina. It was tough for his family to come and see him at Terre Haute and the facility in South Carolina was much closer to Goldsboro. It looked as if the transfer would be a good move for Ike, but he challenged it. 'Why the hell are you sending me to South Carolina?' Ike told the authorities. 'I live in North Carolina. I have a good record. I should be placed closer to my home.' Ike appealed but the Board upheld its decision. Ike refused to go. He thought the BOP was jerking him around. The BOP decided to keep him at Terre Haute. On November 1 1999, a few weeks before he turned 74 years old, Ike got his wish and was transferred to the federal pen at Butner, North Carolina. He was now a few miles from his family and close to his release date from the penitentiary.

IN APRIL 2007, the BOP released the octogenarian and one-time drug kingpin from prison. Ike had spent nearly 32 continuous years in the federal prison system. Both the inmates and guards were happy for Ike but sad to see him go. He had been a mentor to many young inmates as well as a stabilizing force among the prison population and that had helped to make the guard's job easier. Although Ike was well known in the prison, his release from prison went unnoticed by the wider world. No newspapers or media announced his release. Ironically, Ike got out of prison at the time Hollywood was beginning to hype the movie release of *American Gangster,* the fantasy life story of Frank Lucas, his long time nemesis.

SINCE HIS RELEASE, Ike has adapted remarkably well to his new life in mainstream society. He is living quietly and alone in North Carolina in a modest two bedroom apartment. He is always in constant touch by phone and visits with his close although extended family. Ike's son John was ten years old when Ike went off to prison for good. 'I marvel at how dad survived and how his long stay in prison didn't really change him,' John explained. 'Most people would have gone crazy.'

As John pointed out, Ike remains in good mental and physical condition, given his time in prison and despite having to deal with bladder cancer. For a man who once arranged drug deals worth millions of dollars, the pleasures of life are now simple. He has his own 'Stassi' trail in his neighborhood that he hikes every day to stay fit and a 1999 Honda Accord that he uses to stay independent. He loves watching pro football on TV as much as he disliked hearing, seeing or reading about the actions and policies of the Bush-Cheney Administration and the way the country has been going since 2000. He keeps up with political events and is amazed that a black man has become president of the U.S. in his lifetime. Still, Harry Truman remains Ike's favorite president, mainly because of his move to integrate the army in 1948.

His favorite local haunts are a McDonald's restaurant and a Borders bookstore, which he frequents nearly every day. The former 'gentleman' gangster is still polite and courteous to all he meets. He takes his hat off before entering a building and addresses all men and women, no matter their status, as 'Sir' and 'Ma'am.' Ike has made contact with the retirement association of his beloved old army unit, the Triple Nickel, and plans to be active and to attend their annual meetings.

Ike is sad that so many members of the band of brothers who sought adventure with him in Europe and Asia, are no longer with him. William Herman 'Jack' Jackson, Jimmy Smedley and Eddie Wooten are all dead, either from diseases of old age or of modern society—prostrate cancer, Alzheimer's and obesity. Some, like Robert Johnson and John Roy, have faded away. They may be dead or perhaps living out their lives in obscurity. Jasper Myrick is one whom we know for sure is living in obscurity in a small southern town. Freddie Thornton, the associate whom Ike considers his biggest mistake in the drug trade, died in 2001. Ike re-established contact with some of the surviving younger members of his band of brothers, including Dan Burch, and, once again he was enjoying their friendship. Unfortunately for Ike, his pal Scoop Jackson has since passed away.

Ike knows that Luchai Ruviwat returned to Thailand after being released from U.S. prison in 1994. He believes that after Herman Jackson died in 2006, Jack's wife, Nitaya, left California and voluntarily returned to her native Thailand. Ike hopes to re-establish contact with them someday. Interestingly, Nitaya divorced Jack during his imprisonment and married a German man. But once Jack was free, she divorced the German and re-joined Jackson.

Ike lives simply on his military pension and social security benefits. Speculation still abounds, though, about what happened to the millions of dollars he supposedly garnered during his years in the drug trade. Legend has it that Ike may have $80 million stashed in an offshore bank account somewhere.

Legends often breed wild stories. One retired DEA agent familiar with the Ike Atkinson investigation asked me if Ike has two thumbs. As the retired agent explained the rumor, one of Ike's children wanted to take out some of the money Ike had stashed in a Cayman bank account. They needed Ike's thumbprint to do it, but he was in prison. You guessed it. Ike was supposed to have cut off one of his thumbs and sent it to his children for the sake of the family finances. I assured the retired DEA agent that Ike indeed still has two thumbs.

More than a few law enforcement officers and lawyers who once worked to put Ike behind bars have chatted with him on the phone, curious about the likeable ex-gangster who has survived more than a few years in prison. Ike always responds as if he is talking to one of his superior officers in the U.S. military and invariably assures the caller that he holds no grudges against them. 'You were only doing your job, sir,' Ike says.

IKE IS THE first to admit that he has made some big mistakes in his life, but he is not a person who dwells on the past. Nor does he worry about things he has done and cannot change. He believes he has paid his debt to society.

Ike does have one regret, however. As his U.S. Army Service had ended, he began his life of crime and international drug trafficking, which, he says, for many years was one long adrenaline rush crammed with risks. But had he taken advantage of the GI Bill, it would have provided him with the money to go to college, which would have opened up opportunities to pursue an honest living, despite the racism prevailing in America at the time. 'I know I would have done well in school,' Ike confides. 'My life could have gone in a much different direction.'

One thing Ike does not regret, though: the opportunity, through this book, to set the historical record straight. Ike is confident this book has debunked the cadaver heroin connection hoax that has branded him with a kind of 'scarlet letter.' And for better or for worse, our book has reclaimed Ike's life story from Frank Lucas, the man who has impersonated the real *American Gangster*—Leslie 'Ike' Atkinson.

CAST OF CHARACTERS

KINGPIN

Leslie 'Ike' Atkinson—Charismatic retired U.S. Army Sergeant, gambler, adventurer and leader of an African-American drug trafficking organization that, according to U.S. Drug Enforcement Agency (DEA) assessments, evolved into a $400 million heroin smuggling organization. Ike was a partner of William Herman Jackson and was responsible for smuggling heroin from Thailand to the U.S. and for its wholesale distribution within the country. Ike took over the entire operation after the arrest of partner Jackson in 1972. The media and law enforcement dubbed Atkinson 'Sergeant Smack.'

PARTNERS

William Herman Jackson—Nicknamed 'Jack,' Jackson was Atkinson's U.S. Army buddy and partner in crime who talked Atkinson into moving to Bangkok in the late 1960s. Jack established Jack's American Star Bar in Bangkok, Thailand, and with Ike, he launched the heroin smuggling empire that became the largest Asian-U.S. heroin connection ever uncovered. Jackson was busted in Denver in 1972.

Luchai Ruviwat—A Thai-Chinese businessman who was a partner in Jack's American Star Bar in Bangkok, Thailand, and a close drug trafficking partner of Atkinson and his associates.

Luchai became responsible for obtaining drugs for Atkinson after Herman Jackson's arrest. Luchai was arrested in an undercover sting in San Francisco.

James Warren Smedley—An ex-U.S. Army soldier, Ike's buddy, a key member of Ike's drug trafficking organization and partner and manager of Jack's American Star Bar.

BAND OF BROTHERS

'Berlin'—Gambler and hustler who operated in Europe. Real name unknown.

Pratt Benthall—Ike's New Jersey-based friend and drug trafficker.

Dan Burch—Professional gambler and drug dealer from Dayton, Ohio, who taught Ike how to sew false bottom into AWOL bags so they could hide heroin.

Lorenzo Bowers—A Federal prisoner serving a life-term who befriended Ike in prison.

Leon Ellis—Master woodworker from North Carolina who came to Bangkok to help build false bottoms into teakwood furniture so they could hide heroin.

Herman Lee Gaillard—Nicknamed 'Peter Rabbit,' Galliard, from La Grange, North Carolina, was a member of Ike's organization.

Andrew Price—Half brother of William Herman Jackson and a key operative within the Atkinson drug ring in Bangkok.

Rudolph Valentino Jennings—A Bangkok-based operative for Sergeant Smack's heroin ring who came to Bangkok and was responsible for fitting the false bottoms of AWOL bags for heroin shipments.

Robert Johnson—Retired U.S. airman from Greensboro North Carolina, whom Ike considered one of the biggest hustlers in Europe. Johnson later moved to Bangkok.

John Roy—a gambler and hustler who was the only white member of Ike's 'Band of Brothers.'

Ed Russell—Gambler and hustler who became friends with Ike in Europe.

Joe Stasi—Soldier in La Cosa Nostra who became good friends with Ike while they served time together in various prisons.

Ellis Sutton—North Carolina native, drug dealer and Ike's friend and associate with whom Ike had an ambivalent relationship.

Thomas Southerland—Ike's friend whom Ike considered to be like a son and who worked for Ike's organization.

Eddie Wooten—Ike's friend and major drug trafficker from Washington, DC, who used the U.S. military base at Okinawa, Japan, as a base to transport heroin to U.S.

FAMILY

Atha Atkinson—Ike's second wife.

Dallas Atkinson—One of Ike's three older brothers.

Edward Atkinson—One of Ike's three older brothers.

Ezzell Atkinson—One of Ike's three older brothers.

Helen Atkinson—Ike's first wife.

Jimmy Atkinson—Ike's nephew and son of Dallas.

Juanita Atkinson—Wife of Dallas Atkinson.

Larry Atkinson—Ike's nephew and Dallas's son who introduced Ike to Frank Lucas.

Linda Atkinson—Daughter of Dallas Atkinson.

Pearl Parks Atkinson—Ike's sister who lived in NY.

Philip Wade Atkinson—Ike's nephew and Edward's son.

ASSOCIATES

Samuel Arrante—Civilian prison employee at Otisville Federal Penitentiary whom Ike recruited to smuggle letters out of the prison.

Cleophus Batton—Husband of Saveneeya 'Ponsi' Batton.

Saveneeya "Ponsi" Batton—Longtime employee of Jack's American Star Bar whom Ike later recruited for the drug ring he tried to revive while incarcerated at Otisville Federal Penitentiary in Otisville, New York.

William Kelley Brown—U.S. Army Sergeant assigned to the SEATO medical research facility in Thailand who agreed to move heroin in teakwood furniture for Ike's drug ring.

Leon Cohen—Atlanta businessman who successfully scammed Ike out of nearly $1 million while Ike was incarcerated in Atlanta, Georgia's Federal Penitentiary.

Gerald Gainous—U.S. Army Master Sergeant involved with Jackson's Denver heroin smuggling run.

Charles Murphy Gillis—U.S. Army Master Sergeant from Goldsboro, North Carolina, who worked for Ike's drug ring.

Laura Holmes—Goldsboro native and girlfriend of William Herman Jackson who worked for the Ike drug ring.

Herbert Houseton—A Bangkok-based U.S. Army Post Office (APO) employee who helped Ike's drug ring move drugs to the U.S. via the U.S. postal system.

Frank Lucas—Heroin trafficker in the New York and New Jersey area about whom the movie *American Gangster* made famous and who bought drugs from Ike.

Vernon 'Shorty' Lucas—Frank Lucas's brother who bought drugs form Ike's organization.

James McArthur—U.S. Army Sergeant stationed in Bangkok who brought packages for Herbert Houseton to ship to the U.S.

Jasper Myrick—Bangkok-based U.S. Army Sergeant who agreed to ship heroin back to the U.S. in teakwood furniture. Arrested by Thai police at his home with one of the biggest amounts of heroin ever seized in Thailand.

Papa San—Shadowy relative of Nitaya Jackson, William Herman Jackson Thai-Chinese wife, who initially supplied the heroin for Atkinson-Jackson drug ring.

Robert Ernest Patterson—Administrative Specialist in the U.S. Army Post Office in Bangkok.

Chalermphol Phitastrakul—Thai drug courier who, along with Luchai Rubiwat, was busted in San Francisco for heroin trafficking.

Sylvester 'Mumbles' Searles—A Sergeant in the U.S. Air Force assigned to U-Tapao Air Base in Thailand whom Jackson recruited for his Denver heroin drug run.

Freddie Thornton—U.S. Air Force NCO who smuggled heroin for Atkinson while he was on active duty, then became heir apparent to head the Bangkok end of the Atkinson heroin smuggling organization. Thornton was the principle witness against Atkinson at the Federal trial in North Carolina.

Johnny Trice—Sergeant in U.S. military assigned to U-Tapao Air Base whom William Herman Jackson recruited for the Denver heroin drug run.

Martin Trowery—Major drug trafficker from Pittsburgh, Pennsylvania, who bought his heroin from Ike's drug ring.

William 'Dog' Turner—Major drug trafficker from Washington, DC who bought his heroin from Ike's drug ring.

Law Enforcement and U.S. Officials

Don Ashton—A U.S. DEA special agent in charge of the Wilmington, North Carolina office in the early and mid 1970s. Ashton was "field commander" of CENTAC 9, a DEA headquarters-based operation that coordinated the worldwide investigation of Ike Atkinson's international drug network.

Lebert Baxter—Base Commander and Head of Personal Effects Department at Tan Son Nhut Mortuary in Vietnam.

Paul Brown—DEA supervisory special agent assigned to the Agency's Bangkok office from 1970 to 1976.

Gary Fouse—DEA special agent who worked in the Agency's Bangkok office and helped investigate the Jason Myrick heroin seizure in 1975.

Dennis Hart—New York-based U.S. Bureau of Narcotics and Dangerous Drugs (BNDD) special agent and partner of Richard Hart, who was prosecuted in Federal Court in a New York City but was found innocent.

Doug Howard—Deputy Director, U.S. Army Mortuary Affairs Center in Fort Lee, Virginia, who worked at Tan Son Nhut Mortuary in the late 1960s and early 1970s.

Charles 'Chuck' Lutz—U.S. DEA special agent in the Agency's Bangkok office in the mid-1970s who led the investigation of Atkinson's drug ring in Thailand. He also partnered with Lionel Stewart on the Luchai Rubiwat undercover investigation.

Richard Patch—New York City-based BNDD special agent and Dennis Hart's partner who was prosecuted for corruption in a New York court but was found innocent.

Wolfgang Preisler—New York-based DEA special agent, fluent in German, who, posing undercover as a West German diplomat, was hired by Atkinson to revive his drug smuggling operation.

Brian Raftery—DEA special agent who worked in the Bangkok office in the 1970s and assisted in the investigation of the heroin seized from Jasper Myrick.

Lew Rice—New York-based DEA special agent who investigated Frank Lucas.

Michael Schwartz—U.S. Customs agent who investigated William Herman Jackson and the Denver heroin connection.

Lionel Stewart—DEA special agent who was sent to Bangkok to infiltrate the Ike Atkinson organization. Stewart made undercover purchases of heroin from Luchai Rubiwat that led to Luchai's conviction in San Francisco, California. Stewart also contributed evidence to the successful conspiracy prosecution of Atkinson and his associates in North Carolina.

Joe Sullivan—A DEA special agent who worked in Harlem, New York City, in the mid 1970s and investigated drug trafficker Frank Lucas.

Howard Wright—U.S. Customs special agent who investigated Atkinson's drug ring and its alleged cadaver-heroin connection.

PROSECUTORS AND DEFENSE LAWYERS

Joe Cheshire—Raleigh, North Carolina lawyer who represented Ike's brother Edward Atkinson against drug trafficking charges.

Paul Cooper—Assistant U.S. Attorney assigned to the Denver office who successfully prosecuted William Herman Jackson in the Denver heroin case.

Christine Whitcover Dean—Federal Prosecutor who assisted in the prosecution of Ike Atkinson and several of his associates in North Carolina.

Joe Dean—Assistant U.S. Attorney who successfully prosecuted Ike Atkinson and associates in a North Carolina court trial.

Dennis Dillon—Assistant U.S. Attorney from Eastern District of New York who prosecuted Richard Patch and Dennis Hart.

Howard Diller—One of Ike's many lawyers who was based in New York City.

Wilber Cleo Fuller—One of Ike's many lawyers who was based in Atlanta, Georgia.

Stanley Galkin—Atlanta lawyer who represented Leon Cohen in Cohen's successful effort to scam Ike out of nearly $1 million while Ike was incarcerated in Atlanta, Georgia's Federal Penitentiary.

Sterling Johnson—A former Federal judge in New York City who presided over the Frank Lucas trial in the late 1970s and early 1980s. John McConnell—Ike's Raleigh, North Carolina-based lawyer who helped Ike and Frank Lucas launder money in the Grand Cayman Islands.

Tom McNamara—A North Carolina-based Assistant District Attorney who prosecuted Ike.

Mike Nerney—A San Francisco, California-based Assistant U.S. Attorney who assisted DEA agents Charles Lutz and Lionel Stewart in the Luchai Rubiwat drug trafficking investigation and successfully prosecuted Luchai in San Francisco.

Stephen Nimocks—Fayetteville, North Carolina lawyer who represented Ike in North Carolina drug cases.

Tolbert Smith—Another of Ike's many lawyers.

Journalists

Al Dawson—Journalist for *United Press International* who covered rumors of the cadaver-heroin connection but found no evidence it existed.

Peter Finucane—*Bangkok Post* journalist and friend of Jimmy Smedley.

John McBeth—A reporter for *Asian Week* magazine and friend of Jimmy Smedley who covered the takedown of the Ike Atkinson drug ring in Thailand.

Cadaver-Heroin Connection Theorists

Dan Addario—DEA special agent in charge of the Bangkok, Thailand Regional Office in the mid 1970s who wrote about discovering heroin in the body of a dead U.S. GI in a Bangkok hospital in the fall of 1974.

Bob Kirkconnell—Retired Army Master Sergeant who claims that in 1972 or 1973 he was involved in an investigation at the

U.S. Kadena Air Base in Okinawa of heroin being smuggled into the U.S. using 'killed in action human remains.'

Michael Levine—DEA special agent who claims the U.S. CIA (Central Intelligence Agency) was involved in the alleged cadaver-heroin connection.

Michael Marr—Assistant District Attorney for the District of Maryland who suspected Ike of moving heroin in the coffins of dead U.S. servicemen.

Helen Stoeckley—Woman who claimed knowledge of the murder of the family of U.S. Army officer and medical doctor, Jeffrey MacDonald, in 1970. She also claimed that Ike Atkinson's drug ring smuggled heroin in the bodies of dead U.S. servicemen in Vietnam to the U.S. via Fort Bragg.